中国矿业大学双一流建设文化传承创新项目

西方人文思想经典选读
Selected Readings of Western Classics in Humanistic Thoughts

主　编　祖大庆
副主编　刘会民
编　者　杜光明　王翔敏
　　　　周　萍　张　璐

南京大学出版社

图书在版编目(CIP)数据

西方人文思想经典选读:汉文、英文 / 祖大庆主编.
—南京:南京大学出版社,2021.1(2023.8 重印)
ISBN 978-7-305-24173-4

Ⅰ.①西… Ⅱ.①祖… Ⅲ.①思想史-西方国家-高等学校-教材-汉、英 Ⅳ.①B5

中国版本图书馆 CIP 数据核字(2020)第 271178 号

出版发行	南京大学出版社		
社　　址	南京市汉口路 22 号	邮　编	210093
出 版 人	王文军		

书　　名　西方人文思想经典选读
主　　编　祖大庆
责任编辑　裴维维　　　　　联系方式　025-83596997
照　　排　南京紫藤制版印务中心
印　　刷　南京百花彩色印刷广告制作有限责任公司
开　　本　787×1092　1/16　印张 12.25　字数 330 千
版　　次　2021 年 1 月第 1 版　2023 年 8 月第 2 次印刷
ISBN　978-7-305-24173-4
定　　价　43.00 元

网　　址　http://www.njupco.com
官方微博　http://weibo.com/njupco
官方微信　njupress
销售热线　(025)83594756

* 版权所有,侵权必究
* 凡购买南大版图书,如有印装质量问题,请与所购图书销售部门联系调换

前言

随着我国高等学校英语教育的快速发展，长期以来英语专业贯彻的"以技能为导向"的课程建设与教学理念已经暴露出很多问题，诸如英语专业学生知识面狭窄、思辨能力偏弱、综合素质欠缺等。《高等学校英语专业本科教学质量国家标准》强调，英语专业主要以英语语言、英语文学和英语国家的社会文化等为学习和研究对象，教学过程强调实践和应用，人才培养突出人文素质教育，注重开阔学生的国际视野。《普通高等学校本科英语类专业教学指南》指出英语专业核心课程应设置体现人文属性的课程，如西方文明史、中国文化概要等。顺应"国标"的要求，从2016年开始，"西方人文思想经典"被正式确立为中国矿业大学外国语言文化学院英语专业的必修课。同时，该课程被越来越多的国内高校英语专业纳入培养方案，作为专业必修课，成为英语专业人文通识教育的重要组成部分。不仅如此，在国内众多综合性大学，西方人文思想经典阅读之类的课程也被纳入全校通识课程体系。本教材的编写与出版正是为了满足上述的教学之需。

《西方人文思想经典选读》是为通过了英语专业四级、大学英语六级考试或者具有同等水平的学生编写的一部依托专业知识内容，训练学生的语言综合运用能力，扩展学生的知识面，提高学生的多元文化意识，提升学生综合素质的英语教材。这本教材充分利用语言与思想之间的密切关系，分主题引导英语专业学生深度阅读并理解西方人文思想典籍，一方面帮助学生提高篇章理解能力，在更高层次夯实英语专业学生"听说读写译"的语言基本功，提升语言综合运用能力；另一方面帮助学生拓宽其在西方文化、哲学、美学等人文社会科学领域内的知识，增加英语专业学生对西方文化和人文脉络的总体把握，帮助学生了解西方文明的发展历程，掌握不同历史时期的重要人文思想，运用所学知识理性分析西方文明，并对西方文明和东方文明进行比较与思辨。通过思想对比与文化反思、融汇并对比东西方的思想精华，从而拓展文化视野，提升人文素养和逻辑思辨能力、跨文化交际能力和人文素养。本教材在编写时，根据党的二十大精神对具体内容做了一些调整。

本教材共11章，包括：希腊文化、罗马文化、文艺复兴、人文主义、科学革命、法国启蒙运动、美国启蒙运动、自由主义、进化论、社会主义与共产主义、存在主义。

本教材各单元的主要设计内容是：

1. 每一章前面有本章的整体导读，介绍与本章内容相关的历史与文化背景。

2. 每一篇选文前都配有导读（Pre-reading），介绍选文作者的生平、学术贡献、代表著作、主要思想与观点等内容。

3. 每一篇选文之后设计了帮助学生理解选文的拓展性思考题（Questions），可以在课堂讨论和提问时使用。

4. 每一章之后设计了综合性思考题（Questions for further reflection），可以在学生做小组陈述（Presentation）或者组织讨论（Leading the discussion）时使用。

本书建议采用课堂精讲、小组讨论、公开辩论等授课形式，以细读和讨论为主，鼓励学生全程参与。课程阅读量大、内容思想性强，语言有难度，研究性强，故要求学生课前阅读做好预习，课堂积极参与，课后研究，讨论和论文必须独立完成。

　　本书每个单元的教学安排建议如下：

　　1. 介绍本单元的教学内容。

　　2. 相关历史背景简述。

　　3. 2—3 组学生分别就本单元阅读内容向全班做汇报，回答其他同学和老师的提问。每位同学对 presentation 进行评分。

　　4. 教师就关键内容做进一步阐释。

　　5. 一组同学(2—3 人)组织课后问题讨论，其他同学和老师进一步提问或讨论。

　　6. 全班自由提问、讨论。

　　作业：每位学生必须参加汇报，参与课堂讨论，撰写每一章节的 response paper 和期末课程论文，考察其思辨能力和学术写作能力。

　　用英语开设西方人文思想经典、西方文明史等人文通识课程，能够强化英语专业的学科内涵，丰富英语专业的思想内容，彰显英语专业自身的品质与价值。我们并不是站在现代人的高度，带着现代人的傲慢之态来解读经典著作，而是以虔敬的心情对经典文本进行理解、诠释、研究，与古往今来之圣贤促膝交谈，希望通过诠释这些蕴藏着丰富文化资源的原著，获得智慧性的启迪，这也是本教材出版的意义。

Contents

Chapter 1   Greek Culture / 希腊文化 ··· 1
    The Apology / 申辩篇 ·· 2
    The Republic / 理想国 ·· 9

Chapter 2   Roman Culture / 罗马文化 ·· 17
    On Friendship / 谈友谊 ·· 19
    Meditations / 沉思录 ·· 24

Chapter 3   The Renaissance / 文艺复兴 ·· 31
    In Praise of Folly / 愚人颂 ··· 32
    Oration on the Dignity of Man / 论人的尊严 ··· 39

Chapter 4   Humanism / 人文主义 ··· 47
    Critique of Pure Reason / 纯粹理性批判 ··· 48
    A Treatise of Human Nature / 人性论 ·· 58

Chapter 5   Scientific Revolution / 科学革命 ·· 65
    Words / 人类理解新论 ··· 66
    Novum Organum / 新工具 ·· 71

Chapter 6   French Enlightenment / 法国启蒙运动 ··································· 80
    Philosophical Letters / 哲学信件 ··· 81
    The Social Contract / 社会契约论 ··· 89

Chapter 7   American Enlightenment / 美国启蒙运动 ································ 98
    The Age of Reason & Rights of Man / 《理性时代》和《人权宣言》 ················· 99
    The Declaration of Independence / 独立宣言 ·· 108

Chapter 8   Liberalism / 自由主义 ··· 114
    The Wealth of Nations / 国富论 ··· 115

  On Liberty / 论自由 ·· *128*

  Socialism: Utopian and Scientific / 社会主义：乌托邦与科学（历史唯物主义）

  ··· *133*

Chapter 9 *Evolutionism* / 进化论 ·· *149*

  On the Origin of Species / 物种起源 ································ *151*

Chapter 10 *Socialism and Communism* / 社会主义和共产主义 ············· *156*

  Critique of the Gotha Programme / 哥达纲领批判 ···················· *157*

  Socialism: Utopian and Scientific / 社会主义：乌托邦与科学（辨证法） *165*

Chapter 11 *Existentialism* / 存在主义 ···································· *174*

  Existentialism Is a Humanism / 存在主义是一种人道主义 ············ *177*

  Being and Time / 存在与时间 ·· *182*

目 录

第一章　希腊文化 ··· 1
　　申辩篇 ··· 2
　　理想国 ··· 9
第二章　罗马文化 ·· 19
　　谈友谊 ·· 24
　　沉思录 ·· 31
第三章　文艺复兴 ·· 32
　　愚人颂 ·· 39
　　论人的尊严 ·· 47
第四章　人文主义 ·· 47
　　纯粹理性批判 ······································ 48
　　人性论 ·· 58
第五章　科学革命 ·· 65
　　人类理解新论 ······································ 66
　　新工具 ·· 71
第六章　法国启蒙运动 ···································· 80
　　哲学信件 ·· 81
　　社会契约论 ·· 89
第七章　美国启蒙运动 ···································· 98
　　《理性时代》和《人权宣言》 ······················· 99
　　独立宣言 ··· 108
第八章　自由主义 ······································· 114
　　国富论 ··· 115

论自由 ……………………………………………………… 128
　　社会主义:乌托邦与科学(历史唯物主义) …………… 133
第九章　进化论 …………………………………………… 149
　　物种起源 ………………………………………………… 151
第十章　社会主义和共产主义 …………………………… 156
　　哥达纲领批判 …………………………………………… 157
　　社会主义:乌托邦与科学(辨证法) …………………… 165
第十一章　存在主义 ……………………………………… 174
　　存在主义是一种人道主义 ……………………………… 177
　　存在与时间 ……………………………………………… 182

Chapter 1   Greek Culture

Greece has a history of thousands of years, and therefore, its culture developed and evolved throughout this period. Starting during the Ancient Era in Mycenae and Classical Greece, the culture further developed during the Byzantine Era, before falling under Ottoman and Venetian rule.

Ancient Greece is considered the cradle of Western culture, democratic values and free speech. The civilization of the ancient Greeks was the foundation-head of Western culture. The Ancient Greeks made significant breakthroughs in many fields of science and philosophy, and they also developed important cultural means of expression, such as poetry, history, and drama. Socrates, Plato, and Aristotle established the foundations of Western philosophy. Herodotus and Thucydides created the discipline of history. Our literary forms are largely derived from Greek poetry and drama. Greek notions of harmony, proportion, and beauty have remained the touchstones for all subsequent Western art. A rational inquiry, so important to modern science, was conceived in ancient Greece. Many political terms are of Greek origin, and so are our concepts of the rights and duties of citizenship, especially as they were conceived in Athens, the first great democracy. Athens gave the idea of democracy to the Western world. Especially during their classical period, the Greeks raised and debated the fundamental questions about the purpose of human existence, the structure about human society, and the nature of the universe that have concerned Western thinkers ever since. In architecture, buildings fall under one of three categories or orders, based on their aesthetics, the Doric, the Ionic and the Corinthian order. These orders were later adopted by the Romans and were adapted to their tastes, introducing new traits and ornaments and creating their own architectural orders. The Greek language, which is a member of the Indo-European family, emerged during the pre-historic Mycenaean civilization as the Linear B script and evolved to form the Attic Greek, which is very close to Modern Greek.

Greek literature is particularly rich and extends over almost three millennia. Its first recorded works, which are also the first in Western culture, are the epic poems of Homer and Hesiod during the 8th century BC. *The Fables of Aesop* were written two centuries later; theatrical plays were also first created in Ancient Greece, along with the development of the scientific means of recording history, as can be noted in the works of Herodotus and Thucydides. All of the above, along with many other literary works, had a remarkable contribution in the development of literature in Europe in general.

During the antiquity, philosophical and scientific thinking developed considerably in Greece, by such important scholars as Thales, Democritus, Hippocrates, Thales of Miletus, Aristotle and Archimedes. The list is endless and the contribution of these personalities to the development of philosophy and science is immense.

Spanning over three millennia and receiving the influence of numerous other cultures and mentalities through the ages, the Greek culture is truly multi-faceted and unique in nature.

The Apology
Socrates

Pre-reading

The philosophy of ancient Greece reached its highest level of achievement in the works of Socrates, Plato, and Aristotle. The influence of these men on the culture of the Western world can scarcely be overestimated. Each of them made significant contributions to philosophy, and it would be difficult to determine to which one of them we are most indebted. All three were original thinkers and great teachers. In point of time, Socrates was the one who appeared first. Plato became the most distinguished of his pupils, and Aristotle in turn received instruction from Plato. Both Plato and Aristotle were prolific writers, and what we know about them has been derived chiefly from their published works. In contrast to them, Socrates left no writings at all. Consequently, what information we have concerning him comes from the testimony of others who were associated with him and who were influenced both by the moral quality of his living and the significance of the ideas that he expounded.

Although Socrates left no written records concerning himself, it is possible to reconstruct a fairly accurate account of his life from the writings of his Greek contemporaries. Aristophanes caricatured him in a work called *The Clouds*. Xenophon in his *Memorabilia* expressed high praise for Socrates, with special reference to the method that he advocated for selecting the rulers of a state. Plato, to whom we are most indebted for information about Socrates, made him the chief character in many of his famous dialogs. It is generally assumed that in Plato's earlier dialogs, the speeches attributed to Socrates are historical in the sense that they reproduce what Socrates actually said in the conversations he held with fellow Athenians. In the later dialogs, there is reason to believe that, at least in some instances, Plato was setting forth his own ideas by putting them into the mouth of Socrates. To what extent this was done is something that cannot be known with certainty.

Socrates was born in the city of Athens in 469 BC. He was the son of poor parents, his father being a sculptor and his mother a midwife. Early in life, he took up the occupation of his father and continued in it for a relatively brief period of time. Later he volunteered for service as a soldier in the Peloponnesian War. In the campaigns in which he fought, he showed himself to be a brave and loyal member of the fighting force. After his retirement from the army, most of his adult life was spent in response to what he believed to be a divine command to devote his time and energies to the pursuit of wisdom. It was in this connection that he felt called upon to examine himself by questioning other men. Accordingly, it was his custom to engage in conversation with all sorts and conditions of men and women on the streets, in the marketplace, or wherever it was convenient for them to meet. Their discussions covered a wide range of subjects, including such topics as love, marriage, politics, war, friendship, poetry, religion, science, government, and morals. The method that Socrates used in these discussions is known as dialectic. It consisted of conversations, the purpose of which was to bring to light the implications involved in different points of view and thus to expose the errors that they contained. He had a keen mind and was quick to discover the fallacies in an argument, and he was skillful in steering the conversations toward the very heart of the matter.

With regard to his personal appearance, it is said that Socrates was most unattractive. It is reported that he was short, stout, snub-nosed, and careless about his dress. However, these peculiarities were quickly forgotten by those who listened to his conversations. As soon as he began to speak, his listeners were charmed by his wit, his good humor, and his kindly disposition. His brilliant discourses, which covered a wide range of subjects, brought admiration and respect on the part of those who participated in the conversations with him. He was especially concerned with the subject of moral conduct. He not only talked about the virtues that are an essential part of the good life, but he exemplified in his own living the virtues that he taught others should seek for themselves. For example, he possessed to a remarkable degree the virtue of self-control. He never boasted of his own achievements. He was humble and intellectually honest. He was magnanimous in his attitude toward others. He was noble in character, frugal in his living, and a person of great endurance.

He is remembered not only for the quality of his living but for the content of his teachings. He believed that the most important topic that can occupy the mind is the meaning of the good life. He had no quarrel with the physicists and natural scientists of his day, who were trying to obtain a descriptive account of the way things are and the laws that govern their behavior. Important as this type of information might be, it was a matter of far greater significance to understand the meaning of human life and the way that people ought to live. The physical sciences do not reveal anything concerning the purpose for which things exist, nor do they tell us anything about the nature of goodness. They do not reveal what is good or bad, nor do they distinguish between what is morally right and wrong. A far more important type of inquiry has to do with knowledge of what constitutes the good life.

Although he rejected the popular conceptions of the Greek gods and their relation to human beings, Socrates believed that a divine providence had to do with the creation of the world and, further, that the purpose toward which it was directed was the achievement of the good life on the part of human beings. Man was something more than a physical organism. His body was the dwelling place of the soul, and what happens to the soul was vastly more important than what happens to the body.

An epitome of Socrates' moral philosophy can be expressed briefly in the statement "Virtue is knowledge." Virtues, he taught, are acquired through a fulfillment of the purpose for which one exists. In the case of a human, this would mean the harmonious development of the elements found in human nature and would apply to life as a whole rather than just the present moment or the immediate future. The knowledge to which this statement refers is something more than an awareness of facts concerning the order of the material universe. It involves an understanding of the soul in relation to the good life. It was Socrates' conviction that ignorance concerning the good life was the chief cause of the evil that people do. He did not believe that anyone would knowingly do that which was harmful to oneself. Virtue alone is capable of bringing satisfaction to the soul. Although this is the goal toward which everyone strives, not everyone reaches it. Their failures are due to the fact that they do not know what will bring lasting satisfaction. They pursue sensuous pleasures, material wealth, public esteem, and similar goals, thinking that these will bring about the greatest amount of happiness. When any one or all of these goals has been reached, they discover that objectives of this type do not bring about peace of mind, nor do they meet the demands of one's true or real self. It is only through the proper development of the mind in its pursuit of truth, beauty, and goodness that the goal and purpose of human life can be achieved.

With reference to the trial and death of Socrates, there are four dialogs that are especially relevant. They are *The Euthyphro*, *The Apology*, *The Crito*, and *The Phaedo*. *The Apology* is believed to be the most authentic account that has been preserved of Socrates' defense of himself as it was presented before the Athenian Council after he had been charged with being a corrupter of the youth and one who refuses to accept the popular beliefs concerning the gods of the city of Athens. It is generally regarded as the most authentic account on record of what Socrates actually said as he appeared before his judges. *The Apology* is in essential harmony with the references to the trial that occur in Plato's other dialogs and also with the account given in *Xenophon's Memorabilia*. It appears to record, in many instances, the exact words used by Socrates while making his speech in defense of himself. To be sure, the words were not recorded at the time they were spoken, but we know that Plato was present at the trial, and hence we may conclude that the account given in *The Apology* contains the words of Socrates as they were remembered by Plato. However, we should bear in mind that Plato had been both a pupil and an ardent admirer of Socrates, and for this reason his version of the trial may have been somewhat biased in favor of the one whom he regarded as a truly great hero. At any rate, we may be fairly certain that, even though Socrates has been to some extent idealized by his pupil, the account given represents what Plato believed to be true about his teacher. It is also possible that Socrates' defense of himself was even stronger than what has been reported.

The contents of the dialog include a number of different parts. The first one consists of an introductory statement that Socrates makes concerning the manner of his speaking. This is followed by an account of the specific accusations made with reference to his life and daily activities. Socrates replies at some length to each of the charges brought against him. After making his defense, an account is given of his attempt at mitigation of the penalty imposed on him. Finally, Socrates makes a prophetic rebuke of the judges for supposing they will live at ease and with an untroubled conscience after pronouncing sentence as a penalty for his crimes.

Now let's read the text and reflect on the questions that follow.

Text

How you, O Athenians, have been affected by my accusers, I cannot tell; but I know that they almost made me forget who I was—so persuasively did they speak; and yet they have hardly uttered a word of truth. But of the many falsehoods told by them, there was one which quite amazed me; I mean when they said that you should be upon your guard and not allow yourselves to be deceived by the force of my eloquence. To say this, when they were certain to be detected as soon as I opened my lips and proved myself to be anything but a great speaker, did indeed appear to me most shameless—unless by the force of eloquence they mean the force of truth; for if such is their meaning, I admit that I am eloquent. But in how different a way from theirs! Well, as I was saying, they have scarcely spoken the truth at all; but from me you shall hear the whole truth: not, however, delivered after their manner in a set oration duly ornamented with words and phrases. No, by heaven! But I shall use the words and arguments which occur to me at the moment; for I am confident in the justice of my cause (Or, I am certain that I am right in taking this course): at my time of life I ought not to be appearing before you, O men of Athens, in the character of a juvenile orator—let no one expect it of me. And I must beg of you to grant me a favor:—If I defend myself in my accustomed manner, and you hear me using the words which I have been in the habit of using in the agora, at the tables of the money-changers, or anywhere else, I would ask you not to be surprised, and not to interrupt me on this account. For I am more than seventy years of age, and appearing now for the first time in a court of law, I am quite a stranger to the language of the place; and therefore I would have you regard me as if I were really a stranger, whom you would excuse if he spoke in his native tongue, and after the fashion of his country:—Am I making an unfair request of you? Never mind the manner, which may or may not be good; but think only of the truth of my words, and give heed to that: let the speaker speak truly and the judge decide justly.

And first, I have to reply to the older charges and to my first accusers, and then I will go on to the later ones. For of old I have had many accusers, who have accused me falsely to you during many years; and I am more afraid of them than of Anytus and his associates, who are dangerous, too, in their own way. But far more dangerous are the others, who began when you were children, and took possession of your minds with their falsehoods, telling of one Socrates, a wise man, who speculated about the heaven above, and searched into the earth beneath, and made the worse appear the better cause. The disseminators of this tale are the accusers whom I dread; for their hearers are apt to fancy that such enquirers do not believe in the existence of the gods. And they are many, and their charges against me are of ancient date, and they were made by them in the days when you were more impressible than you are now—in childhood, or it may have been in youth—and the cause when heard went by default, for there was none to answer. And hardest of all, I do not know and cannot tell the names of my accusers; unless in the chance case of a Comic poet. All who from envy and malice have persuaded you—some of them having first convinced themselves—all this class of men are most difficult to deal with; for I cannot have them up here, and cross-examine them, and therefore I must simply fight with shadows in my own defence, and argue when there is no one who answers. I will ask you then to assume with me, as I was saying, that my opponents are of two kinds: one recent, the other ancient; and I hope that you will see the propriety of my answering the latter first, for these accusations you heard long before the others, and much oftener.

Well, then, I must make my defence, and endeavour to clear away in a short time, a slander which has lasted a long time. May I succeed, if to succeed be for my good and yours, or likely to avail me in my cause! The task is not an easy one; I quite understand the nature of it. And so leaving the event with God, in obedience to the law I will now make my defence.

I will begin at the beginning, and ask what is the accusation which has given rise to the slander of me, and in fact has encouraged Meletus to proof this charge against me. Well, what do the slanderers say? They shall be my prosecutors, and I will sum up their words in an affidavit: "Socrates is an evil-doer, and a curious person, who searches into things under the earth and in heaven, and he makes the worse appear the better cause; and he teaches the aforesaid doctrines to others." Such is the nature of the accusation: it is just what you have yourselves seen in the comedy of Aristophanes (Aristoph, Clouds), who has introduced a man whom he calls Socrates, going about and saying that he walks in air, and talking a deal of nonsense concerning matters of which I do not pretend to know either much or little—not that I mean to speak disparagingly of any one who is a student of natural philosophy. I should be very sorry if Meletus could bring so grave a charge against me. But the simple truth is, O Athenians, that I have nothing to do with physical speculations. Very many of those here present are witnesses to the truth of this, and to them I appeal. Speak then, you who have heard me, and tell your neighbours whether any of you have ever known me hold forth in few words or in many upon such matters … You hear their answer. And from what they say of this part of the charge you will be able to judge of the truth of the rest.

As little foundation is there for the report that I am a teacher, and take money; this accusation has no more truth in it than the other. Although, if a man were really able to instruct mankind, to receive money for giving instruction would, in my opinion, be an honor to him. There is Gorgias of Leontium, and Prodicus of Ceos, and Hippias of Elis, who go the round of the cities, and are able to persuade the young men to leave their own citizens by whom they might be taught for nothing, and come to them whom they not only pay, but are thankful if they may be allowed to pay them. There is at this time a Parian philosopher residing in Athens, of whom I have heard; and I came to hear of him in this way: — I came across a man who has spent a world of money on the Sophists, Callias, the son of Hipponicus, and knowing that he had sons, I asked him: "Callias," I said, "if your two sons were foals or calves, there would be no difficulty in finding some one to put over them; we should hire a trainer of horses, or a farmer probably, who would improve and perfect them in their own proper virtue and excellence; but as they are human beings, whom are you thinking of placing over them? Is there any one who understands human and political virtue? You must have thought about the matter, for you have sons; is there any one?" "There is," he said. "Who is he?" said I, "and of what country? and what does he charge?" "Evenus the Parian," he replied, "he is the man, and his charge is five minae." Happy is Evenus, I said to myself, if he really has this wisdom, and teaches at such a moderate charge. Had I the same, I should have been very proud and conceited; but the truth is that I have no knowledge of the kind.

I dare say, Athenians, that some one among you will reply, "Yes, Socrates, but what is the origin of these accusations which are brought against you; there must have been something strange which you have been doing? All these rumours and this talk about you would never have arisen if you had been like other men: tell us, then, what is the cause of them, for we should be sorry to judge hastily of you." Now I regard this as a fair challenge, and I will endeavour to explain to you the reason why I am called wise and have such an evil fame. Please to attend then. And although some of you may think that I am joking, I declare that I will tell you the entire truth. Men of Athens, this reputation of mine has come of a certain sort of wisdom which I possess. If you ask me what kind of wisdom, I reply, wisdom such as may perhaps be attained by man, for to that extent I am inclined to believe that I am wise; whereas the persons of whom I was speaking have a superhuman wisdom which I may fail to describe, because I have it not myself; and he who says that I have, speaks falsely, and is taking away my character. And here, O men of Athens, I must beg you not to interrupt me, even if I seem to say something extravagant. For the word which I will speak is not mine. I will refer you to a witness who is worthy of credit; that witness shall be the God of Delphi—he will tell you about my wisdom, if I have any, and of what sort it is. You must have known Chaerephon; he was early a friend of mine, and also a friend of yours, for he shared in the recent exile of the people, and returned with you. Well, Chaerephon, as you know, was very impetuous in all his doings, and he went to Delphi and boldly asked the oracle to tell him whether—as I was saying, I must beg you not to interrupt—he asked the oracle to tell him whether anyone was wiser than I was, and the Pythian prophetess answered, that there was no man wiser. Chaerephon is dead himself; but his brother, who is in court, will confirm the truth of what I am saying.

Why do I mention this? Because I am going to explain to you why I have such an evil name. When I heard the answer, I said to myself, "What can the god mean?" "and what is the interpretation of his riddle?" for I know that I have no wisdom, small or great. What then can he mean when he says that I am the wisest of men? And yet he is a god, and cannot lie; that would be against his nature. After long consideration, I thought of a method of trying the question. I reflected that if I could only find a man wiser than myself, then I might go to the god with a refutation in my hand. I should say to him, "Here is a man who is wiser than I am; but you said that I was the wisest." Accordingly I went to one who had the reputation of wisdom, and observed him—his name I need not mention; he was a politician whom I selected for examination—and the result was as follows: When I began to talk with him, I could not help thinking that he was not really wise, although he was thought wise by many, and still wiser by himself; and thereupon I tried to explain to him that he thought himself wise, but was not really wise; and the consequence was that he hated me, and his enmity was shared by several who were present and heard me. So I left him, saying to myself, as I went away: Well, although I do not suppose that either of us knows anything really beautiful and good, I am better off than he is—for he knows nothing, and thinks that he knows; I neither know nor think that I know. In this latter particular, then, I seem to have slightly the advantage of him. Then I went to another who had still higher pretensions to wisdom, and my conclusion was exactly the same. Whereupon I made another enemy of him, and of many others besides him.

...

At last I went to the artisans. I was conscious that I knew nothing at all, as I may say, and I was sure that they knew many fine things; and here I was not mistaken, for they did know many things of which I was ignorant, and in this they certainly were wiser than I was. But I observed that even the good artisans fell into the same error as the poets;—because they were good workmen they thought that they also knew all sorts of high matters, and this defect in them overshadowed their wisdom; and therefore I asked myself on behalf of the oracle, whether I would like to be as I was, neither having their knowledge nor their ignorance, or like them in both; and I made answer to myself and to the oracle that I was better off as I was.

This inquisition has led to my having many enemies of the worst and most dangerous kind, and has given occasion also to many calumnies. And I am called wise, for my hearers always imagine that I myself possess the wisdom which I find wanting in others: but the truth is, O men of Athens, that God only is wise; and by his answer he intends to show that the wisdom of men is worth little or nothing; he is not speaking of Socrates, he is only using my name by way of illustration, as if he said, He, O men, is the wisest, who, like Socrates, knows that his wisdom is in truth worth nothing. And so I go about the world, obedient to the god, and search and make enquiry into the wisdom of any one, whether citizen or stranger, who appears to be wise; and if he is not wise, then in vindication of the oracle I show him that he is not wise; and my occupation quite absorbs me, and I have no time to give either to any public matter of interest or to any concern of my own, but I am in utter poverty by reason of my devotion to the god.

There is another thing:—young men of the richer classes, who have not much to do, come about me of their own accord; they like to hear the pretenders examined, and they often imitate me, and proceed to examine others; there are plenty of persons, as they quickly discover, who think that they know something, but really know little or nothing; and then those who are examined by them instead of being angry with themselves are angry with me: This confounded Socrates, they say; this villainous misleader of youth!—and then if somebody asks them, Why, what evil does he practise or teach? they do not know, and cannot tell; but in order that they may not appear to be at a loss, they repeat the ready-made charges which are used against all philosophers about teaching things up in the clouds and under the earth, and having no gods, and making the worse appear the better cause; for they do not like to confess that their pretence of knowledge has been detected—which is the truth; and as they are numerous and ambitious and energetic, and are drawn up in battle array and have persuasive tongues, they have filled your ears with their loud and inveterate calumnies. And this is the reason why my three accusers, Meletus and Anytus and Lycon, have set upon me; Meletus, who has a quarrel with me on behalf of the poets; Anytus, on behalf of the craftsmen and politicians; Lycon, on behalf of the rhetoricians; and as I said at the beginning, I cannot expect to get rid of such a mass of calumny all in a moment. And this, O men of Athens, is the truth and the whole truth; I have concealed nothing, I have dissembled nothing. And yet, I know that my plainness of speech makes them hate me, and what is their hatred but a proof that I am speaking the truth? Hence has arisen the prejudice against me; and this is the reason of it, as you will find out either in this or in any future enquiry.

Questions

1. Socrates states that he will reply to two kinds of accusation brought against him. What were they, and why did he find it so difficult to deal with the first one?
2. How did Socrates reconcile the statement made by the oracle at Delphi that he was the wisest man in Athens with his own admittance of ignorance?
3. How did Socrates account for the popular prejudice that led so many people to be suspicious of him and his work?
4. What, according to Meletus, was the crime of which Socrates was accused? What do you think was the real reason why Meletus was opposed to Socrates?
5. How did Socrates reply to the charge that he was a corrupter of the youth? What was it that led people to think he was guilty?
6. Why did Socrates reject many of the popular beliefs concerning the Athenian gods? Was Socrates an atheist? Give reasons for your answer.
7. Why did Socrates believe it would be wrong for him to escape? Did he believe all laws authorized by the state should be obeyed?
8. How did Socrates reconcile his position about obedience to the laws of the state with his conviction that it is morally right to disobey laws that are unjust? Distinguish moral and legal rights.

The Republic

Plato

Pre-reading

Among those who were influenced by the life and teachings of Socrates, no one has done more to perpetuate his memory than Plato, who has long been recognized as one of the greatest philosophers of ancient Greece and one of the most profound thinkers of all time. Plato was too young to have been one of Socrates' most intimate friends. It was not until the last seven or eight years of Socrates' life that Plato came under his influence, but those years made a lasting impression on his life and determined to a large extent the future course of his life. In his later years, Plato is reported to have said, "I thank God that I was born Greek and not barbarian, free and not slave, male and not female, but above all that I was born in the age of Socrates."

Owing to the fact that he was ill at the time, Plato was not present when a group of Socrates' friends came to the prison for their last visit with him. However, he had been so deeply impressed by the moral quality of Socrates' teachings and his devotion to the cause of truth and justice that he determined to perpetuate his memory by writing a series of biographical dialogs in which his true character would be brought to light. Even after Plato's own thought had matured, he continued to make Socrates the protagonist of his dialogs. The result has been such a blending of views that in several instances it is difficult, if not impossible, to tell where the actual historical Socrates leaves off and Plato's own thought begins.

Plato was born in the city of Athens in the year 427 BC. He died in the year 347 BC. He came from an aristocratic family that for a long time had been identified with leadership in Athens. His father, Ariston, was a descendant of King Codrus, and his mother, whose name was Perictione, claimed to have been descended from the famous lawgiver Solon. As a boy, he was named Aristocles, but because of his broad shoulders and forehead he was called Plato, and it is by this name that he has become known to posterity. During his youth, he gained distinction as an athlete and was also recognized for his extraordinary mental abilities. In addition to his achievements along these lines, his social standing and connections would have made him an outstanding individual in any career he might have entered.

He lived during a critical period of Greek history. His youth saw the decline and fall of Athenian power but not of Athenian genius. His early education began under the supervision of private tutors who were well known for their professional skills. Under their guidance, he received instruction in the elementary disciplines, such as gymnastics, music, reading, writing, and the study of numbers. After reaching the age of eighteen or thereabouts, he spent two years in military training, which placed considerable emphasis on physical exercises and the proper care of the body. This training was followed by a more advanced period of study in which he gained familiarity with several of the more prominent schools of Greek philosophy, which gave him an opportunity to become acquainted with many of the Sophists, who were the recognized professional teachers of that time. Finally, Plato spent about seven or eight years as a pupil of Socrates. This experience influenced him, not only to devote the rest of his life to philosophy, but to carry on his career in the spirit and under the guidance of his beloved teacher.

Because Socrates had been put to death under the auspices of the Athenian government, Plato believed that it would not be safe for him to remain in the city and thus expose himself to the same kind of treatment. It was well known that Plato had been one of Socrates' followers and that he was most sympathetic toward the ideas that his teacher had proclaimed. So long as these ideas were regarded as harmful to the state, anyone who subscribed to them would be in danger. For this reason, Plato left the city of Athens for a time and journeyed to a number of different places, where he hoped to become better acquainted with the leaders of a number of philosophical movements. At first he went to Megara, where he carried on conversations with Euclid, the famous mathematician. Later, he made extensive journeys to Egypt, Cyrene, Crete, and southern Italy. These excursions gave him an opportunity to become better acquainted with the leaders of each of the schools founded, respectively, by Pythagoras, Heraclitus, and the Eleatic philosophers.

When Plato was approximately forty years of age, he undertook an experiment in government. From his early youth he had been interested in political affairs. From his associations with Socrates and from his own observations, he had arrived at certain convictions concerning the proper qualifications for those whose duty was to govern the state. He believed that only those persons who possessed intellectual as well as moral qualities should be entrusted with the power to rule over others. Eventually, the opportunity came to him to put his philosophy into practice. At Syracuse, on the coast of the island of Sicily, a friend and pupil by the name of Dion urged him to undertake the education of Dionysius, the tyrant of Syracuse. Dionysius appeared to be willing to take instruction from Plato, which would make it possible for Plato's theory of government to be tried out under actual conditions. The experiment was not a success, for Dionysius was not an apt pupil, and when Plato rebuked him for his stupidity, the tyrant retaliated by having Plato put in chains and sentenced to death. Dion used his influence to get the sentence changed. The result was that Plato's life was spared but at the price of being made a slave. Soon afterward Anniceris, a member of the Cyrenaic school of philosophy, came to Syracuse and purchased Plato's freedom, thus allowing him to return to Athens.

After returning to Athens, Plato established his school, an institution that came to be known as the Academy. It continued for a period of more than eight centuries as a center for the study and evaluation of Platonic philosophy. With the establishment of the Academy, Plato devoted most of his time to teaching and the writing of dialogs. Fortunately, these dialogs have been preserved, and they constitute the chief source of the information we have concerning the various aspects of his philosophy.

The Republic is arguably the most popular and most widely taught of Plato's writings. Although it contains its dramatic moments and it employs certain literary devices, it is not a play, a novel, a story; it is not, in a strict sense, an essay. It is a kind of extended conversation that embraces a central argument, an argument that is advanced by the proponent of the argument, Socrates. *The Republic* may be seen as a kind of debate, a fitting description for most of the Dialogues.

The Republic of Plato is the longest of his works with the exception of the Laws, and is certainly the greatest of them. No other Dialogue of Plato has the same largeness of view and the same perfection of style; no other shows an equal knowledge of the world, or contains more of those thoughts which are new as well as old, and not of one age only but of all. Nowhere in Plato is there a deeper irony or a greater wealth of humor or imagery, or more dramatic power. Nor in any other of his writings is the attempt made to interweave life and speculation, or to connect politics with philosophy. *The Republic* is the center around which the other Dialogues may be grouped; here philosophy reaches the highest point (especially in Books V, VI, VII) to which ancient thinkers ever attained. Plato among the Greeks, like Bacon among the moderns, was the first who conceived a method of knowledge, although neither of them always distinguished the bare outline or form from the substance of truth; and both of them had to be content with an abstraction of science which was not yet realized. He was the greatest metaphysical genius whom the world has seen; and in him, more than in any other ancient thinker, the germs of future knowledge are contained. The sciences of logic and psychology, which have supplied so many instruments of thought to after-ages, are based upon the analyses of Socrates and Plato. The principles of definition, the law of contradiction, the fallacy of arguing in a circle, the distinction between the essence and accidents of a thing or notion, between means and ends, between causes and conditions; also the division of the mind into the rational, concupiscent, and irascible elements, or of pleasures and desires into necessary and unnecessary—these and other great forms of thought are all of them to be found in *The Republic*, and were probably first invented by Plato.

The division into books, like all similar divisions, is probably later than the age of Plato. The natural divisions are five in number—(1) Book I and the first half of Book II down to the paragraph beginning, "I had always admired the genius of Glaucon and Adeimantus," which is introductory; the first book containing a refutation of the popular and sophistical notions of justice, and concluding, like some of the earlier Dialogues, without arriving at any definite result. To this is appended a restatement of the nature of justice according to common opinion, and an answer is demanded to the question—what is justice, stripped of appearances? The second division (2) includes the remainder of the second and the whole of the third and fourth books, which are mainly occupied with the construction of the first State and the first education. The third division (3) consists of the fifth, sixth, and seventh books, in which philosophy rather than justice is the subject of enquiry, and the second State is constructed on principles of communism and ruled by philosophers, and the contemplation of the idea of good takes the place of the social and political virtues. In the eighth and ninth books (4) the perversions of States and of the individuals who correspond to them are reviewed in succession; and the nature of pleasure and the principle of tyranny are further analyzed in the individual man. The tenth book (5) is the conclusion of the whole, in which the relations of philosophy to poetry are finally determined, and the happiness of the citizens in this life, which has now been assured, is crowned by the vision of another.

Now let's read the text and reflect on the questions that follow.

Text

AND now, I said, let me show in a figure how far our nature is enlightened or unenlightened:—Behold! human beings living in a underground den, which has a mouth open towards the light and reaching all along the den; here they have been from their childhood, and have their legs and necks chained so that they cannot move, and can only see before them, being prevented by the chains from turning round their heads. Above and behind them a fire is blazing at a distance, and between the fire and the prisoners there is a raised way; and you will see, if you look, a low wall built along the way, like the screen which marionette players have in front of them, over which they show the puppets.

I see.

And do you see, I said, men passing along the wall carrying all sorts of vessels, and statues and figures of animals made of wood and stone and various materials, which appear over the wall? Some of them are talking, others silent.

You have shown me a strange image, and they are strange prisoners.

Like ourselves, I replied; and they see only their own shadows, or the shadows of one another, which the fire throws on the opposite wall of the cave?

True, he said; how could they see anything but the shadows if they were never allowed to move their heads?

And of the objects which are being carried in like manner they would only see the shadows?

Yes, he said.

And if they were able to converse with one another, would they not suppose that they were naming what was actually before them?

Very true.

The prisoners would mistake the shadows for realities. And suppose further that the prison had an echo which came from the other side, would they not be sure to fancy when one of the passers-by spoke that the voice which they heard came from the passing shadow?

No question, he replied.

To them, I said, the truth would be literally nothing but the shadows of the images.

That is certain.

And now look again, and see what will naturally follow if the prisoners are released and disabused of their error. At first, when any of them is liberated and compelled suddenly to stand up and turn his neck round and walk and look towards the light, he will suffer sharp pains; the glare will distress him, and he will be unable to see the realities of which in his former state he had seen the shadows; and then conceive some one saying to him, that what he saw before was an illusion, but that now, when he is approaching nearer to being and his eye is turned towards more real existence, he has a clearer vision,—what will be his reply? And when released, they would still persist in maintaining the superior truth of the shadows. And you may further imagine that his instructor is pointing to the objects as they pass and requiring him to name them,—will he not be perplexed? Will he not fancy that the shadows which he formerly saw are truer than the objects which are now shown to him?

...

Nothing extraordinary in the philosopher being unable to see in the dark, and is there anything surprising in one who passes from divine contemplations to the evil state of man, misbehaving himself in a ridiculous manner; if, while his eyes are blinking and before he has become accustomed to the surrounding darkness, he is compelled to fight in courts of law, or in other places, about the images or the shadows of images of justice, and is endeavoring to meet the conceptions of those who have never yet seen absolute justice?

Anything but surprising, he replied.

The eyes may be blinded in two ways, by excess or by defect of light. Any one who has common sense will remember that the bewilderments of the eyes are of two kinds, and arise from two causes, either from coming out of the light or from going into the light, which is true of the mind's eye, quite as much as of the bodily eye; and he who remembers this when he sees any one whose vision is perplexed and weak, will not be too ready to laugh; he will first ask whether that soul of man has come out of the brighter life, and is unable to see because unaccustomed to the dark, or having turned from darkness to the day is dazzled by excess of light. And he will count the one happy in his condition and state of being, and he will pity the other; or, if he have a mind to laugh at the soul which comes from below into the light, there will be more reason in this than in the laugh which greets him who returns from above out of the light into the den.

That, he said, is a very just distinction.

The conversion of the soul is the turning round of the eye from darkness to light. But then, if I am right, certain professors of education must be wrong when they say that they can put a knowledge into the soul which was not there before, like sight into blind eyes.

They undoubtedly say this, he replied.

Whereas, our argument shows that the power and capacity of learning exists in the soul already; and that just as the eye was unable to turn from darkness to light without the whole body, so too the instrument of knowledge can only by the movement of the whole soul be turned from the world of becoming into that of being, and learn by degrees to endure the sight of being, and of the brightest and best of being, or in other words, of the good.

Very true.

And must there not be some art which will effect conversion in the easiest and quickest manner; not implanting the faculty of sight, for that exists already, but has been turned in the wrong direction, and is looking away from the truth?

Yes, he said, such an art may be presumed.

The virtue of wisdom has a divine power which may be turned either towards good or towards evil. And whereas the other so-called virtues of the soul seem to be akin to bodily qualities, for even when they are not originally innate they can be implanted later by habit and exercise, the virtue of wisdom more than anything else contains a divine element which always remains, and by this conversion is rendered useful and profitable; or, on the other hand, hurtful and useless. Did you never observe the narrow intelligence flashing from the keen eye of a clever rogue—how eager he is, how clearly his paltry soul sees the way to his end; he is the reverse of blind, but his keen eye-sight is forced into the service of evil, and he is mischievous in proportion to his cleverness?

Very true, he said.

But what if there had been a circumcision of such natures in the days of their youth; and they had been severed from those sensual pleasures, such as eating and drinking, which, like leaden weights, were attached to them at their birth, and which drag them down and turn the vision of their souls upon the things that are below—if, I say, they had been released from these impediments and turned in the opposite direction, the very same faculty in them would have seen the truth as keenly as they see what their eyes are turned to now.

Very likely.

Neither the uneducated nor the overeducated will be good servants of the State. Yes, I said; and there is another thing which is likely, or rather a necessary inference from what has preceded, that neither the uneducated and uninformed of the truth, nor yet those who never make an end of their education, will be able ministers of State; not the former, because they have no single aim of duty which is the rule of all their actions, private as well as public; nor the latter, because they will not act at all except upon compulsion, fancying that they are already dwelling apart in the islands of the blest.

Very true, he replied.

Then, I said, the business of us who are the founders of the State will be to compel the best minds to attain that knowledge which we have already shown to be the greatest of all—they must continue to ascend until they arrive at the good; but when they have ascended and seen enough we must not allow them to do as they do now.

What do you mean?

Men should ascend to the upper world, but they should also return to the lower. I mean that they remain in the upper world: but this must not be allowed; they must be made to descend again among the prisoners in the den, and partake of their labors and honors, whether they are worth having or not.

But is not this unjust? he said; ought we to give them a worse life, when they might have a better?

You have again forgotten, my friend, I said, the intention of the legislator, who did not aim at making any one class in the State happy above the rest; the happiness was to be in the whole State, and he held the citizens together by persuasion and necessity, making them benefactors of the State, and therefore benefactors of one another; to this end he created them, not to please themselves, but to be his instruments in binding up the State.

...

No question.

Who then are those whom we shall compel to be guardians? Surely they will be the men who are wisest about affairs of State, and by whom the State is best administered, and who at the same time have other honors and another and a better life than that of politics?

They are the men, and I will choose them, he replied.

And now shall we consider in what way such guardians will be produced, and how they are to be brought from darkness to light,—as some are said to have ascended from the world below to the gods?

By all means, he replied.

Questions

1. What is the main argument in Plato's *Republic*, Book Ⅶ?
2. What is the conventional interpretation of "Allegory of the Cave" in Plato's *Republic*?
3. How does one better understand Plato's "Myth of the Cave"?
4. In Plato's "Allegory of the Cave," in what types of activities are the prisoners engaged?
5. How does the allegory of the cave relate to the theory of form?
6. How do the doctrines of Determinism and Free Will contrast, and how does one use either Determinism or Free Will to interpret Plato's myth?

Questions for Further Reflection

1. Why is ancient Greek Civilization the cradle of Western Civilization? How is it different from other ancient civilizations in the world?
2. Why was Socrates sentenced to death? Why did Plato criticize democracy?
3. How was Plato significant in Western Civilization? How were his wittings influential on societies: Ethics, Politics, The Republic, Symposium and Socrates dialogues?
4. How would you explain Aristotle views on pleasure with reference to the ethics and Plato's view on pleasure?
5. As a towering figure in ancient Greek philosophy, Why did Aristotle fail to anticipate the great success of Alexander?

References and Further Reading

1. Aristotle.(1999). *Metaphysics*. (Joe Sachs, trans.). Santa Fe: Green Lion Press.
2. Aristotle.(2002). *Nicomachean Ethics*. (Joe Sachs, trans.). Focus Philosophical Library, Pullins Press.
3. Aristotle.(2006) *On the Soul*. (Joe Sachs, trans.). Santa Fe: Green Lion Press.
4. Aristotle.(2006). *Poetics*. (Joe Sachs, trans.). Newburyport, M.A.: Focus Philosophical Library/ Pullins Press.
5. Aristotle.(1995). *Physics*. (Joe Sachs, trans.). Piscataway, N.J.: Rutgers U. P.
6. Benson, H. H. (ed.).(1992). *Essays on the Philosophy of Socrates*. New York: Oxford University Press.
7. Brickhouse, T. C. & Smith, N. D.(1994). *Plato's Socrates*. New York: Oxford University Press.
8. Brickhouse, T. C. & Smith, N. D. (2000). *The Philosophy of Socrates*. Boulder: Westview.
9. Morrison, D. R.(2012). *The Cambridge Companion to Socrates*. Cambridge: Cambridge University Press.
10. Rudebusch, G.(2009). *Socrates*. Malden, MA: Wiley-Blackwell.

Chapter 2   Roman Culture

According to legend, Ancient Rome was founded by the two brothers, and demigods, Romulus and Remus, on 21 April 753 BCE. The legend claims that in an argument over who would rule the city (or, in another version, where the city would be located), Romulus killed Remus and named the city after himself.

Originally a small town on the banks of the Tiber, Rome grew in size and strength, early on, through trade. The location of the city provided merchants with an easily navigable waterway on which to traffic their goods. The city was ruled by seven kings, from Romulus to Tarquin, as it grew in size and power. Greek culture and civilization, which came to Rome via Greek colonies to the south, provided the early Romans with a model on which to build their own culture. From the Greeks they borrowed literacy and religion as well as the fundamentals of architecture.

From the start, the Romans showed a talent for borrowing and improving upon the skills and concepts of other cultures. The Kingdom of Rome grew rapidly from a trading town to a prosperous city between the 8th and 6th centuries BCE. When the last of the seven kings of Rome, Tarquin the Proud, was deposed in 509 BCE, his rival for power, Lucius Junius Brutus, reformed the system of government and established the Roman Republic.

In the late 6th century BCE, the small city-state of Rome overthrew the shackles of monarchy and created a republican government that, in theory if not always in practice, represented the wishes of its citizens. From this basis the city would go on to conquer all of the Italian peninsula and large parts of the Mediterraean world and beyond. The Republic and its institutions of government would endure for five centuries, until, wrecked by civil wars, it would transform into a Principate ruled by emperors.

During the early Roman Republic, important new political offices and institutions were created, and old ones were adapted to cope with the changing needs of the state. The two consuls (who had come to replace the king) were primarily generals whose task was to lead Rome's armies in war. The Senate, which may have existed under the monarchy and served as an advisory council for the king, now advised both magistrates and the Roman people. During the republic there were two different popular assemblies, the centuriate assembly and the tribal assembly. In 451 BCE Rome received its first written law code, inscribed upon 12 bronze tablets and publicly displayed in the forum. This so-called *Law of the Twelve Tables* was to form the basis of all subsequent Roman private law.

During the 6th century BCE, Rome became one of the more important states in Latium.

Toward the end of the 5th century BCE, the Romans began to expand at the expense of the Etruscan states, possibly propelled by population growth. The ensuing Latin War (340 – 338 BCE) was quickly decided in Rome's favour. Rome was now the master of central Italy and spent the next decade pushing forward its frontier through conquest and colonization. The Romans occupied Carthage and eventually destroyed it completely in 146. The Romans organized the conquered peoples into provinces—under the control of appointed governors with absolute power over all non-Roman citizens—and stationed troops in each, ready to exercise appropriate force if necessary. The ensuing period of unrest and revolution marked the transition of Rome from a republic to an empire.

The Roman Empire, at its height, was the most extensive political and social structure in western civilization. By 285 CE the empire had grown too vast to be ruled from the central government at Rome and so was divided by Emperor Diocletian (r. 284 – 305 CE) into a Western and an Eastern Empire. The Roman Empire began when Augustus Caesar (r. 27 BCE – 14 CE) became the first emperor of Rome and ended, in the west, when the last Roman emperor, Romulus Augustulus (r. 475 – 476 CE), was deposed by the Germanic King Odoacer (r. 476 – 493 CE). In the east, it continued as the Byzantine Empire until the death of Constantine XI (r. 1449 – 1453 CE) and the fall of Constantinople to the Ottoman Turks in 1453 CE. The influence of the Roman Empire on western civilization was profound in its lasting contributions to virtually every aspect of western culture.

The inventions and innovations which were generated by the Roman Empire profoundly altered the lives of the ancient people and continue to be used in cultures around the world today. Advancements in the construction of roads and buildings, indoor plumbing, aqueducts, and even fast-drying cement were either invented or improved upon by the Romans. The calendar used in the West derives from the one created by Julius Caesar, and the names of the days of the week (in the romance languages) and months of the year also come from Rome. Even the practice of returning some purchase one finds one does not want come from Rome whose laws made it legal for a consumer to bring back some defective or unwanted merchandise to the seller.

Apartment complexes (known as insula), public toilets, locks and keys, newspapers, even socks, all were developed by the Romans as were shoes, a postal system (modeled after the Persians), cosmetics, the magnifying glass, and the concept of satire in literature. During the time of the empire, significant developments were also advanced in the fields of medicine, law, religion, government, and warfare. The Romans were adept at borrowing from, and improving upon those inventions or concepts they found among the indigenous populace of the regions they conquered. It is therefore difficult to say what is an "original" Roman invention and what is an innovation on a pre-existing concept, technique, or tool. It can safely be said, however, that the Roman Empire left an enduring legacy which continues to affect the way in which people live in the present day.

On Friendship

Marcus Tullius Cicero

Pre-reading

Marcus Tullius Cicero (106 – 43 BCE) was a Roman statesman, orator, lawyer and philosopher, who served as consul in the year 63 BCE. He came from a wealthy municipal family of the Roman equestrian order, and is considered one of Rome's greatest orators and prose stylists.

His influence on the Latin language was so immense that the subsequent history of prose, not only in Latin but in European languages up to the 19th century, was said to be either a reaction against or a return to his style. Cicero introduced the Romans to the chief schools of Greek philosophy and created a Latin philosophical vocabulary distinguishing himself as a translator and philosopher.

Though he was an accomplished orator and successful lawyer, Cicero believed his political career was his most important achievement. It was during his consulship that the second Catilinarian conspiracy attempted to overthrow the government through an attack on the city by outside forces, and Cicero suppressed the revolt by summarily and controversially executing five conspirators. During the chaotic latter half of the 1st century BCE marked by civil wars and the dictatorship of Gaius Julius Caesar, Cicero championed a return to the traditional republican government. Following Julius Caesar's death, Cicero became an enemy of Mark Antony in the ensuing power struggle, attacking him in a series of speeches. He was proscribed as an enemy of the state by the Second Triumvirate and consequently executed by soldiers operating on their behalf in 43 BCE after having been intercepted during an attempted flight from the Italian peninsula. His severed hands and head were then, as a final revenge of Mark Antony, displayed on the rostra.

The peak of Cicero's authority and prestige came during the 18th-century Enlightenment, and his impact on leading Enlightenment thinkers and political theorists was substantial. His works rank among the most influential in European culture, and today still constitute one of the most important bodies of primary material for the writing and revision of Roman history, especially the last days of the Roman Republic.

As a philosopher, Cicero's most important function was to make his countrymen familiar with the main schools of Greek thought. Much of this writing is thus of secondary interest to us in comparison with his originals, but in the fields of religious theory and of the application of philosophy to life he made important first-hand contributions. From these works have been selected the two treatises, *On Old Age* and *On Friendship*, which have proved of most permanent and widespread interest to posterity, and which give a clear impression of the way in which a high-minded Roman thought about some of the main problems of human life.

Now let's read the text and reflect on the questions that follow.

Text

5. Laelius. I should certainly have no objection if I felt confidence in myself. For the theme is a noble one, and we are (as Fannius has said) at leisure. But who am I and what ability have I? What you propose is all very well for professional philosophers, who are used, particularly if Greeks, to have the subject for discussion proposed to them on the spur of the moment. It is a task of considerable difficulty, and requires no little practice. Therefore for a set discourse on friendship you must go, I think, to professional lecturers. All I can do is to urge on you to regard friendship as the greatest thing in the world; for there is nothing which so fits in with our nature, or is so exactly what we want in prosperity or adversity.

But I must at the very beginning lay down this principle—friendship can only exist between good men. I do not, however, press this too closely, like the philosophers who push their definitions to a superfluous accuracy. They have truth on their side, perhaps, but it is of no practical advantage. Those, I mean, who say that no one but the "wise" is "good." Granted, by all means. But the "wisdom" they mean is one to which no mortal ever yet attained. We must concern ourselves with the facts of everyday life as we find it—not imaginary and ideal perfections. Even Gaius Fannius, Manius Curius, and Tiberius Coruncanius, whom our ancestors decided to be "wise," I could never declare to be so according to their standard. Let them, then, keep this word "wisdom" to themselves. Everybody is irritated by it; no one understands what it means. Let them but grant that the men I mentioned were "good." No, they won't do that either. No one but the "wise" can be allowed that title, say they. Well, then, let us dismiss them and manage as best we may with our own poor mother wit, as the phrase is.

We mean then by the "good" those whose actions and lives leave no question as to their honour, purity, equity, and liberality; who are free from greed, lust, and violence; and who have the courage of their convictions. The men I have just named may serve as examples. Such men as these being generally accounted "good," let us agree to call them so, on the ground that to the best of human ability they follow nature as the most perfect guide to a good life.

Now this truth seems clear to me, that nature has so formed us that a certain tie unites us all, but that this tie becomes stronger from proximity. So it is that fellow-citizens are preferred in our affections to foreigners, relations to strangers; for in their case Nature herself has caused a kind of friendship to exist, though it is one which lacks some of the elements of permanence. Friendship excels relationship in this, that whereas you may eliminate affection from relationship, you cannot do so from friendship. Without it relationship still exists in name, friendship does not. You may best understand this friendship by considering that, whereas the merely natural ties uniting the human race are indefinite, this one is so concentrated, and confined to so narrow a sphere, that affection is ever shared by two persons only or at most by a few.

6. Now friendship may be thus defined: a complete accord on all subjects human and divine, joined with mutual goodwill and affection. And with the exception of wisdom, I am inclined to think nothing better than this has been given to man by the immortal gods. There are people who give the palm to riches or to good health, or to power and office, many even to sensual pleasures. This last is the ideal of brute beasts; and of the others we may say that they are frail and uncertain, and depend less on our own prudence than on the caprice of fortune. Then there are those who find the "chief good" in virtue. Well, that is a noble doctrine. But the very virtue they talk of is the parent and preserver of friendship, and without it friendship cannot possibly exist.

Let us, I repeat, use the word virtue in the ordinary acceptation and meaning of the term, and do not let us define it in high-flown language. Let us account as good the persons usually considered so, such as Paulus, Cato, Gallus, Scipio, and Philus. Such men as these are good enough for everyday life; and we need not trouble ourselves about those ideal characters which are nowhere to be met with.

Well, between men like these, the advantages of friendship are almost more than I can say. To begin with, how can life be worth living, to use the words of Ennius, which lacks that repose which is to be found in the mutual good-will of a friend? What can be more delightful than to have some one to whom you can say everything with the same absolute confidence as to yourself? Is not prosperity robbed of half its value if you have no one to share your joy? On the other hand, misfortunes would be hard to bear if there were not some one to feel them even more acutely than yourself. In a word, other objects of ambition serve for particular ends—riches for use, power for securing homage, office for reputation, pleasure for enjoyment, health for freedom from pain and the full use of the functions of the body. But friendship embraces innumerable advantages. Turn which way you please, you will find it at hand. It is everywhere; and yet never out of place, never unwelcome. Fire and water themselves, to use a common expression, are not of more universal use than friendship. I am not now speaking of the common or modified form of it, though even that is a source of pleasure and profit, but of that true and complete friendship which existed between the select few who are known to fame. Such friendship enhances prosperity, and relieves adversity of its burden by halving and sharing it.

7. And great and numerous as are the blessings of friendship, this certainly is the sovereign one, that it gives us bright hopes for the future and forbids weakness and despair. In the face of a true friend a man sees as it were a second self. So that where his friend is he is; if his friend be rich, he is not poor; though he be weak, his friend's strength is his; and in his friend's life he enjoys a second life after his own is finished. This last is perhaps the most difficult to conceive. But such is the effect of the respect, the loving remembrance, and the regret of friends which follow us to the grave. While they take the sting out of death, they add a glory to the life of the

survivors. Nay, if you eliminate from nature the tie of affection, there will be an end of house and city, nor will so much as the cultivation of the soil be left. If you don't see the virtue of friendship and harmony, you may learn it by observing the effects of quarrels and feuds. Was any family ever so well established, any State so firmly settled, as to be beyond the reach of utter destruction from animosities and factions? This may teach you the immense advantage of friendship.

They say that a certain philosopher of Agrigentum, in a Greek poem, pronounced with the authority of an oracle the doctrine that whatever in nature and the universe was unchangeable was so in virtue of the binding force of friendship; whatever was changeable was so by the solvent power of discord. And indeed this is a truth which everybody understands and practically attests by experience. For if any marked instance of loyal friendship in confronting or sharing danger comes to light, every one applauds it to the echo. What cheers there were, for instance, all over the theatre at a passage in the new play of my friend and guest Pacuvius; where the king, not knowing which of the two was Orestes, Pylades declared himself to be Orestes, that he might die in his stead, while the real Orestes kept on asserting that it was he. The audience rose en masse and clapped their hands. And this was at an incident in fiction: what would they have done, must we suppose, if it had been in real life? You can easily see what a natural feeling it is, when men who would not have had the resolution to act thus themselves, shewed how right they thought it in another.

I don't think I have any more to say about friendship. If there is any more, and I have no doubt there is much, you must, if you care to do so, consult those who profess to discuss such matters.

...

8. Laclius. Now you are really using force. It makes no difference what kind of force you use: force it is. For it is neither easy nor right to refuse a wish of my sons-in-law, particularly when the wish is a creditable one in itself.

Well, then, it has very often occurred to me when thinking about friendship, that the chief point to be considered was this: is it weakness and want of means that make friendship desired? I mean, is its object an interchange of good offices, so that each may give that in which he is strong, and receive that in which he is weak? Or is it not rather true that, although this is an advantage naturally belonging to friendship, yet its original cause is quite other, prior in time, more noble in character, and springing more directly from our nature itself? The Latin word for friendship—amicitia—is derived from that for love—amor; and love is certainly the prime mover in contracting mutual affection. For as to material advantages, it often happens that those are obtained even by men who are courted by a mere show of friendship and treated with respect from interested motives. But friendship by its nature admits of no feigning, no pretence: as far as it goes it is both genuine and spontaneous. Therefore I gather that friendship springs from a natural impulse rather than a wish for help: from an inclination of the heart, combined with a certain instinctive feeling of love, rather than from a deliberate calculation of the material advantage it was likely to confer. The strength of this feeling you may notice in certain animals. They show such love to their offspring for a certain period, and are so beloved by them, that they clearly have a share in this natural, instinctive affection. But of course it is more evident in the case of man: first, in the natural affection between children and their parents, an affection which only shocking wickedness can sunder; and next, when the passion of love has attained to a like strength—on our finding, that is, some one person with whose character and nature we are in full sympathy, because we think that we perceive in him what I may call the beacon-light of virtue. For nothing inspires love, nothing conciliates affection, like virtue. Why, in a certain sense we may be said to feel affection even for men we have never seen, owing to their honesty and virtue. Who, for instance, fails to dwell on the memory of Gaius Fabricius and Manius Curius with some affection and warmth of feeling, though he has never seen them? Or who but loathes Tarquinius Superbus, Spurius Cassius, Spurius Maelius? We have fought for empire in Italy with two great generals, Pyrrhus and Hannibal. For the former, owing to his probity, we entertain no great feelings of enmity: the latter, owing to his cruelty, our country has detested and always will detest.

9. Now, if the attraction of probity is so great that we can love it not only in those whom we have never seen, but, what is more, actually in an enemy, we need not be surprised if men's affections are roused when they fancy that they have seen virtue and goodness in those with whom a close intimacy is possible. I do not deny that affection is strengthened by the actual receipt of benefits, as well as by the perception of a wish to render service, combined with a closer intercourse. When these are added to the original impulse of the heart, to which I have alluded, a quite surprising warmth of feeling springs up. And if any one thinks that this comes from a sense of weakness, that each may have some one to help him to his particular need, all I can say is that, when he maintains it to be born of want and poverty, he allows to friendship an origin very base, and a pedigree, if I may be allowed the expression, far from noble. If this had been the case, a man's inclination to friendship would be exactly in proportion to his low opinion of his own resources. Whereas the truth is quite the other way. For when a man's confidence in himself is greatest, when he is so fortified by virtue and wisdom as to want nothing and to feel absolutely self-dependent, it is then that he is most conspicuous for seeking out and keeping up friendships. Did Africanus, for example, want anything of me? Not the least in the world! Neither did I of him. In my case it was an admiration of his virtue, in his an opinion, may be, which he entertained of my character, that caused our affection. Closer intimacy added to the warmth of our feelings. But though many great material advantages did ensue, they were not the source from which our affection proceeded. For as we are not beneficent and liberal with any view of extorting gratitude, and do not regard an act of kindness as an investment, but follow a natural inclination to liberality; so we look on friendship as worth trying for, not because we are attracted to it by the expectation of ulterior gain, but in the conviction that what it has to give us

is from first to last included in the feeling itself.

Far different is the view of those who, like brute beasts, refer everything to sensual pleasure. And no wonder. Men who have degraded all their powers of thought to an object so mean and contemptible can of course raise their eyes to nothing lofty, to nothing grand and divine. Such persons indeed let us leave out of the present question. And let us accept the doctrine that the sensation of love and the warmth of inclination have their origin in a spontaneous feeling which arises directly the presence of probity is indicated. When once men have conceived the inclination, they of course try to attach themselves to the object of it, and move themselves nearer and nearer to him. Their aim is that they may be on the same footing and the same level in regard to affection, and be more inclined to do a good service than to ask a return, and that there should be this noble rivalry between them. Thus both truths will be established. We shall get the most important material advantages from friendship; and its origin from a natural impulse rather than from a sense of need will be at once more dignified and more in accordance with fact. For if it were true that its material advantages cemented friendship, it would be equally true that any change in them would dissolve it. But nature being incapable of change, it follows that genuine friendships are eternal.

So much for the origin of friendship. But perhaps you would not care to hear any more.

Questions

1. What is Cicero's "Laelius, on Friendship" really about? Does it contain principles that benefit any people at any time?
2. How do you understand what Cicero claims "One's real friend is his other self"?
3. Why does friendship only exist between people with virtues?

Meditations

Marcus Aurelius

Pre-reading

Marcus Aurelius (121-180) (Full name Marcus Aurelius Antoninus) is the Roman emperor and philosopher. Aurelius was born in Rome in 121. His father, Annius Verus, was a consular who had stemmed from a long line of nobles; his mother, Domitia Lucilla, was well educated, fluent in Greek, extremely wealthy, and also of aristocratic birth. Incorporated into their son's early education in character, culture, poetry, and public speaking, was an emphasis on instilling in him an appreciation for simplicity. Aurelius's studies continued at home after his father died, and he benefitted from the best tutors in geometry, music, and in Greek and Latin grammar.

Aurelius soon came under the care of the childless Hadrian, who became emperor of Rome in 117. In 136 Marcus was betrothed to the daughter of the current consul, Lucius Ceionius Commodus, who was next in line to be emperor. Upon Ceionius's death in 138, Hadrian adopted Antoninus Pius and made him adopt both Aurelius and Ceionius's son Lucius Verus. During Pius's reign as emperor from 138 to 161, Aurelius studied rhetoric and law and served in numerous important government positions. His first betrothal having been put aside—probably reflecting political realities—Aurelius married Pius's daughter Faustina in 145. The couple had a daughter the following year. They also had a son, Commodus, in 161. Although Aurelius's claim to the position of emperor was superior to Verus's, Aurelius insisted they rule together, which they did from 161 until 169, when Verus died. It was during the following years of solo rule that Aurelius wrote the bulk of the *Meditations*. Although during this time the empire was troubled with invasions, nearly constant warfare, and internal strife, early historians soon called it a Golden Age because Aurelius's eminently just rule contrasted so greatly with that of his son, the savage Commodus, who reigned from 180 to 192.

Aurelius is one of the most remembered of the Roman emperors because of his *Meditations*, a classic work of Stoic philosophy consisting of a collection of his private notes gathered posthumously under one title. As the last of the five "good emperors," as head of the Roman Empire from 161 to 180, and because he was revered for centuries after as the perfect emperor, Aurelius continues to be of great interest to historians.

While ruler of the Roman Empire during its greatest period, Marcus Aurelius practiced a simple, even austere personal lifestyle based on the sincere belief in Stoic philosophy, which emphasized the overwhelming importance of spiritual and intellectual values over physical or material pleasures. Noted publicly for his restraint, modesty, and nobility, Marcus Aurelius devoted many of his private hours to writing his *Meditations*, which contained the essence of his version of Stoic ethics. The core of his ethical beliefs may be summed up in a few basic rules: forgive others for their wrongs; be aware of the harm done to people by their own bad actions; avoid judging others; be conscious of your own faults; consider that you cannot know the inner thoughts of others; avoid anger, for life is brief; anger and grief can be worse than actual physical harm; and kindness and friendship are best for all. Although these rules are hardly revolutionary in theory, they assumed and retain importance because they were held by a Roman emperor.

Marcus Aurelius, a stoic in his personal life, was also a Stoic, heir to the philosophic tradition initiated by Zeno of Citium and expanded and continued by Chrysippus of Soloi, Panaetius of Rhodes, Posidonius, Seneca the Younger, and Epictetus. What is central to Stoicism is not a stonelike stubbornness in a world of suffering but a strengthening faith in the way of nature. Nature is one, the substance of God. God is a divine fire that periodically consumes all things. However, although the divine conflagration turns all things and persons to fire—thus effectively uniting all in the purest form possible—things and persons will exist in the next cycle of existence; the cycles of existence and conflagration will succeed each other forever. Virtue for humankind is in willing to be in harmony with the way of nature. Pleasure and pain are irrelevant, if the only good is nature's way and obedience to that way. Thus, the stoical attitude is the consequence of a dedication to the Stoical ideal; it is not itself the essence of that ideal.

So conceived, Stoicism can be recognized as close in spirit to Daoism, the philosophy and religion of ancient China, in which obedience to the Dao, the "way" of the universe, is the highest virtue. Like Daoism, Stoicism involves the belief that nature, because it is the matter of God, works only toward the good—although the Chinese did not identify the cosmic power as fire or as God. Finally, to fix the idea of Stoicism, it is helpful to distinguish between Stoicism and Epicureanism. Although both the Stoics and the Epicureans fostered a life of moderation in which the passions would be controlled by will and reason, the Epicureans regarded pleasure as the highest good. Contrary to common belief, they did not endorse a program of wine, women, and song but rather a life of moderation in which the desire for peace and contemplation would take precedence over the desire for gratification of the senses. For the Stoics, virtue itself was the highest good, although it was generally believed that a modest kind of happiness would be the virtuous person's natural reward. Although there are other important differences, one can come to understand the essential distinction between Stoicism and Epicureanism by realizing that for the Stoics, virtue was the highest good, and for the Epicureans, happiness was the highest good and virtue only the means.

In Stoicism, particularly in the later philosophy as exemplified in the *Meditations*, the ethical elements received more emphasis than the metaphysical. The early philosophy was a pantheistic materialism—because it held that God is fire, and all nature is God—but later Stoics were not interested in developing these ideas, and insofar as fire was mentioned it was in a metaphorical, rather than a metaphysical way.

Now let's read the text and reflect on the questions that follow.

Text

Book One
From my governor, to be neither of the green nor of the blue party at the games in the Circus, nor a partizan either of the Parmularius or the Scutarius at the gladiators' fights; from him too I learned endurance of labour, and to want little, and to work with my own hands, and not to meddle with other people's affairs, and not to be ready to listen to slander.

From Diognetus, not to busy myself about trifling things, and not to give credit to what was said by miracle-workers and jugglers about incantations and the driving away of daemons and such things; and not to breed quails for fighting, nor to give myself up passionately to such things; and to endure freedom of speech; and to have become intimate with philosophy.

...

From Apollonius I learned freedom of will and undeviating steadiness of purpose; and to look to nothing else, not even for a moment, except to reason; and to be always the same, in sharp pains, on the occasion of the loss of a child, and in long illness; and to see clearly in a living example that the same man can be both most resolute and yielding, and not peevish in giving his instruction; and to have had before my eyes a man who clearly considered his experience and his skill in expounding philosophical principles as the smallest of his merits; and from him I learned how to receive from friends what are esteemed favours, without being either humbled by them or letting them pass unnoticed.

From Sextus, a benevolent disposition, and the example of a family governed in a fatherly manner, and the idea of living conformably to nature; and gravity without affectation, and to look carefully after the interests of friends, and to tolerate ignorant persons, and those who form opinions without consideration: he had the power of readily accommodating himself to all, so that intercourse with him was more agreeable than any flattery; and at the same time he was most highly venerated by those who associated with him: and he had the faculty both of discovering and ordering, in an intelligent and methodical way, the principles necessary for life; and he never showed anger or any other passion, but was entirely free from passion, and also most affectionate; and he could express approbation without noisy display, and he possessed much knowledge without ostentation.

Book Two
Begin the morning by saying to thyself, I shall meet with the busy-body, the ungrateful, arrogant, deceitful, envious, unsocial. All these things happen to them by reason of their ignorance of what is good and evil. But I who have seen the nature of the good that it is beautiful, and of the bad that it is ugly, and the nature of him who does wrong, that it is akin to me, not only of the same blood or seed, but that it participates in the same intelligence and the same portion of the divinity, I can neither be injured by any of them, for no one can fix on me what is ugly, nor can I be angry with my kinsman, nor hate him, for we are made for co-operation, like feet, like hands, like eyelids, like the rows of the upper and lower teeth. To act against one another then is contrary to nature; and it is acting against one another to be vexed and to turn away.

Whatever this is that I am, it is a little flesh and breath, and the ruling part. Throw away thy books; no longer distract thyself: it is not allowed; but as if thou wast now dying, despise the flesh; it is blood and bones and a network, a contexture of nerves, veins, and arteries. See the breath also, what kind of a thing it is, air, and not always the same, but every moment sent out and again sucked in. The third then is the ruling part: consider thus: Thou art an old man; no longer let this be a slave, no longer be pulled by the strings like a puppet to unsocial movements, no longer either be dissatisfied with thy present lot, or shrink from the future.

...

Do the things external which fall upon thee distract thee? Give thyself time to learn something new and good, and cease to be whirled around. But then thou must also avoid being carried about the other way. For those too are triflers who have wearied themselves in life by their activity, and yet have no object to which to direct every movement, and, in a word, all their thoughts.

Through not observing what is in the mind of another a man has seldom been seen to be unhappy; but those who do not observe the movements of their own minds must of necessity be unhappy.

How quickly all things disappear, in the universe the bodies themselves, but in time the remembrance of them; what is the nature of all sensible things, and particularly those which attract with the bait of pleasure or terrify by pain, or are noised abroad by vapoury fame; how worthless, and contemptible, and sordid, and perishable, and dead they are—all this it is the part of the intellectual faculty to observe. To observe too who these are whose opinions and voices give reputation; what death is, and the fact that, if a man looks at it in itself, and by the abstractive power of reflection resolves into their parts all the things which present themselves to the imagination in it, he will then consider it to be nothing else than an operation of nature; and if any one is afraid of an operation of nature, he is a child. This, however, is not only an operation of nature, but it is also a thing which conduces to the purposes of nature. To observe too how man comes near to the deity, and by what part of him, and when this part of man is so disposed.

Book Three

We ought to consider not only that our life is daily wasting away and a smaller part of it is left, but another thing also must be taken into the account, that if a man should live longer, it is quite uncertain whether the understanding will still continue sufficient for the comprehension of things, and retain the power of contemplation which strives to acquire the knowledge of the divine and the human. For if he shall begin to fall into dotage, perspiration and nutrition and imagination and appetite, and whatever else there is of the kind, will not fail; but the power of making use of ourselves, and filling up the measure of our duty, and clearly separating all appearances, and considering whether a man should now depart from life, and whatever else of the kind absolutely requires a disciplined reason, all this is already extinguished. We must make haste then, not only because we are daily nearer to death, but also because the conception of things and the understanding of them cease first.

...

Body, soul, intelligence: to the body belong sensations, to the soul appetites, to the intelligence principles. To receive the impressions of forms by means of appearances belongs even to animals; to be pulled by the strings of desire belongs both to wild beasts and to men who have made themselves into women, and to a Phalaris and a Nero: and to have the intelligence that guides to the things which appear suitable belongs also to those who do not believe in the gods, and who betray their country, and do their impure deeds when they have shut the doors. If then everything else is common to all that I have mentioned, there remains that which is peculiar to the good man, to be pleased and content with what happens, and with the thread which is spun for him; and not to defile the divinity which is planted in his breast, nor disturb it by a crowd of images, but to preserve it tranquil, following it obediently as a god, neither saying anything contrary to the truth, nor doing anything contrary to justice. And if all men refuse to believe that he lives a simple, modest, and contented life, he is neither angry with any of them, nor does he deviate from the way which leads to the end of life, to which a man ought to come pure, tranquil, ready to depart, and without any compulsion perfectly reconciled to his lot.

...

Book Seven

What is badness? It is that which thou hast often seen. And on the occasion of everything which happens keep this in mind, that it is that which thou hast often seen. Everywhere up and down thou wilt find the same things, with which the old histories are filled, those of the middle ages and those of our own day; with which cities and houses are filled now. There is nothing new: all things are both familiar and short-lived.

...

How many after being celebrated by fame have been given up to oblivion; and how many who have celebrated the fame of others have long been dead.

Be not ashamed to be helped; for it is thy business to do thy duty like a soldier in the assault on a town. How then, if being lame thou canst not mount up on the battlements alone, but with the help of another it is possible?

Let not future things disturb thee, for thou wilt come to them, if it shall be necessary, having with thee the same reason which now thou usest for present things.

Book Eight

Thou hast not leisure or ability to read. But thou hast leisure or ability to check arrogance: thou hast leisure to be superior to pleasure and pain: thou hast leisure to be superior to love of fame, and not to be vexed at stupid and ungrateful people, nay even to care for them.

...

If thou canst see sharp, look and judge wisely, says the philosopher.

In the constitution of the rational animal I see no virtue which is opposed to justice; but I see a virtue which is opposed to love of pleasure, and that is temperance.

Questions

1. Why do we say Marcus Aurelius, a stoic in his personal life, was also a Stoic philosopher?
2. It is claimed that Stoicism can be recognized as close in spirit to Daoism? What do you think?
3. From a modern perspective, Marcus Aurelius is certainly not in the first rank of ancient philosophers. What's the function and the philosophical value of Marcus's *Meditations*?

Questions for Further Reflection

1. Why is Roman Civilization related to the ancient Greek Civilization?
2. How did the Roman Empire flourish?
3. Why was Roman Republic replaced by Roman Empire?
4. Was it the Slave Uprising led by Spartacus that led to the decline of Roman Empire?

5. Why was Roman Empire divided into Eastern and Western Roman Empire?
6. Why did Roman Empire collapse?

References and Further Reading

1. Crossley, H. (1882). *The Fourth Book of the Meditations of Marcus Aurelius Antoninus*. (A Revised Text with Translation and Commentary). London: Macmillan.

2. Everitt, A. (2002). *Cicero: The Life and Times of Rome's Greatest Politician*. New York: Random House. Places Cicero's life and career amid the context of the political intrigue and civil unrest of the Roman Republic.

3. Hadot, P. (1998). *The Inner Citadel: The Meditations of Marcus Aurelius*. (M. Chase, Trans.). Cambridge, MA: Harvard University Press; a translation of La Citadelle Intérieure (Paris, 1992).

4. Mitchell, T. N. (1991). *Cicero: The Senior Statesman*. New Haven, Conn.: Yale University Press. This two-volume biography is considered one of the most reliable, insightful, and thorough studies available.

5. Steel, C. E. W. (2002). *Cicero, Rhetoric, and Empire*. New York: Oxford University Press. A close reading of Cicero's speeches, dissecting his rhetorical strategies, examining the role of political oratory, and placing Cicero's attitude toward empire in the context of his contemporaries.

6. Sellars, J. (2015). Marcus Aurelius. In D. Pritchard, (ed.), *Oxford Bibliographies in Philosophy*. New York: Oxford University Press. Doi 10.1093/obo/9780195396577-0278

7. 西塞罗思想介绍: https://iep.utm.edu/cicero/
https://plato.stanford.edu/entries/ancient-political/#CicLif

8. 奥勒留思想介绍: https://iep.utm.edu/marcus/
https://plato.stanford.edu/entries/marcus-aurelius/

Chapter 3　The Renaissance

Renaissance, which literally means "rebirth", generally refers to a dramatic period in European civilization following immediately after the Medieval Ages, which dawned on the collapse of the Roman Empire around the 5th century, and extending to the 17th century of a multitude of convulsions and transformations, giving way to the Age of Enlightenment. It bridged the gap between the Middle Ages and modern-day civilization in the Western. Originally the belief that Europeans had eventually rediscovered the superiority of Greek and Roman culture after hundreds of years of intellectual and cultural decline that ignited Europeans' passion for new innovations in many fields. It is characterized by a series of literary and cultural movements in the 14th, 15th and 16th centuries, beginning in Italy and eventually expanding into Germany, France, England, and other pockets of Europe. Those engaged were convinced of the possibility of improving human society via classical education, mainly composed of teachings from ancient texts and involving a wide range of disciplines, including poetry, history, rhetoric and moral philosophy. This set the tone for the Renaissance: humanism, which is expounded in the next chapter.

This period exhibits several characteristics that deserve special recognition. Firstly, Renaissance works of art and literature were studied largely for their own sake and were hailed as objects of ideal beauty or learning instead of rigid teachings for its religious significance by theologians, philosophers, and writers in the Middle Ages, though sharing a lively interest in classical literature, especially Latin and Latin translations of Greek. Secondly, public interest shifted from abstract speculations, a prominent feature of the Middle Ages, to the visible world and sensory experience. Human curiosity and objectivity were highly celebrated and advanced. Thirdly, perhaps most importantly, the unique talents and potential of the individuals were much more highly developed than previous ages, placing a new emphasis on education with a goal intended to nurture the individual's talents in all intellectual and physical areas.

Some prominent figures have contributed enormously to the progression of the Renaissance:

Leonardo da Vinci (1452 – 1519), Italian painter, architect, inventor, and "Renaissance man" well-known for paintings *The Mona Lisa* and *The Last Supper*;

Desiderius Erasmus (1466 – 1536), scholar from Holland who defined the humanist movement in Northern Europe and translator of the New Testament into Greek;

Rene Descartes (1596 – 1650), French philosopher and mathematician, father of modern philosophy;

Galileo (1564 – 1642), Italian astronomer, physicist and engineer;

Nicolaus Copernicus (1473 – 1543), mathematician and astronomer;

Thomas Hobbes (1588 – 1679), English philosopher and author of *Leviathan*;

Geoffrey Chaucer (1343 – 1400), English poet and author of *Canterbury Tales*;

Dante (1265 – 1321), Italian philosopher, poet, writer and political thinker, author of *The Divine Comedy*;

John Milton (1608 – 1674), English poet and historian, author of epic peom *Paradise Lost*;

William Shakespeare (1564 – 1616), England's "national poet" and playwright famous for his sonnets and plays;

Donatello (1386 – 1466), Italian sculptor celebrated for lifelike sculptures like *David*;

Michelangelo (1483 – 1520), Italian sculptor, painter, and architect who painted the *Sistine Chapel in Rome*.

The two pieces of writings presented here are designed to help readers gain some insight into what is the true spirit of Renaissance: *In Praise of Folly* written by Desiderius Erasmus and *Oration on the Dignity of Man* by Giovanni Pico della Mirandola. The first one is an excerpt from a half-satirical work *In Praise of Folly*, in which the character of "Folly" praises herself and all her "followers", criticizes a lot of social classes and the church itself. It came out quite as a shock in 1509 when religious establishment still dominated each one's daily life. The second one is a famous public discourse composed in 1486 by Giovanni Pico della Mirandola, an Italian scholar and philosopher. In this discourse Pico attempted to direct our attention on human capacity and human perspective, the importance of liberal arts and human quest for knowledge and his enthusiasm for seeking truth beyond religious instructions.

In Praise of Folly

Desiderius Erasmus

Pre-reading

Desiderius Erasmus is a Dutch writer, scholar, and humanist. He is also the chief interpreter to northern Europe of the intellectual currents of the Italian Renaissance.

Written in 1509 and printed in 1511, *In Praise of Folly*, was translated from Latin and has long been the best-known work of Desiderius Erasmus. According to the letter sent to Thomas More, Erasmus chose Folly as the narrator "... And therefore, being satisfied that something was to be done, and that that time was no wise proper for any serious matter, I resolved to make some sport with the praise of folly. But who the devil put that in your head? You'll say. The first thing was your surname of More, which comes so near the word Moriae (folly) as you are far from the thing." It is a satirical criticism of many traditions held by European society, especially those of the Roman Catholic Church and contributed significantly to the beginning of the Protestant Reformation.

In Praise of Folly is often divided into three distinct sections, though without any subheading or chapter head. The first section centers on her intention to admire and commend her own virtues and merits, from which this text is excerpted. Several attendants are introduced as personified characteristics, including Philautia (Self Love), Kolakia (Flattery), Lethe (Oblivion), Anoia (Madness), etc. The second section continues with Folly criticizing various classes, social and academic. In the third section, Folly turns her attack on Christianity.

Now let's read the text and reflect on the questions that follow.

Text

An oration of feigned matter spoken by Folly in her own person

At what rate so ever the world talks of me (for I am not ignorant what an ill report Folly has got, even among the most foolish), yet that I am that she, that only she, whose deity recreates both gods and men, even this is a sufficient argument, that I no sooner stepped up to speak to this full assembly than all your faces put on a kind of new and unwonted pleasantness. So suddenly have you cleared your brows, and with so frolic and hearty a laughter given me your applause, that in truth as many of you as I behold on every side of me seem to me no less than Homer's gods drunk with nectar and nepenthe; whereas before, you sat as lumpish and pensive as if you had come from consulting an oracle. And as it usually happens when the sun begins to show his beams, or when after a sharp winter the spring breathes afresh on the earth, all things immediately get a new face, new color, and recover as it were a certain kind of youth again: in like manner, by but beholding me you have in an instant gotten another kind of countenance; and so what the otherwise great rhetoricians with their tedious and long-studied orations can hardly effect, to wit, to remove the trouble of the mind, I have done it at once with my single look.

But if you ask me why I appear before you in this strange dress, be pleased to lend me your ears, and I'll tell you; not those ears, I mean, you carry to church, but abroad with you, such as you are wont to prick up to jugglers, fools, and buffoons, and such as our friend Midas once gave to Pan. For I am disposed awhile to play the sophist with you; not of their sort who nowadays boozle young men's heads with certain empty notions and curious trifles, yet teach them nothing but a more than womanish obstinacy of scolding: but I'll imitate those ancients who, that they might the better avoid that infamous appellation of sophi or wise, chose rather to be called sophists. Their business was to celebrate the praises of the gods and valiant men. And the like encomium shall you hear from me, but neither of Hercules nor Solon, but my own dear self, that is to say, Folly.

Nor do I esteem a rush that call it a foolish and insolent thing to praise one's self. Be it as foolish as they would make it, so they confess it proper: and what can be more than that Folly be her own trumpet? For who can set me out better than myself, unless perhaps I could be better known to another than to myself? Though yet I think it somewhat more modest than the general practice of our nobles and wise men who, throwing away all shame, hire some flattering orator or lying poet from whose mouth they may hear their praises, that is to say, mere lies; and yet, composing themselves with a seeming modesty, spread out their peacock's plumes and erect their crests, while this impudent flatterer equals a man of nothing to the gods and proposes him as an absolute pattern of all virtue that's wholly a stranger to it, sets out a pitiful jay in other's feathers, washes the blackamoor white, and lastly swells a gnat to an elephant. In short, I will follow that old proverb that says, "He may lawfully praise himself that lives far from neighbors." Though, by the way, I cannot but wonder at the ingratitude, shall I say, or negligence of men who, notwithstanding they honor me in the first place and are willing enough to confess my bounty, yet not one of them for these so many ages has there been who in some thankful oration has set out the praises of Folly; when yet there has not wanted them whose elaborate endeavors have extolled tyrants, agues, flies, baldness, and such other pests of nature, to their own loss of both time and sleep.

And now you shall hear from me a plain extempory speech, but so much the truer. Nor would I have you think it like the rest of orators, made for the ostentation of wit; for these, as you know, when they have been beating their heads some thirty years about an oration and at last perhaps produce somewhat that was never their own, shall yet swear they composed it in three days, and that too for diversion: whereas I ever liked it best to speak whatever came first out. But let none of you expect from me that after the manner of rhetoricians I should go about to define what I am, much less use any division; for I hold it equally unlucky to circumscribe her whose deity is universal, or make the least division in that worship about which everything is so generally agreed. Or to what purpose, think you, should I describe myself when I am here present before you, and you behold me speaking? For I am, as you see, that true and only giver of wealth whom the Greeks call Moria, the Latins Stultitia, and our plain English Folly.

Or what need was there to have said so much, as if my very looks were not sufficient to inform you who I am? Or as if any man, mistaking me for wisdom, could not at first sight convince himself by my face the true index of my mind? I am no counterfeit, nor do I carry one thing in my looks and another in my breast. No, I am in every respect so like myself that neither can they dissemble me who arrogate to themselves the appearance and title of wise men and walk like asses in scarlet hoods, though after all their hypocrisy Midas' ears will discover their master. A most ungrateful generation of men that, when they are wholly given up to my party, are yet publicly ashamed of the name, as taking it for a reproach; for which cause, since in truth they are morotatoi, fools, and yet would appear to the world to be wise men and Thales, we'll even call them morosophous, wise fools.

...

And as to the place of my birth, forasmuch as nowadays that is looked upon as a main point of nobility, it was neither, like Apollo's, in the floating Delos, nor Venus-like on the rolling sea, nor in any of blind Homer's as blind caves: but in the Fortunate Islands, where all things grew without plowing or sowing; where neither labor, nor old age, nor disease was ever heard of; and in whose fields neither daffodil, mallows, onions, beans, and such contemptible things would ever grow, but, on the contrary, rue, angelica, bugloss, marjoram, trefoils, roses, violets, lilies, and all the gardens of Adonis invite both your sight and your smelling. And being thus born, I did not begin the world, as other children are wont, with crying; but straight perched up and smiled on my mother. Nor do I envy to the great Jupiter the goat, his nurse, forasmuch as I was suckled by two jolly nymphs, to wit, Drunkenness, the daughter of Bacchus, and Ignorance, of Pan. And as for such my companions and followers as you perceive about me, if you have a mind to know who they are, you are not like to be the wiser for me, unless it be in Greek: this here, which you observe with that proud cast of her eye, is Philautia, Self-love; she with the smiling countenance, that is ever and anon clapping her hands, is Kolakia, Flattery; she that looks as if she were half asleep is Lethe, Oblivion; she that sits leaning on both elbows with her hands clutched together is Misoponia, Laziness; she with the garland on her head, and that smells so strong of perfumes, is Hedone, Pleasure; she with those staring eyes, moving here and there, is Anoia, Madness; she with the smooth skin and full pampered body is Tryphe, Wantonness; and, as to the two gods that you see with them, the one is Komos, Intemperance, the other Negretos hypnos, Dead Sleep. These, I say, are my household servants, and by their faithful counsels I have subjected all things to my dominion and erected an empire over emperors themselves.

Thus have you had my lineage, education, and companions. And now, lest I may seem to have taken upon me the name of goddess without cause, you shall in the next place understand how far my deity extends, and what advantage by it I have brought both to gods and men. For, if it was not unwisely said by somebody, that this only is to be a god, to help men; and if they are deservedly enrolled among the gods that first brought in corn and wine and such other things as are for the common good of mankind, why am not I of right the alpha, or first, of all the gods? Who being but one, yet bestow all things on all men.

For first, what is more sweet or more precious than life? And yet from whom can it more properly be said to come than from me? For neither the crab-favoured Pallas' spear nor the cloud-gathering Jupiter's shield either beget or propagate mankind; but even he himself, the father of gods and king of men at whose very beck the heavens shake, must lay by his forked thunder and those looks wherewith he conquered the giants and with which at pleasure he frightens the rest of the gods, and like a common stage player put on a disguise as often as he goes about that, which now and then he does, that is to say the getting of children: And the Stoics too, that conceive themselves next to the gods, yet show me one of them, nay the veriest bigot of the sect, and if he do not put off his beard, the badge of wisdom, though yet it be no more than what is common with him and goats; yet at least he must lay by his supercilious gravity, smooth his forehead, shake off his rigid principles, and for some time commit an act of folly and dotage. In fine, that wise man whoever he be, if he intends to have children, must have recourse to me. But tell me, I beseech you, what man is that would submit his neck to the noose of wedlock, if, as wise men should, he did but first truly weigh the inconvenience of the thing? Or what woman is there would ever go to it did she seriously consider either the peril of childbearing or the trouble of bringing them up? So then, if you owe your beings to wedlock, you owe that wedlock to this my follower, Madness; and what you owe to me I have already told you. Again, she that has but once tried what it is, would she, do you think, make a second venture if it were not for my other companion, Oblivion? Nay, even Venus herself, notwithstanding whatever Lucretius has said, would not deny but that all her virtue were lame and fruitless without the help of my deity. For out of that little, odd, ridiculous May-game came the supercilious philosophers, in whose room have succeeded a kind of people the world calls monks, cardinals, priests, and the most holy popes. And lastly, all that rabble of the poets' gods, with which heaven is so thwacked and thronged, that though it be of so vast an extent, they are hardly able to crowd one by another.

But I think it is a small matter that you thus owe your beginning of life to me, unless I also show you that whatever benefit you receive in the progress of it is of my gift likewise. For what other is this? Can that be called life where you take away pleasure? Oh! Do you like what I say? I knew none of you could have so little wit, or so much folly, or wisdom rather, as to be of any other opinion. For even the Stoics themselves that so severely cried down pleasure did but handsomely dissemble, and railed against it to the common people to no other end but that having discouraged them from it, they might the more plentifully enjoy it themselves. But tell me, by Jupiter, what part of man's life is that that is not sad, crabbed, unpleasant, insipid, troublesome, unless it be seasoned with pleasure, that is to say, folly? For the proof of which the never sufficiently praised Sophocles in that his happy elegy of us, "To know nothing is the only happiness," might be authority enough, but that I intend to take every particular by itself.

And first, who knows not but a man's infancy is the merriest part of life to himself, and most acceptable to others? For what is that in them which we kiss, embrace, cherish, nay enemies succor, but this witchcraft of folly, which wise Nature did of purpose give them into the world with them that they might the more pleasantly pass over the toil of education, and as it were flatter the care and diligence of their nurses? And then for youth, which is in such reputation everywhere, how do all men favor it, study to advance it, and lend it their helping hand? And whence, I pray, all this grace? Whence but from me? by whose kindness, as it understands as little as may be, it is also for that reason the higher privileged from exceptions; and I am mistaken if, when it is grown up and by experience and discipline brought to savor something like man, if in the same instant that beauty does not fade, its liveliness decay, its pleasantness grow flat, and its briskness fail. And by how much the further it runs from me, by so much the less it lives, till it comes to the burden of old age, not only hateful to others, but to itself also.

Which also were altogether insupportable did not I pity its condition, in being present with it, and, as the poets' gods were wont to assist such as were dying with some pleasant metamorphosis, help their decrepitness as much as in me lies by bringing them back to a second childhood, from whence they are not improperly called twice children. Which, if you ask me how I do it, I shall not be shy in the point. I bring them to our River Lethe (for its springhead rises in the Fortunate Islands, and that other of hell is but a brook in comparison), from which, as soon as they have drunk down a long forgetfulness, they wash away by degrees the perplexity of their minds, and so wax young again. But perhaps you'll say they are foolish and doting. Admit it; 'tis the very essence of childhood; as if to be such were not to be a fool, or that that condition had anything pleasant in it, but that it understood nothing. For who would not look upon that child as a prodigy that should have as much wisdom as a man?—according to that common proverb, "I do not like a child that is a man too soon." Or who would endure a converse or friendship with that old man who to so large an experience of things had joined an equal strength of mind and sharpness of judgment? And therefore for this reason it is that old age dotes; and that it does so, it is beholding to me. Yet, notwithstanding, is this dotard exempt from all those cares that distract a wise man; he is not the less pot companion, nor is he sensible of that burden of life which the more manly age finds enough to do to stand upright under it. And sometimes too, like Plautus' old man, he returns to his three letters, A.M.O., the most unhappy of all things living, if he rightly understood what he did in it.

And yet, so much do I befriend him that I make him well received of his friends and no unpleasant companion; for as much as, according to Homer, Nestor's discourse was pleasanter than honey, whereas Achilles' was both bitter and malicious; and that of old men, as he has it in another place, florid. In which respect also they have this advantage of children, in that they want the only pleasure of the others' life, we'll suppose it prattling. Add to this that old men are more eagerly delighted with children, and they, again, with old men. "Like to like," quoted the Devil to the collier. For what difference between them, but that the one has more wrinkles and years upon his head than the other? Otherwise, the brightness of their hair, toothless mouth, weakness of body, love of mild, broken speech, chatting, toying, forgetfulness, inadvertency, and briefly, all other their actions agree in everything. And by how much the nearer they approach to this old age, by so much they grow backward into the likeness of children, until like them they pass from life to death, without any weariness of the one, or sense of the other.

And now, let him that will compare the benefits they receive by me, the metamorphoses of the gods, of whom I shall not mention what they have done in their pettish humors but where they have been most favorable: turning one into a tree, another into a bird, a third into a grasshopper, serpent, or the like. As if there were any difference between perishing and being another thing! But I restore the same man to the best and happiest part of his life. And if men would but refrain from all commerce with wisdom and give up themselves to be governed by me, they should never know what it were to be old, but solace themselves with a perpetual youth. Do but observe our grim philosophers that are perpetually beating their brains on knotty subjects, and for the most part you'll find them grown old before they are scarcely young. And whence is it, but that their continual and restless thoughts insensibly prey upon their spirits and dry up their radical moisture? Whereas, on the contrary, my fat fools are as plump and round as a Westphalian hog, and never sensible of old age, unless perhaps, as sometimes it rarely happens, they come to be infected with wisdom, so hard a thing it is for a man to be happy in all things.

And to this purpose is that no small testimony of the proverb, that says, "Folly is the only thing that keeps youth at a stay and old age afar off;" as it is verified in the Brabanders, of whom there goes this common saying, "That age, which is wont to render other men wiser, makes them the greater fools." And yet there is scarce any nation of a more jocund converse, or that is less sensible of the misery of old age, than they are. And to these, as in situation, so for manner of living, come nearest my friends the Hollanders. And why should I not call them mine, since they are so diligent observers of me that they are commonly called by my name?—of which they are so far from being ashamed, they rather pride themselves in it. Let the foolish world then be packing and seek out Medeas, Circes, Venuses, Auroras, and I know not what other fountains of restoring youth. I am sure I am the only person that both can, and have, made it good. 'Tis I alone that have that wonderful juice with which Memnon's daughter prolonged the youth of her grandfather Tithon. I am that Venus by whose favor Phaon became so young again that Sappho fell in love with him. Mine are those herbs, if yet there be any such, mine those charms, and mine that fountain that not only restores departed youth but, which is more desirable, preserves it perpetual. And if you all subscribe to this opinion, that nothing is better than youth or more execrable than age, I conceive you cannot but see how much you are indebted to me, that have retained so great a good and shut out so great an evil.

Questions

1. Why does Folly try to celebrate herself instead of the Gods or valiant men in this oration?
2. What does Erasmus mean by saying "For who can set me out better than myself, unless perhaps I could be better known to another than to myself"?
3. Who might be called morosophous or wise fools? What are the differences between Folly and them?
4. Who are her companions in the Fortunate Islands? What do they embody in real life?
5. What does Folly try to convey by quoting "To know nothing is the only happiness?"
6. How does Folly prove the pervasiveness of folly whether in gods or ordinary men?
7. What is Folly's attitude towards education especially of children?
8. What is suggested of old age when Folly quotes "Folly is the only thing that keeps youth at a stay and old age afar off"? How does she prove that?

Chapter 3   The Renaissance

Oration on the Dignity of Man

Giovanni Pico della Mirandola

Pre-reading

Giovanni Pico della Mirandola is an Italian humanist philosopher. At the age of 23 or in December, 1486, he publicized a list of 900 theses or propositions concerning all subjects and even offered to defend them in public after he returned from his visits of famous universities in Italy and France. The Church was outraged by some of his theses and forbade him to continue his discussions. Pico was not frustrated and invited all interested scholars to dispute them with him the following month. *Oration on the Dignity of Man* served as an introduction to his defense. Pitifully Pico became increasingly religious after in conflict with the Catholic Church for several years. This discourse was never published in his lifetime.

This text is divided into two sections. The first section presents and deals with the speaker's philosophical basis. It begins by praising human beings not as a function of their unique place in Creation, but as an individual of potential thinking capacity. In the second section, Pico announces and justifies the topics to be disputed. He exhibits great courage in defying the so called scholars and the Church.

Now let's read the text and reflect on the questions that follow.

Text

Most esteemed Fathers, I have read in the ancient writings of the Arabians that Abdala the Saracen on being asked what, on this stage, so to say, of the world, seemed to him most evocative of wonder, replied that there was nothing to be seen more marvelous than man. And that celebrated exclamation of Hermes Trismegistus, "What a great miracle is man, Asclepius" confirms this opinion.

And still, as I reflected upon the basis assigned for these estimations, I was not fully persuaded by the diverse reasons advanced for the pre-eminence of human nature; that man is the intermediary between creatures, that he is the familiar of the gods above him as he is the lord of the beings beneath him; that, by the acuteness of his senses, the inquiry of his reason and the light of his intelligence, he is the interpreter of nature, set midway between the timeless unchanging and the flux of time; the living union (as the Persians say), the very marriage hymn of the world, and, by David's testimony but little lower than the angels. These reasons are all, without question, of great weight; nevertheless, they do not touch the principal reasons, those, that is to say, which justify man's unique right for such unbounded admiration. Why, I asked, should we not admire the angels themselves and the beatific choirs more? At long last, however, I feel that I have come to some understanding of why man is the most fortunate of living things and, consequently, deserving of all admiration; of what may be the condition in the hierarchy of beings assigned to him, which draws upon him the envy, not of the brutes alone, but of the astral beings and of the very intelligences which dwell beyond the confines of the world. A thing surpassing belief and smiting the soul with wonder. Still, how could it be otherwise? For it is on this ground that man is, with complete justice, considered and called a great miracle and a being worthy of all admiration.

Hear then, oh Fathers, precisely what this condition of man is; and in the name of your humanity, grant me your benign audition as I pursue this theme.

God the Father, the Mightiest Architect, had already raised, according to the precepts of His hidden wisdom, this world we see, the cosmic dwelling of divinity, a temple most august. He had already adorned the supercelestial region with Intelligences, infused the heavenly globes with the life of immortal souls and set the fermenting dung-heap of the inferior world teeming with every form of animal life. But when this work was done, the Divine Artificer still longed for some creature which might comprehend the meaning of so vast an achievement, which might be moved with love at its beauty and smitten with awe at its grandeur. When, consequently, all else had been completed (as both Moses and Timaeus testify), in the very last place, He bethought Himself of bringing forth man. Truth was, however, that there remained no archetype according to which He might fashion a new offspring, nor in His treasure-houses the wherewithal to endow a new son with a fitting inheritance, nor any place, among the seats of the universe, where this new creature might dispose himself to contemplate the world. All space was already filled; all things had been distributed in the highest, the middle and the lowest orders. Still, it was not in the nature of the power of the Father to fail in this last creative élan; nor was it in the nature of that supreme Wisdom to hesitate through lack of counsel in so crucial a matter; nor, finally, in the nature of His beneficent love to compel the creature destined to praise the divine generosity in all other things to find it wanting in himself.

At last, the Supreme Maker decreed that this creature, to whom He could give nothing wholly his own, should have a share in the particular endowment of every other creature. Taking man, therefore, this creature of indeterminate image, He set him in the middle of the world and thus spoke to him:

"We have given you, O Adam, no visage proper to yourself, nor endowment properly your own, in order that whatever place, whatever form, whatever gifts you may, with premeditation, select, these same you may have and possess through your own judgement and decision. The nature of all other creatures is defined and restricted within laws which we have laid down; you, by contrast, impeded by no such restrictions, may, by your own free will, to whose custody we have assigned you, trace for yourself the lineaments of your own nature. I have placed you at the very center of the world, so that from that vantage point you may with greater ease glance round about you on all that the world contains. We have made you a creature neither of heaven nor of earth, neither mortal nor immortal, in order that you may, as the free and proud shaper of your own being, fashion yourself in the form you may prefer. It will be in your power to descend to the lower, brutish forms of life; you will be able, through your own decision, to rise again to the superior orders whose life is divine."

Oh unsurpassed generosity of God the Father, Oh wondrous and unsurpassable felicity of man, to whom it is granted to have what he chooses, to be what he wills to be! The brutes, from the moment of their birth, bring with them, as Lucilius says, "from their mother's womb" all that they will ever possess. The highest spiritual beings were, from the very moment of creation, or soon thereafter, fixed in the mode of being which would be theirs through measureless eternities. But upon man, at the moment of his creation, God bestowed seeds pregnant with all possibilities, the germs of every form of life. Whichever of these a man shall cultivate, the same will mature and bear fruit in him. If vegetative, he will become a plant; if sensual, he will become brutish; if rational, he will reveal himself a heavenly being; if intellectual, he will be an angel and the son of God. And if, dissatisfied with the lot of all creatures, he should recollect himself into the center of his own unity, he will there become one spirit with God, in the solitary darkness of the Father, Who is set above all things, himself transcend all creatures.

Who then will not look with awe upon this our chameleon, or who, at least, will look with greater admiration on any other being? This creature, man, whom Asclepius the Athenian, by reason of this very mutability, this nature capable of transforming itself, quite rightly said was symbolized in the mysteries by the figure of Proteus. This is the source of those metamorphoses, or transformations, so celebrated among the Hebrews and among the Pythagoreans; for even the esoteric theology of the Hebrews at times transforms the holy Enoch into that angel of divinity which is sometimes called malakh-ha-shekhinah and at other times transforms other personages into divinities of other names; while the Pythagoreans transform men guilty of crimes into brutes or even, if we are to believe Empedocles, into plants; and Mohammed, imitating them, was known frequently to say that the man who deserts the divine law becomes a brute. And he was right; for it is not the bark that makes the tree, but its insensitive and unresponsive nature; nor the hide which makes the beast of burden, but its brute and sensual soul; nor the orbicular form which makes the heavens, but their harmonious order. Finally, it is not freedom from a body, but its spiritual intelligence, which makes the angel. If you see a man dedicated to his stomach, crawling on the ground, you see a plant and not a man; or if you see a man bedazzled by the empty forms of the imagination, as by the wiles of Calypso, and through their alluring solicitations made a slave to his own senses, you see a brute and not a man. If, however, you see a philosopher, judging and distinguishing all things according to the rule of reason, him shall you hold in veneration, for he is a creature of heaven and not of earth; if, finally, a pure contemplator, unmindful of the body, wholly withdrawn into the inner chambers of the mind, here indeed is neither a creature of earth nor a heavenly creature, but some higher divinity, clothed in human flesh.

Who then will not look with wonder upon man, upon man who, not without reason in the sacred Mosaic and Christian writings, is designated sometimes by the term "all flesh" and sometimes by the term "every creature," because he molds, fashions and transforms himself into the likeness of all flesh and assumes the characteristic power of every form of life? This is why Evantes the Persian in his exposition of the Chaldean theology, writes that man has no inborn and proper semblance, but many which are extraneous and adventitious: whence the Chaldean saying: "Enosh hu shinnujim vekammah tebhaoth haj"—"man is a living creature of varied, multiform and ever-changing nature."

But what is the purpose of all this? That we may understand—since we have been born into this condition of being what we choose to be—that we ought to be sure above all else that it may never be said against us that, born to a high position, we failed to appreciate it, but fell instead to the estate of brutes and uncomprehending beasts of burden; and that the saying of Aspah the Prophet, "You are all Gods and sons of the Most High," might rather be true; and finally that we may not, through abuse of the generosity of a most indulgent Father, pervert the free option which he has given us from a saving to a damning gift. Let a certain saving ambition invade our souls so that, impatient of mediocrity, we pant after the highest things and (since, if we will, we can) bend all our efforts to their attainment. Let us disdain things of earth, hold as little worth even the astral orders and, putting behind us all the things of this world, hasten to that court beyond the world, closest to the most exalted Godhead. There, as the sacred mysteries tell us, the Seraphim, Cherubim and Thrones occupy the first places; but, unable to yield to them, and impatient of any second place, let us emulate their dignity and glory. And, if we will it, we shall be inferior to them in nothing.

How must we proceed and what must we do to realize this ambition? Let us observe what they do, what kind of life they lead. For if we lead this kind of life (and we can), we shall attain their same estate. The Seraphim burns with the fire of charity; from the Cherubim flashes forth the splendor of intelligence; the Thrones stand firm with the firmness of justice. If, consequently, in the pursuit of the active life we govern inferior things by just criteria, we shall be established in the firm position of the Thrones. If, freeing ourselves from active care, we devote our time to contemplation, meditating upon the Creator in His work, and the work in its Creator, we shall be resplendent with the light of the Cherubim. If we burn with love for the Creator only, his consuming fire will quickly transform us into the flaming likeness of the Seraphim. Above the Throne, that is, above the just judge, God sits, judge of the ages. Above the Cherub, that is, the contemplative spirit, He spreads His wings, nourishing him, as it were, with an enveloping warmth. For the spirit of the Lord moves upon the waters, those waters which are above the heavens and which, according to Job, praise the Lord in pre-aurorial hymns. Whoever is a Seraph, that is a lover, is in God and God is in him; even, it may be said, God and he are one. Great is the power of the Thrones, which we attain by right judgement, highest of all the sublimity of the Seraphim which we attain by loving.

But how can anyone judge or love what he does not know? Moses loved the God whom he had seen and as judge of his people he administered what he had previously seen in contemplation on the mountain. Therefore the Cherub is the intermediary and by his light equally prepares us for the fire of the Seraphim and the judgement of the Thrones. This is the bond which unites the highest minds, the Palladian order which presides over contemplative philosophy; this is then the bond which before all else we must emulate, embrace and comprehend, whence we may be rapt to the heights of love or descend, well instructed and prepared, to the duties of the practical life. But certainly it is worth the effort, if we are to form our life on the model of the Cherubim, to have familiarly before our eyes both its nature and its quality as well as the duties and the functions proper to it. Since it is not granted to us, flesh as we are and knowledgeable only the things of earth, to attain such knowledge by our own efforts, let us have recourse to the ancient Fathers. They can give us the fullest and most reliable testimony concerning these matters because they had an almost domestic and connatural knowledge of them.

Let us ask the Apostle Paul, that vessel of election, in what activity he saw the armies of the Cherubim engaged when he was rapt into the third heaven. He will answer, according to the interpretation of Dionysius, that he saw them first being purified, then illuminated, and finally made perfect. We, therefore, imitating the life of the Cherubim here on earth, by refraining the impulses of our passions through moral science, by dissipating the darkness of reason by dialectic—thus washing away, so to speak, the filth of ignorance and vice—may likewise purify our souls, so that the passions may never run rampant, nor reason, lacking restraint, range beyond its natural limits. Then may we suffuse our purified souls with the light of natural philosophy, bringing it to final perfection by the knowledge of divine things.

Lest we be satisfied to consult only those of our own faith and tradition, let us also have recourse to the patriarch, Jacob, whose likeness, carved on the throne of glory, shines out before us. This wisest of the Fathers who though sleeping in the lower world, still has his eyes fixed on the world above, will admonish us. He will admonish, however, in a figure, for all things appeared in figures to the men of those times: a ladder rises by many rungs from earth to the height of heaven and at its summit sits the Lord, while over its rungs the contemplative angels move, alternately ascending and descending. If this is what we, who wish to imitate the angelic life, must do in our turn, who, I ask, would dare set muddied feet or soiled hands to the ladder of the Lord? It is forbidden, as the mysteries teach, for the impure to touch what is pure. But what are these hands, these feet, of which we speak? The feet, to be sure, of the soul: that is, its most despicable portion by which the soul is held fast to earth as a root to the ground; I mean to say, it alimentary and nutritive faculty where lust ferments and voluptuous softness is fostered. And why may we not call "the hand" that irascible power of the soul, which is the warrior of the appetitive faculty, fighting for it and foraging for it in the dust and the sun, seizing for it all things which, sleeping in the shade, it will devour? Let us bathe in moral philosophy as in a living stream, these hands, that is, the whole sensual part in which the lusts of the body have their seat and which, as the saying is, holds the soul by the scruff of the neck, let us be flung back from that ladder as profane and polluted intruders. Even this, however, will not be enough, if we wish to be the companions of the angels who traverse the ladder of Jacob, unless we are first instructed and rendered able to advance on that ladder duly, step by step, at no point to stray from it and to complete the alternate ascensions and descents. When we shall have been so prepared by the art of discourse or of reason, then, inspired by the spirit of the Cherubim, exercising philosophy through all the rungs of the ladder—that is, of nature—we shall penetrate being from its center to its surface and from its surface to its center. At one time we shall descend, dismembering with titanic force the "unity" of the "many," like the members of Osiris; at another time, we shall ascend, recollecting those same members, by the power of Phoebus, into their original unity. Finally, in the bosom of the Father, who reigns above the ladder, we shall find perfection and peace in the felicity of theological knowledge.

Let us also inquire of the just Job, who made his covenant with the God of life even before he entered into life, what, above all else, the supreme God desires of those tens of thousands of beings which surround Him. He will answer, without a doubt: peace, just as it is written in the pages of Job: He establishes peace in the high reaches of heaven. And since the middle order interprets the admonitions of the higher to the lower orders, the words of Job the theologian may well be interpreted for us by Empedocles the philosopher. Empedocles teaches us that there is in our souls a dual nature; the one bears us upwards toward the heavenly regions; by the other we are dragged downward toward regions infernal, through friendship and discord, war and peace; so witness those verses in which he laments that, torn by strife and discord, like a madman, in flight from the gods, he is driven into the depths of the sea. For it is a patent thing, O Fathers, that many forces strive within us, in grave, intestine warfare, worse than the civil wars of states. Equally clear is it that, if we are to overcome this warfare, if we are to establish that peace which must establish us finally among the exalted of God, philosophy alone can compose and allay that strife. In the first place, if our man seeks only truce with his enemies, moral philosophy will restrain the unreasoning drives of the protean brute, the passionate violence and wrath of the lion within us. If, acting on wiser counsel, we should seek to secure an unbroken peace, moral philosophy will still be at hand to fulfill our desires abundantly; and having slain either beast, like sacrificed sows, it will establish an inviolable compact of peace between the flesh and the spirit. Dialectic will compose the disorders of reason torn by anxiety and uncertainty amid the conflicting hordes of words and captious reasonings. Natural philosophy will reduce the conflict of opinions and the endless debates which from every side vex, distract and lacerate the disturbed mind. It will compose this conflict, however, in such a manner as to remind us that nature, as Heraclitus wrote, is generated by war and for this reason is called by Homer, "strife." Natural philosophy, therefore, cannot assure us a true and unshakable peace. To bestow such peace is rather the privilege and office of the queen of the sciences, most holy theology. Natural philosophy will at best point out the way to theology and even accompany us along the path, while theology, seeing us from afar hastening to draw close to her, will call out: "Come unto me you who are spent in labor and I will restore you; come to me and I will give you the peace which the world and nature cannot give."

...

Let us also seek the opinion of Pythagoras, that wisest of men, known as a wise man precisely because he never thought himself worthy of that name. His first precept to us will be: "Never sit on a bushel;" never, that is, through slothful inaction to lose our power of reason, that faculty by which the mind examines, judges and measures all things; but rather unremittingly by the rule and exercise of dialectic, to direct it and keep it agile. Next he will warn us of two things to be avoided at all costs: Neither to make water facing the sun, nor to cut our nails while offering sacrifice. Only when, by moral philosophy, we shall have evacuated the weakening appetites of our too-abundant pleasures and pared away, like nail clippings, the sharp points of anger and wrath in our souls, shall we finally begin to take part in the sacred rites, that is, the mysteries of Bacchus of which we have spoken and to dedicate ourselves to that contemplation of which the Sun is rightly called the father and the guide. Finally, Pythagoras will command us to "Feed the cock"; that is, to nourish the divine part of our soul with the knowledge of divine things as with substantial food and heavenly ambrosia. This is the cock whose visage is the lion, that is, all earthly power, holds in fear and awe. This is the cock to whom, as we read in Job, all understanding was given. At this cock's crowing, erring man returns to his senses. This is the cock which every day, in the morning twilight, with the stars of morning, raises a Te Deum to heaven. This is the cock which Socrates, at the hour of his death, when he hoped he was about to join the divinity of his spirit to the divinity of the higher world and when he was already beyond danger of any bodily illness, said that he owed to Asclepius, that is, the healer of souls.

...

Questions

1. What are the principal reasons for the pre-eminence of humans over other beings according to Pico?
2. Why did "God bestow seeds pregnant with all possibilities" for humans?
3. Can Humans elevate themselves to be Gods? Why or why not?
4. Why does Pico have recourse to some ancient Fathers, such Apostle Paul, Jacob, Job, Moses, Apollo, and the Chaldeans?
5. Is it appropriate to dispute in public the most subtle mysteries of Christian theology? Why or why not?

Questions for Further Reflection

1. Is it true that "A man of great wisdom often appears slow-witted(大智若愚)"? Then what is true wisdom?
2. As a token of the Renaissance, individualism is highly celebrated in the two texts. Then what is individualism? What does it mean in socialistic context?
3. In the early period of Renaissance, God was not to be disposed of but served as a guide for self-liberation or as a means to the end of spiritual freedom. Is it true? Why or why not?
4. Pico demonstrated enormous courage and confidence by proposing the study of philosophy instead of theology and exhibited a high degree of diplomacy in delivering this speech. What can be learned from him?
5. Is it possible for China to initiate the rebirth of its ancient classic literature? What lessons can be recapped from the Renaissance?

References and Further Reading

伊拉斯谟. 愚人颂. 许崇信,译. 沈阳:辽宁教育出版社,2001.

Chapter 4   Humanism

Humanism, as a predominant set of beliefs, is the fundamental force that empowered artists, scholars, artists, philosophers and even ordinary Europeans to seek truth and the value of the individual beyond the teachings of the Catholic Church in the Renaissance. It was developed in Norther Italy during the 13th and 14th centuries and later spread to other parts of continental Europe and England. It places humans in a pivotal position instead of the Creator. Though it has been touched upon in Chapter 3, it requires further investigation and appreciation of its profound effect on modern western civilization after the end of the Renaissance. This is why a single chapter is reserved for it.

According to Encyclopedia Britannica, early Humanism embraces the following basic principles and attitudes, which may offer some illuminous guide to insight into humanist movement itself. Firstly, early humanists initiated a new conversation with the classics by referring to an inherent and lasting human reality. They achieved this by returning to the classics or translations of Latin works from ancient Rome. Secondly, they engaged themselves in a realism that discarded religious conventions and began to focus on an objective analysis of their sensory experience, which in turn gave rise to the modern social science. Thirdly, humanists exhibited a high degree of independent critical thinking and meticulous attention to details, which was showcased by the great artists Da Vinci. And finally, they cried for personal autonomy and sung the dignity of man, as is shown in *Oration on the Dignity of Man*. It can be safely concluded that humanism offered a fertile soil for human development in various fields, such as literature, philosophy, art, religion, social science and even natural science.

The two pieces of philosophical discourses presented here are intended for a glimpse of humanism, as it is an impossible mission to cover a topic of such scale and profoundness in such limited space and time. As Kant wrote in Preface to the first edition of *Critique of Pure Reason*, "it can be said many a book that it would be much shorter if it were not so short." The ultimate goal of these selections is to kindle their inner sensibilities to converse with these giants. The first text, written by Kant in 1781, is the two prefaces to *Critique of Pure Reason*, a monumental book in the history of Western philosophy. Kant introduced the historic and academic background to his book in these two prefaces and some prerequisite crucial concepts required to comprehend his thoughts. The second text is an excerpt from *A Treatise of Human Nature* by David Hume in 1739, a book generally considered as Hume's most important work and one of the most influential works in the history of philosophy. Hume shifted his foundation of analysis from empirical investigation, a predominant format at that time, to that of human nature. He also attempted to apply the experimental method of reasoning, widespread in the physical sciences, to the study of human psychology to reveal the extent and force of human understanding. His book can help us gain certain insight into cognitive science. Many theories proposed by Hume have proved valid and solid by modern technologies.

Critique of Pure Reason

Immanuel Kant

Pre-reading

Immanuel Kant is a leading figure in the evolution of modern Western philosophy. His systematic effort in the theory of knowledge, ethics and aesthetics laid the foundation for all subsequent studies of philosophy. Here two prefaces to his much-debated book of *Critique of Pure Reason* were severed for convenience of study or succession of learning as his philosophical doctrines advanced from those of Humanism, though it would be more appropriate to categorize them in our discussion of Enlightenment.

Critique of Pure Reason (1781) was one of Kant's series of monumental works, including *Critique of Practical Reason* (1788) and *Critique of Judgment* (1790). In this book, Kant attempted to criticize some metaphysics as they claimed that human mind can find truth by pure thought without referring to the objects of experience. According to Kant, knowledge should not rely on judgments analytically contained in what one already knows but the ones that are a priori, as they are separated from the contingencies of required and synthetic experience. This is what Kant calls Pure Reason. The two prefaces center on the controversies that rose over metaphysics and some basic concepts and their conceptions that occur in this book. They can offer certain pathway to the comprehension of his ideas and book.

Now let's read the text and reflect on the questions that follow.

Text

Preface to the first edition

Human reason has the peculiar fate in one species of its cognitions that it is burdened with questions which it cannot dismiss, since they are given to it as problems by the nature of reason itself, but which it also cannot answer, since they transcend every capacity of human reason.

Reason falls into this perplexity through no fault of its own. It begins from principles whose use is unavoidable in the course of experience and at the same time sufficiently warranted by it. With these principles it rises (as its nature also requires) ever higher, to more remote conditions. But since it becomes aware in this way that its business must always remain incomplete because the questions never cease, reason sees itself necessitated to take refuge in principles that overstep all possible use in experience, and yet seem so unsuspicious that even ordinary common sense agrees with them. But it thereby falls into obscurity and contradictions, from which it can indeed surmise that it must somewhere be proceeding on the ground of hidden errors; but it cannot discover them, for the principles on which it is proceeding, since they surpass the bounds of all experience, no longer recognize any touchstone of experience. The battlefield of these endless controversies is called **metaphysics**.

There was a time when metaphysics was called the **queen** of all the sciences, and if the will be taken for the deed, it deserved this title of honor, on account of the preeminent importance of its object. Now, in accordance with the fashion of the age, the queen proves despised on all sides; and the matron, outcast and forsaken, mourns like Hecuba: *Modo maxima rerum, tot generis natisque potens—nunc trahor exul, inops—*Ovid, Metamorphoses. (Greatest of all by race and birth, I now am cast out, powerless)

In the beginning, under the administration of the **dogmatists**, her rule was **despotic**. Yet because her legislation still retained traces of ancient barbarism, this rule gradually degenerated through internal wars into complete **anarchy**; and the skeptics, a kind of nomads who abhor all permanent cultivation of the soil, shattered civil unity from time to time. But since there were fortunately only a few of them, they could not prevent the dogmatists from continually attempting to rebuild, though never according to a plan unanimously accepted among themselves. Once in recent times it even seemed as though an end would be put to all these controversies, and the lawfulness of all the competing claims would be completely decided, through a certain **physiology** of the human understanding (by the famous Locke); but it turned out that although the birth of the purported queen was traced to the rabble of common experience and her pretensions would therefore have been rightly rendered suspicious, nevertheless she still asserted her claims, because in fact this **genealogy** was attributed to her falsely; thus metaphysics fell back into the same old worm-eaten **dogmatism**, and thus into the same position of contempt out of which the science was to have been extricated. Now after all paths (as we persuade ourselves) have been tried in vain, what rules is tedium and complete **indifferentism**, the mother of chaos and night in the sciences, but at the same time also the origin, or at least the prelude, of their incipient transformation and enlightenment, when through ill-applied effort they have become obscure, confused, and useless.

For it is pointless to affect **indifference** with respect to such inquiries, to whose object human nature **cannot** be **indifferent**. Moreover, however much they may think to make themselves unrecognizable by exchanging the language of the schools for a popular style, these so-called **indifferentists**, to the extent that they think anything at all, always unavoidably fall back into metaphysical assertions, which they yet professed so much to despise. Nevertheless this indifference, occurring amid the flourishing of all sciences, and directed precisely at those sciences whose results (if such are to be had at all) we could least do without, is a phenomenon deserving our attention and reflection. This is evidently the effect not of the thoughtlessness of our age, but of its ripened **power of judgment** (Now and again one hears complaints about the superficiality of our age's way of thinking, and about the decay of well-grounded science. Yet I do not see that those sciences whose grounds are well laid, such as mathematics, physics, etc., in the least deserve this charge; rather, they maintain their old reputation for well-groundedness, and in the case of natural science, even surpass it. This same spirit would also prove itself effective in other species of cognition if only care had first been taken to correct their principles. In the absence of this, indifference, doubt, and finally strict criticism are rather proofs of a well-grounded way of thinking. Our age is the genuine age of **criticism**, to which everything must submit. **Religion** through its **holiness** and **legislation** through its **majesty** commonly seek to exempt themselves from it. But in this way they excite a just suspicion against themselves, and cannot lay claim to that unfeigned respect that reason grants only to that which has been able to withstand its free and public examination.), which will no longer be put off with illusory knowledge, and which demands that reason should take on anew the most difficult of all its tasks, namely, that of self-knowledge, and to institute a court of justice, by reason may secure its rightful claims while dismissing all its groundless pretensions, and this not by mere decrees but according to its own eternal and unchangeable laws; and this court is none other than the **critique of pure reason** itself.

Yet by this I do not understand a critique of books and systems, but a critique of the faculty of reason in general, in respect of all the cognitions after which reason might strive **independently of all experience**, and hence the decision about the possibility or impossibility of a metaphysics in general, and the determination of its sources, as well as its extent and boundaries, all, however, from principles.

It is on this path, the only one left, that I have set forth, and I flatter myself that in following it I have succeeded in removing all those errors that have so far put reason into dissension with itself in its non-experiential use. I have not avoided reason's questions by pleading the incapacity of human reason as an excuse; rather I have completely specified these questions according to principles, and after discovering the point where reason has misunderstood itself, I have resolved them to reason's full satisfaction. To be sure, the answer to these questions has not turned out just as dogmatically enthusiastic lust for knowledge might have expected; for the latter could not be satisfied except through magical powers in which I am not an expert. Yet this was also not the intent of our reason's natural vocation; and the duty of philosophy was to abolish the semblance arising from misinterpretation, even if many prized and beloved delusions have to be destroyed in the process. In this business I have made comprehensiveness my chief aim in view, and I make bold to say that there cannot be a single metaphysical problem that has not been solved here, or at least to the solution of which the key has not been provided. In fact pure reason is such a perfect unity that if its principle were insufficient for even a single one of the questions that are set for it by its own nature, then this [principle] might as well be discarded, because then it also would not be up to answering any of the other questions with complete reliability.

While I am saying this I believe I perceive in the face of the reader an indignation mixed with contempt at claims that are apparently so pretentious and immodest; and yet they are incomparably more moderate than those of any author of the commonest program who pretends to prove the simple nature of the **soul** or the necessity of a first **beginning of the world**. For such an author pledges himself to extend human cognition beyond all bounds of possible experience, of which I humbly admit that this wholly surpasses my capacity; instead I have to do merely with reason itself and its pure thinking; to gain exhaustive acquaintance with them I need not seek far beyond myself, because it is in myself that I encounter them, and common logic already also gives me an example of how the simple acts of reason may be fully and systematically enumerated; only here the question is raised how much I may hope to settle with these simple acts if all the material and assistance of experience are taken away from me.

So much for the **completeness** in reaching **each** of the ends, and for the **comprehensiveness** in reaching **all** of them together, which ends are not proposed arbitrarily, but are set up for us by the nature of cognition itself, as the **matter** of our critical investigation.

Furthermore, **certainty** and **clarity**, two things that concern the **form** of the investigation, are to be viewed as essential demands, which may rightly be made on the author who ventures upon so slippery an undertaking.

As far as **certainty** is concerned, I have myself pronounced the judgment that in this kind of inquiry it is in no way allowed to **hold opinions**, and that anything that even looks like an hypothesis is a forbidden commodity, which should not be put up for sale even at the lowest price but must be confiscated as soon as it is discovered. For every cognition that is supposed to be certain *a priori* proclaims that it wants to be held for absolutely necessary, and even more is this true of a determination of all pure cognitions *a priori*, which is to be the standard and thus even the example of all apodictic (philosophical) certainty. Whether I have performed what I have just pledged in that respect remains wholly to the judgment of the reader, since it is appropriate for an author only to present the grounds, but not to judge about their effect on his judges. But in order that he should not inadvertently be the cause of weakening his own arguments, the author may be permitted to note himself those places that, even though they pertain only to the incidental end of the work, may be the occasion for some mistrust, in order that he may in a timely manner counteract the influence that even the reader's slightest reservation on this point may have on his judgment over the chief end.

I am acquainted with no investigations more important for getting to the bottom of that faculty we call the understanding, and at the same time for the determination of the rules and boundaries of its use, than those I have undertaken in the second chapter of the Transcendental Analytic, under the title **Deduction of the Pure Concepts of the Understanding**; they are also the investigations that have cost me the most, but I hope not unrewarded, effort. This inquiry, which goes rather deep, has two sides. One side refers to the objects of the pure understanding, and is supposed to demonstrate and make comprehensible the objective validity of its concepts *a priori*; thus it belongs essentially to my ends. The other side deals with the pure understanding itself, concerning its possibility and the powers of cognition on which it itself rests; thus it considers it in a subjective relation, and although this exposition is of great importance in respect of my chief end, it does not belong essentially to it; because the chief question always remains: "What and how much can understanding and reason cognize free of all experience?" and not:

"How is the **faculty of thinking** itself possible?" Since the latter question is something like the search for the cause of a given effect, and is therefore something like a hypothesis (although, as I will elsewhere take the opportunity to show, this is not in fact how matters stand), it appears as if I am taking the liberty in this case of expressing an **opinion**, and that the reader might therefore be free to hold another **opinion**. In view of this I must remind the reader in advance that even in case my subjective deduction does not produce the complete conviction that I expect, the objective deduction that is my primary concern would come into its full strength, on which what is said at pages [A]92–3 should even be sufficient by itself.

Finally, as regards **clarity**, the reader has a right to demand first **discursive** (logical) **clarity**, **through concepts**, but then also intuitive (aesthetic) clarity, through **intuitions**, that is, through examples or other illustrations *in concreto*. I have taken sufficient care for the former. That was essential to my undertaking but was also the contingent cause of the fact that I could not satisfy the second demand, which is less strict but still fair. In the progress of my labor I have been almost constantly undecided how to deal with this matter. Examples and illustrations always appeared necessary to me, and hence actually appeared in their proper place in my first draft. But then I looked at the size of my task and the many objects with which I would have to do, and I became aware that this alone, treated in a dry, merely **scholastic** manner, would suffice to fill an extensive work; thus I found it inadvisable to swell it further with examples and illustrations, which are necessary only for a **popular** aim, especially since this work could never be made suitable for popular use, and real experts in this science do not have so much need for things to be made easy for them; although this would always be agreeable, here it could also have brought with it something counter-productive. The Abbe Terrasson says that if the size of a book is measured not by the number of pages but by the time needed to understand it, then it can be said of many a book **that it would be much shorter if it were not so short**. But on the other hand, if we direct our view toward the intelligibility of a whole of speculative cognition that is wide-ranging and yet is connected in principle, we could with equal right say that **many a book would have been much clearer if it had not been made quite so clear**. For the aids to clarity help in the parts but often confuse in the **whole**, since the reader cannot quickly enough attain a survey of the whole; and all their bright colors paint over and make unrecognizable the articulation or structure of the system, which yet matters most when it comes to judging its unity and soundness.

It can, as it seems to me, be no small inducement for the reader to unite his effort with that of the author, when he has the prospect of carrying out, according to the outline given above, a great and important piece of work, and that in a complete and lasting way. Now metaphysics, according to the concepts we will give of it here, is the only one of all the sciences that may promise that little but unified effort, and that indeed in a short time, will complete it in such a way that nothing remains to posterity except to adapt it in a **didactic** manner to its intentions, yet without being able to add to its content in the least. For it is nothing but the **inventory** of all we possess through **pure reason**, ordered systematically. Nothing here can escape us, because what reason brings forth entirely out of itself cannot be hidden, but is brought to light by reason itself as soon as reason's common principle has been discovered. The perfect unity of this kind of cognition, and the fact that it arises solely out of pure concepts without any influence that would extend or increase it from experience or even **particular intuition**, which would lead to a determinate experience, make this unconditioned completeness not only feasible but also necessary. *Tecum habita, et naris quam sit tibi curta supellex.*—Persius.(Dwell in your own house, and you will know how simple your possessions are.)

Such a system of pure (speculative) reason I hope myself to deliver under the title **Metaphysics of Nature**, which will be not half so extensive but will be incomparably richer in content than this critique, which had first to display the sources and conditions of its possibility, and needed to clear and level a ground that was completely overgrown. Here I expect from my reader the patience and impartiality of a **judge**, but there I will expect the cooperative spirit and assistance of a **fellow worker**; for however completely the **principles** of the system may be expounded in the critique, the comprehensiveness of the system itself requires also that no **derivative** concepts should be lacking, which, however, cannot be estimated *a priori* in one leap, but must be gradually sought out; likewise, just as in the former the whole **synthesis** of concepts has been exhausted, so in the latter it would be additionally demanded that the same thing should take place in respect of their **analysis**, which would be easy and more entertainment than labor.

I have only a few more things to remark with respect to the book's printing. Since the beginning of the printing was somewhat delayed, I was able to see only about half the proof sheets, in which I have come upon a few printing errors, though none that confuse the sense except the one occurring at page [A] 379, fourth line from the bottom, where **specific** should be read in place of **skeptical**. The Antinomy of Pure Reason, from page [A] 425 to page [A] 461, is arranged in the manner of a table, so that everything belonging to the **thesis** always continues on the left side and what belongs to the **antithesis** on the right side, which I did in order to make it easier to compare proposition and counter-proposition with one another.

Preface to the second edition

Whether or not the treatment of the cognitions belonging to the concern of reason travels the secure course of a science is something which can soon be judged by its success. If after many preliminaries and preparations are made, a science gets stuck as soon as it approaches its end, or if in order to reach this end it must often go back and set out on a new path; or likewise if it proves impossible for the different co-workers to achieve unanimity as to the way in which they should pursue their common aim; then we may be sure that such a study is merely groping about, that it is still far from having entered upon the secure course of a science; and it is already a service to reason if we can possibly find that path for it, even if we have to give up as futile much of what was included in the end previously formed without deliberation.

That from the earliest times **logic** has traveled this secure course can be seen from the fact that since the time of Aristotle it has not had to go a single step backwards, unless we count the abolition of a few dispensable subtleties or the more distinct determination of its presentation, which improvements belong more to the elegance than to the security of that science. What is further remarkable about logic is that until now it has also been unable to take a single step forward, and therefore seems to all appearance to be finished and complete. For if some moderns have thought to enlarge it by interpolating **psychological** chapters about our different cognitive powers (about imagination, wit), or **metaphysical** chapters about the origin of cognition or the different kinds of certainty in accordance with the diversity of objects (about idealism, skepticism, etc.), or **anthropological** chapters about our prejudice (about their causes and remedies), then this proceeds only from their ignorance of the peculiar nature of this science. It is not an improvement but a deformation of the sciences when their boundaries are allowed to run over into one another; the boundaries of logic, however, are determined quite precisely by the fact that logic is the science that exhaustively presents and strictly proves nothing but the formal rules of all thinking (whether this thinking be empirical or *a priori*, whatever origin or object it may have, and whatever contingent or natural obstacles it may meet with in our minds).

For the advantage that has made it so successful, logic has solely its own limitation to thank, since it is thereby justified in abstracting—is indeed obliged to abstract—from all objects of cognition and all the distinctions between them; and in logic, therefore, the understanding has to do with nothing further than itself and its own form. How much more difficult, naturally, must it be for reason to enter upon the secure path of a science if it does not have to do merely with itself, but has to deal with objects too; hence logic as a propadeutic constitutes only the outer courtyard, as it were, to the sciences; and when it comes to information, a logic may indeed be presupposed in judging about the latter, but its acquisition must be sought in the sciences properly and objectively so called.

Insofar as there is to be reason in these sciences, something in them must be cognized *a priori*, and this cognition can relate to its object in either of two ways, either merely **determining** the object and its concept (which must be given from elsewhere), or else also **making** the object **actual**. The former is **theoretical**, the latter **practical** cognition of reason. In both the **pure** part, the part in which reason determines its object wholly *a priori*, must be expounded all by itself, however much or little it may contain, and that part that comes from other sources must not be mixed up with it; for it is bad economy to spend blindly whatever comes in without being able later, when the economy comes to a standstill, to distinguish the part of the revenue that can cover the expenses from the part that must be cut.

Mathematics and **physics** are the two theoretical cognitions of reason that are supposed to determine their **objects** *a priori*, the former entirely purely, the latter at least in part purely but also following the standards of sources of cognition other than reason.

Mathematics has, from the earliest times to which the history of human reason reaches, in that admirable people the Greeks, traveled the secure path of a science. Yet it must not be thought that it was as easy for it as for logic—in which reason has to do only with itself—to find that royal path, or rather itself to open it up; rather, I believe that mathematics was left groping about for a long time (chiefly among the Egyptians), and that its transformation is to be ascribed to a **revolution**, brought about by the happy inspiration of a single man in an attempt from which the road to be taken onward could no longer be missed, and the secure course of a science was entered on and prescribed for all time and to an infinite extent. The history of this revolution in the way of thinking—which was far more important than the discovery of the way around the famous Cape Ⅱ and of the lucky one who brought it about, has not been preserved for us. But the legend handed down to us by Diogenes Laertius—who names the reputed inventor of the smallest elements of geometrical demonstrations, even of those that, according to common judgment, stand in no need of proof—proves that the memory of the alteration wrought by the discovery of this new path in its earliest footsteps must have seemed exceedingly important to mathematicians, and was thereby rendered unforgettable. A new light broke upon the first person who demonstrated the isoscelesa triangle (whether he was called "Thales" or had some other name). For he found that what he had to do was not to trace what he saw in this figure, or even trace its mere concept, and read off, as it were, from the properties of the figure; but rather that he had to produce the latter from what he himself thought into the object and presented (through construction) according to *a priori* concepts, and that in order to know something securely *a priori* he had to ascribe to the thing nothing except what followed necessarily from what he himself had put into it in accordance with its concept.

It took natural science much longer to find the highway of science; for it is only about one and a half centuries since the suggestion of the ingenious Francis Bacon partly occasioned this discovery and partly further stimulated it, since one was already on its tracks—which discovery, therefore, can just as much be explained by a sudden revolution in the way of thinking. Here I will consider natural science only insofar as it is grounded on **empirical** principles.

When Galileo rolled balls of a weight chosen by himself down an inclined plane, or when Torricelli' made the air bear a weight that he had previously thought to be equal to that of a known column of water, or when in a later time Stahl's changed metals into calyx and then changed the latter back into metal by first removing something and then putting it back again (Here I am not following exactly the thread of the history of the experimental method, whose first beginnings are also not precisely known.), a light dawned on all those who study nature. They comprehended that reason has insight only into what it itself produces according to its own design; that it must take the lead with principles for its judgments according to constant laws and compel nature to answer its questions, rather than letting nature guide its movements by keeping reason, as it were, in leading-strings; for otherwise accidental observations, made according to no previously designed plan, can never connect up into a necessary law, which is yet what reason seeks and requires. Reason, in order to be taught by nature, must approach nature with its principles in one hand, according to which alone the agreement among appearances can count as laws, and, in the other hand, the experiments thought out in accordance with these principles—yet in order to be instructed by nature not like a pupil, who has recited to him whatever the teacher wants to say, but like an appointed judge who compels witnesses to answer the questions he puts to them. Thus even physics owes the advantageous revolution in its way of thinking to the inspiration that what reason would not be able to know of itself and has to learn from nature, it has to seek in the latter (though not merely ascribe to it) in accordance with what reason itself puts into nature. This is how natural science was first brought to the secure course of a science after groping about for so many centuries.

Metaphysics—a wholly isolated speculative cognition of reason that elevates itself entirely above all instruction from experience, and that through mere concepts (not, like mathematics, through the application of concepts to intuition), where reason thus is supposed to be its own pupil—has up to now not been so favored by fate as to have been able to enter upon the secure course of a science, even though it is older than all other sciences, and would remain even if all the others were swallowed up by an all-consuming barbarism. For in it reason continuously gets stuck, even when it claims *a priori* insight (as it pretends) into those laws confirmed by the commonest experience. In metaphysics we have to retrace our path countless times, because we find that it does not lead where we want to go, and it is so far from reaching unanimity in the assertions of its adherents that it is rather a battlefield, and indeed one that appears to be especially determined for testing one's powers in mock combat; on this battlefield no combatant has ever gained the least bit of ground, nor has any been able to base any lasting possession on his victory. Hence there is no doubt that up to now the procedure of metaphysics has been a mere groping, and what is the worst, a groping among mere concepts.

Now why is it that here the secure path of science still could not be found? Is it perhaps impossible? Why then has nature afflicted our reason with the restless striving for such a path, as if it were one of reason's most important occupations? Still more, how little cause have we to place trust in our reason if in one of the most important parts of our desire for knowledge it does not merely forsake us but even entices us with delusions and in the end betrays us! Or if the path has merely eluded us so far, what indications may we use that might lead us to hope that in renewed attempts we will be luckier than those who have gone before us?

I should think that the examples of mathematics and natural science, which have become what they now are through a revolution brought about all at once, were remarkable enough that we might reflect on the essential element in the change in the ways of thinking that has been so advantageous to them, and, at least as an experiment, imitate it insofar as their analogy with metaphysics, as rational cognition, might permit. Up to now it has been assumed that all our cognition must conform to the objects; but all attempts to find out something about them *a priori* through concepts that would extend our cognition have, on this presupposition, come to nothing. Hence let us once try whether we do not get farther with the problems of metaphysics by assuming that the objects must conform to our cognition, which would agree better with the requested possibility of an *a priori* cognition of them, which is to establish something about objects before they are given to us. This would be just like the first thoughts of Copernicus, who, when he did not make good progress in the explanation of the celestial motions if he assumed that the entire celestial host revolves around the observer, tried to see if he might not have greater success if he made the observer revolve and left the stars at rest. Now in metaphysics we can try in a similar way regarding the intuition of objects. If intuition has to conform to the constitution of the objects, then I do not see how we can know anything of them *a priori*; but if the object (as an object of the senses) conforms to the constitution of our faculty of intuition, then I can very well represent this possibility to myself. Yet because I cannot stop with these intuitions, if they are to become cognitions, but must refer them as representations to something as their object and determine this object through them, I can assume either that the concepts through which I bring about this determination also conform to the objects, and then I am once again in the same difficulty about how I could know anything about them *a priori*, or else I assume that the objects, or what is the same thing, the experience in which alone they can be cognized (as given objects) conforms to those concepts, in which case I immediately see an easier way out of the difficulty, since experience itself is a kind of cognition requiring the understanding, whose rule I have to presuppose in myself before any object is given to me, hence *a priori*, which rule is expressed in concepts *a priori*, to which all objects of experience must therefore necessarily conform, and with which they must agree. As for objects insofar as they are thought merely through reason, and necessarily at that, but that (at least as reason thinks them) cannot be given in experience at all—the attempt to think them (for they must be capable of being thought) will provide a splendid touchstone of what we assume as the altered method of our way of thinking, namely that we can cognize of things *a priori* only what we ourselves have put into them.

Questions

1. What are principles? How do they contribute to human reason?
2. Does Kant despise metaphysics? Why or why not?
3. How does power of judgment influence pure reason?
4. What kind of relationship is supposed to be established between reason and experience?
5. Why does Kant say that "there cannot be a single metaphysical problem that has not been solved here, or at least to the solution of which the key has not been provided"? What is "key"?
6. What does Kant mean when he says "certainty does not allow us to hold opinions"?
7. What does Kant try to convey by saying that "In the progress of my labor I have been almost constantly undecided how to deal with this matter(clarity) ?"
8. What is the secure course of a science according to Kant?
9. What different roles does reason play in metaphysics and mathematics?
10. According to Kant, does all our cognition have to conform to the objects?
11. What does Kant mean by saying "all appearances is the conditioned"?
12. Is pure reason static or dynamic according to Kant?
13. What is knowledge?
14. What does Kant do to tackle the misunderstandings invited on the first edition of *Critique of Pure Reason*?
15. Can you find the differences and similarities between the two prefaces?

A Treatise of Human Nature

David Hume

Pre-reading

This text is selected from *A Treatise of Human Nature* (1739) by David Hume. He is a philosopher, especially famous for his work in philosophical empiricism and skepticism, though his great achievements in historical study, economics and essay writing could be at least at abreast. Inspired by Isaac Newton's scientific method and John Locke's epistemology, Hume attempted to theorize the process of knowledge acquisition by human mind, which is primarily contained in our selected excerpt. He even endeavored to prove that reason and rational judgments are natural responses prompted by distinct sensations and experiences.

David Hume, in contrast with Kant, concluded that humans are more of sensitive, practical and sentimental creatures than that of reason. This text is an exemplary discourse in demonstrating his standpoint. It is logically presented, complete with its own system, though it might seem to be loosely organized.

Now let's read the text and reflect on the questions that follow.

Text

PART I
Of ideas, their origin, composition, connection, abstraction, etc.

Section I Of the origin of our ideas

All the perceptions of the human mind resolve themselves into two distinct kinds, which I shall call Impressions and Ideas. The difference betwixt these consists in the degrees of force and liveliness with which they strike upon the mind, and make their way into our thought or consciousness. Those perceptions, which enter with most force and violence, we may name impressions, and under this name I comprehend all our sensations, passions and emotions, as they make their first appearance in the soul. By ideas I mean the faint images of these in thinking and reasoning, such as, for instance, are all the perceptions excited by the present discourse, excepting only, those which arise from the sight and touch, and excepting the immediate pleasure or uneasiness it may occasion. I believe it will not be very necessary to employ many words in explaining this distinction. Every one of himself will readily perceive the difference betwixt feeling and thinking. The common degrees of these are easily distinguished; though it is not impossible but in particular instances they may very nearly approach to each other. Thus in sleep, in a fever, in madness, or in any very violent emotions of soul, our ideas may approach to our impressions: As on the other hand it sometimes happens, that our impressions are so faint and low, that we cannot distinguish them from our ideas. But notwithstanding this near resemblance in a few instances, they are in general so very different, that no one can make a scruple to rank them under distinct heads, and assign to each a peculiar name to mark the difference.

There is another division of our perceptions, which it will be convenient to observe, and which extends itself both to our impressions and ideas. This division is into Simple and Complex. Simple perceptions or impressions and ideas are such as admit of no distinction nor separation. The complex are the contrary to these, and may be distinguished into parts. Though a particular colour, taste, and smell are qualities all united together in this apple, it is easy to perceive they are not the same, but are at least distinguishable from each other.

Having by these divisions given an order and arrangement to our objects, we may now apply ourselves to consider with the more accuracy their qualities and relations. The first circumstance, that strikes my eye, is the great resemblance betwixt our impressions and ideas in every other particular, except their degree of force and vivacity. The one seem to be in a manner the reflection of the other; so that all the perceptions of the mind are double, and appear both as impressions and ideas. When I shut my eyes and think of my chamber, the ideas I form are exact representations of the impressions I felt; nor is there any circumstance of the one, which is not to be found in the other. In running over my other perceptions, I find still the same resemblance and representation. Ideas and impressions appear always to correspond to each other. This circumstance seems to me remarkable, and engages my attention for a moment.

Upon a more accurate survey I find I have been carried away too far by the first appearance and that I must make use of the distinction of perceptions into simple and complex, to limit this general decision, that all our ideas and impressions are resembling. I observe, that many of our complex ideas never had impressions that corresponded to them, and that many of our complex impressions never are exactly copied in ideas. I can imagine to myself such a city as the New Jerusalem, whose pavement is gold and walls are rubies, though I never saw any such. I have seen Paris; but shall I affirm I can form such an idea of that city, as will perfectly represent all its streets and houses in their real and just proportions?

I perceive, therefore, that though there is in general a great resemblance betwixt our complex impressions and ideas, yet the rule is not universally true, that they are exact copies of each other. We may next consider how the case stands with our simple perceptions. After the most accurate examination, of which I am capable, I venture to affirm, that the rule here holds without any exception, and that every simple idea has a simple impression, which resembles it; and every simple impression a correspondent idea. That idea of red, which we form in the dark, and that impression, which strikes our eyes in sun-shine, differ only in degree, not in nature. That the case is the same with all our simple impressions and ideas, it's impossible to prove by a particular enumeration of them. Every one may satisfy himself in this point by running over as many as he pleases. But if anyone should deny this universal resemblance, I know no way of convincing him, but by desiring him to show a simple impression, that has not a correspondent idea, or a simple idea, that has not a correspondent impression. If he does not answer this challenge, as it is certain he cannot, we may from his silence and our own observation establish our conclusion.

Thus we find, that all simple ideas and impressions resemble each other; and as the complex are formed from them, we may affirm in general, that these two species of perception are exactly correspondent. Having discovered this relation, which requires no further examination, I am curious to find some other of their qualities. Let us consider how they stand with regard to their existence, and which of the impressions and ideas are causes, and which effects.

The full examination of this question is the subject of the present treatise; and therefore we shall here content ourselves with establishing one general proposition, That all our simple ideas in their first appearance are derived from simple impressions, which are correspondent to them, and which they exactly represent.

In seeking for phenomena to prove this proposition, I find only those of two kinds; but in each kind the phenomena are obvious, numerous, and conclusive. I first make myself certain, by a new review, of what I have already asserted, that every simple impression is attended with a correspondent idea, and every simple idea with a correspondent impression. From this constant conjunction of resembling perceptions I immediately conclude, that there is a great connection betwixt our correspondent impressions and ideas, and that the existence of the one has a considerable influence upon that of the other. Such a constant conjunction, in such an infinite number of instances, can never arise from chance; but clearly proves a dependence of the impressions on the ideas, or of the ideas on the impressions. That I may know on which side this dependence lies, I consider the order of their first appearance; and find by constant experience, that the simple impressions always take the precedence of their correspondent ideas, but never appear in the contrary order. To give a child an idea of scarlet or orange, of sweet or bitter, I present the objects, or in other words, convey to him these impressions; but proceed not so absurdly, as to endeavor to produce the impressions by exciting the ideas. Our ideas upon their appearance produce not their correspondent impressions, nor do we perceive any colour, or feel any sensation merely upon thinking of them. On the other hand we find, that any impressions either of the mind or body is constantly followed by an idea, which resembles it, and is only different in the degrees of force and liveliness. The constant conjunction of our resembling perceptions, is a convincing proof, that the one are the causes of the other; and this priority of the impressions is an equal proof, that our impressions are the causes of our ideas, not our ideas of our impressions.

……

But besides this exception, it may not be amiss to remark on this head, that the principle of the priority of impressions to ideas must be understood with another limitation, viz. that as our ideas are images of our impressions, so we can form secondary ideas, which are images of the primary; as appears from this very reasoning concerning them. This is not, properly speaking, an exception to the rule so much as an explanation of it. Ideas produce the images of themselves in new ideas; but as the first ideas are supposed to be derived from impressions, it still remains true, that all our simple ideas proceed either mediately or immediately from their correspondent impressions.

This then is the first principle I establish in the science of human nature; nor ought we to despise it because of the simplicity of its appearance. Forit is remarkable, that the present question concerning the precedency of our impressions or ideas, is the same with what has made so much noise in other terms, when it has been disputed whether there be any innate ideas, or whether all ideas be derived from sensation and reflection. We may observe, that in order to prove the ideas of extension and colour not to be innate, philosophers do nothing but show, that they are conveyed by our senses. To prove the ideas of passion and desire not to be innate, they observe that we have a preceding experience of these emotions in ourselves. Now if we carefully examine these arguments, we shall find that they prove nothing but that ideas are preceded by other more lively perceptions, from which they are derived, and which they represent. I hope this clear stating of the question will remove all disputes concerning it, and will render this principle of more use in our reasonings, than it seems hitherto to have been.

Section II Division of the subject

Since it appears, that our simple impressions are prior to their correspondent ideas, and that the exceptions are very rare, method seems to require we should examine our impressions, before we consider our ideas. Impressions may be divided into two kinds, those of Sensation and those of Reflection. The first kind arises in the soul originally, from unknown causes. The second is derived in a great measure from our ideas, and that in the following order. An impression first strikes upon the senses, and makes us perceive heat or cold, thirst or hunger, pleasure or pain of some kind or other. Of this impression there is a copy taken by the mind, which remains after the impression ceases; and this we call an idea. This idea of pleasure or pain, when it returns upon the soul, produces the new impressions of desire and aversion, hope and fear, which may properly be called impressions of reflection, because derived from it. These again are copied by the memory and imagination, and become ideas which perhaps in their turn give rise to other impressions and ideas. So the impressions of reflection are only antecedent to their correspondent ideas, but posterior to those of sensation, and derived from them. The examination of our sensations belongs more to anatomists and natural philosophers than to moral; and therefore shall not at present be entered upon. And as the impressions of reflection, viz. passions, desires, and emotions, which principally deserve our attention, arise mostly from ideas, it will be necessary to reverse that method, which at first sight seems most natural; and in order to explain the nature and principles of the human mind, give a particular account of ideas, before we proceed to impressions. For this reason I have here chosen to begin with ideas.

Section III Of the ideas of the memory and imagination

We find by experience, that when any impression has been present with the mind, it again makes its appearance there as an idea; and this it may do after two different ways: either when in its new appearance it retains a considerable degree of its first vivacity, and is somewhat intermediate betwixt an impression and an idea; or when it entirely loses that vivacity, and is a perfect idea. The faculty, by which we repeat our impressions in the first manner, is called the Memory, and the other the Imagination.It is evident at first sight, that the ideas of the memory are much more lively and strong than those of the imagination, and that the former faculty paints its objects in more distinct colours, than any which are employed by the latter. When we remember any past event, the idea of it flows in upon the mind in a forcible manner; whereas in the imagination the perception is faint and languid, and cannot without difficulty be preserved by the mind steady and uniform for any considerable time. Here then is a sensible difference betwixt one species of ideas and another. But of this more fully hereafter.

There is another difference betwixt these two kinds of ideas, which is no less evident, namely that though neither the ideas of the memory nor imagination, neither the lively nor faint ideas can make their appearance in the mind, unless their correspondent impressions have gone before to prepare the way for them, yet the imagination is not restrained to the same order and form with the original impressions; while the memory is in a manner tied down in that respect, without any power of variation.

It is evident, that the memory preserves the original form, in which its objects were presented, and that wherever we depart from it in recollecting anything, it proceeds from some defect or imperfection in that faculty. An historian may, perhaps, for the more convenient carrying on of his narration, relate an event before another, to which it was in fact posterior; but then he takes notice of this disorder, if he be exact; and by that means replaces the idea in its due position. It is the same case in our recollection of those places and persons, with which we were formerly acquainted. The chief exercise of the memory is not to preserve the simple ideas, but their order and position. In short, this principle is supported by such a number of common and vulgar phenomena, that we may spare ourselves the trouble of insisting on it any farther.

The same evidence follows us in our second principle, of the liberty of the imagination to transpose and change its ideas. The fables we meet with in poems and romances put this entirely out of question. Nature there is totally confounded, and nothing mentioned but winged horses, fiery dragons, and monstrous giants. Nor will this liberty of the fancy appear strange, when we consider, that all our ideas are copied from our impressions, and that there are not any two impressions which are perfectly inseparable. Not to mention, that this is an evident consequence of the division of ideas into simple and complex. Where-ever the imagination perceives a difference among ideas, it can easily produce a separation.

Section IV Of the connection or association of ideas

As all simple ideas may be separated by the imagination, and may be united again in what form it pleases, nothing would be more unaccountable than the operations of that faculty, were it not guided by some universal principles, which render it, in some measure, uniform with itself in all times and places. Were ideas entirely loose and unconnected, chance alone would join them; andit is impossible the same simple ideas should fall regularly into complex ones (as they commonly do) without some bond of union among them, some associating quality, by which one idea naturally introduces another. This uniting principle among ideas is not to be considered as an inseparable connection; for that has been already excluded from the imagination: nor yet are we to conclude, that without it the mind cannot join two ideas; for nothing is more free than that faculty: but we are only to regard it as a gentle force, which commonly prevails, and is the cause why, among other things, languages so nearly correspond to each other; nature in a manner pointing out to everyone those simple ideas, which are most proper to be united into a complex one. The qualities, from which this association arises, and by which the mind is after this manner conveyed from one idea to another, are three, viz. Resemblance, Contiguity in time or place, and Cause and Effect.

I believe it will not be very necessary to prove, that these qualities produce an association among ideas, and upon the appearance of one idea naturally introduce another. It is plain, that in the course of our thinking, and in the constant revolution of our ideas, our imagination runs easily from one idea to any other that resembles it, and that this quality alone is to the fancy a sufficient bond and association. It is likewise evident, that as the senses, in changing their objects, are necessitated to change them regularly, and take them as they lie contiguous to each other, the imagination must by long custom acquire the same method of thinking, and run along the parts of space and time in conceiving its objects. As to the connection, that is made by the relation of cause and effect. We shall have occasion afterwards to examine it to the bottom, and therefore shall not at present insist upon it. It is sufficient to observe, that there is no relation, which produces a stronger connection in the fancy, and makes one idea more readily recall another, than the relation of cause and effect betwixt their objects.

That we may understand the full extent of these relations, we must consider, that two objects are connected together in the imagination, not only when the one is immediately resembling, contiguous to, or the cause of the other, but also when there is interposed betwixt them a third object, which bears to both of them any of these relations. This may be carried on to a great length; though at the same time we may observe, that each remove considerably weakens the relation. Cousins in the fourth degree are connected by causation, if I may be allowed to use that term; but not so closely as brothers, much less as child and parent. In general we may observe, that all the relations of blood depend upon cause and effect, and are esteemed near or remote, according to the number of connecting causes interposed betwixt the persons.

Of the three relations above-mentioned this of causation is the most extensive. Two objects may be considered as placed in this relation, as well when one is the cause of any of the actions or motions of the other, as when the former is the cause of the existence of the latter. For as that action or motion is nothing but the object itself, considered in a certain light, and as the object continues the same in all its different situations, it is easy to imagine how such an influence of objects upon one another may connect them in the imagination.

Questions

1. Does Hume agree that "many of our complex ideas never had impressions that corresponded to them, and that many of our complex impressions never are exactly copied in ideas"? Why or why not?
2. How are impressions related to ideas? What kind of relationship is established between them?
3. What does Hume think of innate ideas?
4. What are the differences between impressions of Sensation and those of Reflection?
5. What is the proper way to distinguish the ideas of memory from the ideas of imagination according to Hume?

6. By what means are ideas logically connected to each other? What qualities are employed by human mind to convey from idea to another? Try to explain each of them in your own words.

7. Why does Hume say that of the three relations of ideas that of causation is the most extensive?

Questions for Further Reflection

1. Both Kant and Hume discussed reason. What do they refer to respectively? Is it possible to reconcile the two?
2. Reason is and will remain to be a hot topic for philosophers. Can you recognize any differences in the mode of reasoning between western philosophers and Chinese scholars?
3. Numerous scholars have attempted to explain the creation of thoughts and ideas. Does Hume's illustration or theorization make sense to you? Why or why not?
4. Humanism is the centerpiece of modern western philosophy. Has humanism found its place in Chinese philosophy? What might be the differences between Western humanism and humanism of China?
5. President Xi has advocated the building of a community with a shared future for mankind. How is humanism related to or utilized to facilitate its realization?

References and Further Reading

1. Kant, I.(1998). *Critique of Pure Reason.* Cambridge: Cambridge University Press.
2. 人文主义历史 https://rlp.hds.harvard.edu/religions/humanism/history-humanism
3. 人文主义背景 https://www.newworldencyclopedia.org/entry/Humanism
4. 人文主义概念 https://americanhumanist.org/what-is-humanism/edwords-what-is-humanism/
5. 人文主义介绍 https://www.britannica.com/topic/humanism

Chapter 5　Scientific Revolution

This chapter presents two excerpts of the classical works of scientific revolution, the purpose of which is to help readers establish a basic framework of this historical period in the science.

The Scientific Revolution is traditionally assumed to start with the Copernican Revolution (initiated in 1543) and to be complete in the "grand synthesis" of Isaac Newton's 1687 *Principia*. Much of the change of attitude came from Francis Bacon whose "confident and emphatic announcement" in the modern progress of science inspired the creation of scientific societies such as the Royal Society, and Galileo who championed Copernicus and developed the science of motion. In the 20th century, Alexandre Koyré introduced the term "scientific revolution", centering his analysis on Galileo. The term was popularized by Butterfield in his *Origins of Modern Science*.

The period saw a fundamental transformation in scientific ideas across mathematics, physics, astronomy, and biology in institutions supporting scientific investigation and in the more widely held picture of the universe. The new kind of scientific activity emerged only in a few countries of Western Europe, and it was restricted to that small area for about two hundred years. Since the 19th century, scientific knowledge has been assimilated by the rest of the world.

The two works selected in this chapter are "Words" from Gottfried Wilhelm Leibniz's *New Essays on Human Understanding* and "Aphorisms concerning the interpretation of nature" from Sir Francis Bacon's *Novum Organum*. The first one, mainly as the critique against the John Locke's *An Essay Concerning Human Understanding*, was written by Gottfried Wilhelm Leibniz after he read Locke's book in 1690s. But the book was never published when Leibniz was alive until Raspe started to edit and publish Leibniz's works in 1765. The second one was written by Sir Francis Bacon. The *Novum Organum*, fully *Novum Organum, sive indicia vera de Interpretatione Naturae* (*New organon, or true directions concerning the interpretation of nature*), is a philosophical work by Francis Bacon, written in Latin and published in 1620. The title is a reference to Aristotle's work *Organon*, which was his treatise on logic and syllogism. In *Novum Organum*, Bacon details a new system of logic he believes to be superior to the old ways of syllogism. This is now known as the Baconian method.

Words

Gottfried Wilhelm Leibniz

Pre-reading

Leibniz's lifelong concern with language and signs in general is well known: his contributions to mathematical notation, his endeavor to create a universal "characteristic" or a "philosophical" language, his attempts to develop a symbolism for logic, his studies in comparative, historical, and "rational" grammar—all are often mentioned as forerunners of contemporary efforts in their respective fields.

The essays here collected bring to light aspects of Leibniz's work on these and related issues which have been so far neglected. As a rule, they take as their starting point Leibniz's early writings on characters and cognition, on definition, on truth, on memory, on grammar, on the specific problems of religious discourse, and so on. But an effort has been made to relate the views expressed in these writings both to Leibniz's more mature views, and to the conceptions prevailing in his time, as well as in the preceding and following periods. In spite of the apparent diversity of topics, there is a common thread running through all the essays. All of them try to investigate to what extent language and signs, in their most varied forms, are related to cognitive processes, according to Leibniz and some of his contemporaries.

Now let's read the text and reflect on the questions that follow.

Text

Foreword

The *Essay on the Understanding*, produced by the illustrious John Locke, is one of the finest and most admired works of the age. It's true that my opinions often differ from his, but far from denying Locke's merit I testify in his favour by showing where and why I differ from him when I find that on certain significant points I have to prevent his authority from prevailing over reason. Indeed, although Locke says hundreds of fine things that I applaud, our systems are very different. His is closer to Aristotle and mine to Plato, although each of us parts company at many points from the teachings of both these ancient writers. He writes in a more informal style whereas I am sometimes forced to be a little more technical and abstract—which is no advantage for me, particularly when writing in a living language. However, I think that by using two speakers, one presenting opinions drawn from Locke's Essay and the other adding my comments, the confrontation will be more to your taste than a dry commentary from which you would have to be continually turning back to Locke's book in order to understand mine.

Part I Of words and language in general

Philalethes: God having designed man to be a sociable creature, made him not only with an inclination and indeed a need to associate with those of his own kind, but also with the ability to speak—which was to be the great instrument, and common tie of society. This is the origin of words, which serve to represent and even to explicate ideas.

Theophilus: I'm happy to find you far removed from Hobbes's view. He didn't agree that man was designed for society, and imagined that we have merely been forced into it by necessity and by the wickedness of the members of our species. But he didn't take into account that the best of men, free from all wickedness, would join together the better to accomplish their goal, just as birds flock together the better to travel in company. Or as beavers congregate by the hundreds to construct great dams, which couldn't be achieved by a small number of them: they need these dams to create reservoirs or ponds in which they build their lodges and catch the fish on which they feed. That is the basis of society amongst social animals, and not fear of their kind, which hardly occurs among the beasts.

Phil: Just so; and, the better to promote such society, man's organs were shaped by nature so as to be fit to make articulate sounds, which we call "words".

Theo: As regards organs, those of monkeys are apparently just as well adapted as ours for forming speech, yet they don't show the slightest progress in this direction. So they must lack something that doesn't appear on the surface. We should also bear in mind that one could speak—i.e. make oneself understood by sounds from one's mouth—without forming "articulate sounds", instead employing musical tones for this purpose. But it would take great skill to design a language of tones, whereas a language of words has been able to be formed and perfected gradually by people in a state of natural simplicity. Yet there are peoples, such as the Chinese, who use tones and accents to vary their words, of which they have only a small number. This led one... authority on languages to think that the Chinese language is artificial—that is, invented all at once by some ingenious man in order to enable the many different peoples occupying the great land of China to communicate verbally, although this language might by now be changed through long usage.

Phil: Just as orang-outangs and other monkeys have the organs for speech, but don't form words, parrots and certain other birds may be said to have words but no language. For parrots and some other birds can be taught to make distinct enough sounds, but they are by no means capable of language. Only man is in a position to use these sounds as signs of internal conceptions—signs through which a man can make his thoughts known to others.

Theo: If we didn't want to make ourselves understood we indeed wouldn't ever have created language—I agree about that. But once it has been created, it serves also for purposes other than communication; for it also enables man to reason to himself, both because words provide the means for remembering abstract thoughts and also because symbols and "blind thoughts" are useful in reasoning, as it would take too long to lay everything out and always replace terms by definitions.

Phil: But if every particular thing needed a distinct name to be signified by, there would be so many words that it would be hard to manage them; and so language was further improved by the use of general terms standing for general ideas.

Theo: General terms don't merely improve languages; they are required for their essential structure. (**1**) If by "particular" things you mean individual ones, then if we only had words that applied to them—only proper names and no descriptive terms—we wouldn't be able to say anything. This is because new items are being encountered at every moment—new individuals and accidents and (what we talk about most) events. (**2**) But if by "particular things" you mean the lowest species—the ultimately detailed and specific kinds of things—then… it is obvious that these are themselves universals, based on similarity. So what we have here is just a matter of more or less widespread similarity, depending on whether one is speaking of large classes or of smaller ones; and it's natural to mark linguistically all sorts of similarities or agreements, thus employing terms having every degree of generality. Indeed the most general ones, though they have a wider spread over individuals to which they apply, carry a lighter load of ideas or essences; they were very often the easiest to form, and are the most useful. Thus you will see children and people who are trying to speak an unfamiliar language, or to speak about unfamiliar matters, employ general terms like "thing", "plant" and "animal" in place of the more specific terms that they don't know. And it is certain that all proper or individual names were originally descriptive or general.

Phil: There are even words that men use not to signify any idea but to signify the lack or absence of some idea—words such as "nothing", "ignorance" and "barrenness".

Theo: I don't see what's wrong with saying that there are negative ideas, just as there are negative truths, since the act of denial is positive. I have already mentioned this.

Phil: I shan't argue with you about that. It will be more useful in leading us a little way towards understanding the source of all our notions and knowledge if we notice how words that are used to conceive events and notions far removed from the senses arise from sensible ideas, from which they are carried across to more abstruse meanings.

Theo: The situation is that our specifically human needs have forced us to abandon the natural order of ideas, for the natural order would be common to angels and men and intelligences in general. It would be the one for us to follow if we had no concern for our own interests. As things stand, however, our specifically human needs have forced us to abandon the natural order in favour of the order that was provided by the incidents and episodes to which our species is subject; this order represents the history of our discoveries, as it were, rather than the origin of notions.

Phil: Just so; and this historical order, which can't (for the reason you have given) be learned through the analysis of notions, can be learned from names themselves through the analysis of words. Thus the following words:

imagine,
comprehend,
adhere,
conceive,

instill,
disgust,
disturbance,
tranquillity,

and so on are all words taken from the operations of sensible things and applied to certain ways of thinking. "Spirit" in its primary meaning is breath; "angel" in its primary meaning is messenger. Facts like these enable us to make some kind of guess about what kind of notions filled the minds of those who first launched languages; and about how nature used the names themselves to suggest to men—without the men being aware of what was happening—the sources and drivers of all their knowledge.

Theo: In the Hottentots' Creed the Holy Spirit is called by a word that signifies a mild, gentle puff of air. It is the same with most other words—sometimes without its even being recognized, because most of the true etymologies are lost... This analogy between sensible and insensible things, which has been the basis for figures of speech, is worth exploring. We will understand it better if we consider the very widespread examples provided by the use of prepositions, such as "to", "with", "of", "before", "in", "out", "by", "for", "on", "toward", which were all derived from place, distance and motion and were subsequently carried across to all kinds of changes, orders, sequences, differences, and conformities. "**To**" signifies *approach*, as when we say "I am going to Rome". But also to tie something down we make it *approach* the thing we want to join it to, and so we say that one thing is tied **to** another. Also, since there is an immaterial tie (so to speak) when one thing follows from another according to moral reasons, we say that what results from someone's movements or decisions belongs or attaches **to** him, as if it tended to cling to and *go along* with him... If someone is **of** [= "from"] a certain place, the place has been an object for him by virtue of the sensible things with which it has confronted him, and it is still an object of his memory, which continues to be full of it; with the result that objects of thought are signified by the preposition "**of**", as when we say: it is a question **of** this, he is speaking **of** that; as though the person were **of** [= "from"] the item in question. [He adds two more examples: "in" and "on".] Since these analogies are extremely variable and don't depend on any determinate notions, languages vary greatly in their use of these particles...

Part II The signification of words

Philalethes: Since words are used by men as signs of their ideas, we can begin by asking how these words came to be settled as such—i.e. how it came about that this word signified that idea. This much is generally agreed: particular articulate sounds aren't naturally connected with certain ideas, for if they were there would be only one human language; rather, sounds are connected with ideas through human decisions, in which this word is voluntarily made the mark of that idea.

Theophilus: I know that the Scholastics and everyone else are given to saying that the meanings of words are chosen, and it's true they aren't settled by natural necessity. But they are settled by reasons—sometimes natural ones in which chance plays some part, sometimes moral ones that involve choice. [Theophilus continues with this theme at great length, including a theory that an individual syllable or sound can have the same meaning in many languages. He concludes by saying:] I myself have presented some thoughts on this subject... Most inquiries into European origins, customs and antiquities have to do with the Teutonic language and antiquities. I wish that learned men would do as much with regard to Walloon, Biscayan, Slavonic, Finnish, Turkish, Persian, Armenian, Georgian, and others, the better to reveal their harmony—which, as I have said, would especially help to make clear the origin of nations.

Phil: This proposal is important; but now the time has come to set aside material aspects of a word and return to formal ones, i.e. to the aspects of meaning that are common to different languages. You will grant me in the first place that when one man speaks to another, what he wants to give signs of are his own ideas, since he can't apply words to things he doesn't know. Until he has some ideas of his own, he can't suppose them to correspond with the qualities of things or with the conceptions of another man.

Theo: Nevertheless, he very often claims to be indicating what others think rather than what he thinks on his own account. This happens only too often with laymen [here = "people who aren't clerics"] who have an unquestioning faith, which leads them to spout doctrines without properly grasping what they mean. But I agree that the speaker, however "blind" and vacuous his thought may be, always does mean something of a general sort by what he says. At least he takes care to put the words in the order that others customarily do, and without really knowing the meaning of what he is saying, he contents himself with the belief that he could grasp its sense if the need arose. Thus a person is sometimes—oftener indeed than he thinks—a mere passer-on of thoughts, a carrier of someone else's message, as though it were a letter.

Phil: You are right to add that a person always has something general in mind, however dense he may be. In the metal he hears called "gold", a child notices nothing but the bright shining yellow colour; so he applies the word "gold" to this same colour when he sees it in a peacock's tail. Others will add great weight, fusibility and malleability.

Theo: I agree; but our idea of the object we are talking about is often even more general than this child's. I have no doubt that a man born blind could speak aptly about colours, and make a speech in praise of light without being acquainted with it, just from having learned about its effects and about the conditions in which it occurs.

Phil: This observation of yours is very true. It often happens that men focus their thoughts more on words than on things. Indeed, because most words are learned before the ideas for which they stand are known, some people—not only children but adults—often speak as parrots do. However, men usually think they are revealing their own thoughts, and in addition they credit their words with secretly referring also to other people's ideas and to things themselves. For if two conversing people attached different ideas to the same sounds, they would be speaking two languages. It is true that men don't pause long to examine what the ideas of others are; we assume that our idea is the one that the majority and the intelligent people in our country attach to the word in question. This assumption that our words stand also for ideas in the minds of others occurs especially with regard to simple ideas and modes; but with regard to substances it is more especially believed that our words stand also for the reality of things.

Theo: Ideas represent substances and modes equally, and in each case words indicate the things as well as the ideas. So I don't see much difference, except that ideas of substantial things and of sensible qualities are more settled. Another point: It sometimes happens that our ideas and thoughts are what we are talking about, and are the very things we want to signify; and notions of thoughts enter more than one might think into notions of things...

Questions

1. According to the dialogue between Philalethes and Theophilus, how can we define "word" and "language" respectively? Please give your definition by illustrating the function and features of "words" and "language".
2. Can you make an assumption about John Locke's idea on words and language based on the dialogue between Phi and Theo?
3. What are the differences between the words "gold" and "color"?
4. What is Leibniz's opinion on Chinese? Do you agree with him? Please give your reasons or examples to illustrate your idea.
5. In what sense does Leibniz use the word "general"? Please demonstrate your understanding to this word by translating this word into Chinese.

Novum Organum

Francis Bacon

Pre-reading

Bacon is often studied through a comparison to his contemporary René Descartes. Both thinkers were, in a sense, some of the first to question the philosophical authority of the ancient Greeks. Bacon and Descartes both believed that a critique of preexisting natural philosophy was necessary, but their respective critiques proposed radically different approaches to natural philosophy.

In a basic sense the central difference between the philosophical methods of Descartes and those of Bacon can be reduced to an argument between deductive and inductive reasoning and whether to trust or doubt the senses. However, there is another profound difference between the two thinkers' positions on the accessibility of Truth. Descartes professed to be aiming at absolute Truth. It is questionable whether Bacon believed such a Truth can be achieved. In his opening remarks, he proposes "to establish progressive stages of certainty." For Bacon, a measure of truth was its power to allow predictions of natural phenomena (although Bacon's forms come close to what we might call "Truth" because they are universal, immutable laws of nature).

The *Novum Organum*, fully *Novum Organum, sive indicia vera de Interpretatione Naturae* (*New organon, or true directions concerning the interpretation of nature*), is a philosophical work by Francis Bacon, written in Latin and published in 1620. The title is a reference to Aristotle's work *Organon*, which was his treatise on logic and syllogism. In *Novum Organum*, Bacon details a new system of logic he believes to be superior to the old ways of syllogism. This is now known as the Baconian method.

Bacon's work was instrumental in the historical development of the scientific method. His technique bears a resemblance to the modern formulation of the scientific method in the sense that it is centered on experimental research. Bacon's emphasis on the use of artificial experiments to provide additional observances of a phenomenon is one reason that he is often considered "the Father of the Experimental Philosophy" (for example famously by Voltaire). Modern scientific method does not follow Bacon's methods in its details, but more in the spirit of being methodical and experimental, and so his position in this regard can be disputed. Importantly though, Bacon set the scene for science to develop various methodologies, because he made the case against older Aristotelian approaches to science, arguing that method was needed because of the natural biases and weaknesses of the human mind, including the natural bias it has to seek metaphysical explanations which are not based on real observations. Bacon begins the work with a rejection of pure a priori deduction as a means of discovering truth in natural philosophy. Of his philosophy, he stated that his plan was as easy to describe as it was difficult to effect. For it was to establish degrees of certainty, take care of the sense by a kind of reduction, but to reject for the most part the work of the mind that follows upon sense. And Bacon was mean to open up and lay down a new and certain pathway from the perceptions of the senses themselves to the mind.

Novum Organum was actually published as part of a much larger work, *Instauratio Magna*— "the great instauration". The word "instauration" was intended to show that the state of human knowledge was to simultaneously press forward while also returning to that enjoyed by man before the Fall. Originally intending *Instauratio Magna* to contain six parts (of which *Novum Organum* constituted the second), Bacon did not come close to completing this series, as parts V and VI were never written at all. *Novum Organum*, written in Latin and consisting of two books of aphorisms, was included in the volume that Bacon published in 1620; however, it was also unfinished, as Bacon promised several additions to its content which ultimately remained unprinted.

Now let's read the text and reflect on the questions that follow.

Text

Foreword

Those who have taken it on themselves to lay down the law of nature as something that has already been discovered and understood, whether they have spoken in simple confidence or in a spirit of professional posturing, have done great harm to philosophy and the sciences. As well as succeeding in producing beliefs in people, they have been effective in squashing and stopping inquiry; and the harm they have done by spoiling and putting an end to other men's efforts outweighs any good their own efforts have brought. Some people on the other hand have gone the opposite way, asserting that absolutely nothing can be known—having reached this opinion through dislike of the ancient sophists, or through uncertainty and fluctuation of mind, or even through being crammed with some doctrine or other. They have certainly advanced respectable reasons for their view; but zeal and posturing have carried them much too far: they haven't started from true premises or ended at the right conclusion. The earlier of the ancient Greeks (whose writings are lost) showed better judgment in taking a position between one extreme: presuming to pronounce on everything, and the opposite extreme: despairing of coming to understand anything. Often they complained bitterly about how hard investigation is and how dark everything is, and were like impatient horses champing at the bit; but they did pursue their objective and came to grips with nature, apparently thinking that the way to settle this question of whether anything can be known was not by arguing but by trying—testing, experimenting. Yet they too, trusting entirely to the power of their intellect, didn't bring any rules to bear and staked everything on hard thinking and continuous mental effort. My method is hard to practice but easy to explain. I propose to establish degrees of certainty, to retain the evidence of the senses subject to certain constraints, but mostly to reject ways of thinking that track along after sensation. In place of that, I open up a new and certain path for the mind to follow, starting from sense-perception. The need for this was felt, no doubt, by those who gave such importance to dialectics; their emphasis on dialectics showed that they were looking for aids to the intellect, and had no confidence in the innate and spontaneous process of the mind. [Bacon's dialectica, sometimes translated as "logic", refers more narrowly to the formalized and rule-governed use of logic, especially in debates.] But this remedy did no good, coming as it did after the processes of everyday life had filled the mind with hearsay and debased doctrines and infested it with utterly empty idols. (I shall explain "idols" in 39 – 45 below.) The upshot was that the art of dialectics, coming (I repeat) too late to the rescue and having no power to set matters right, was only good for fixing errors rather than for revealing truth. [Throughout this work, "art" will refer to any human activity that involves techniques and requires skills.] We are left with only one way to health—namely to start the work of the mind all over again. In this, the mind shouldn't be left to its own devices, but right from the outset should be guided at every step, as though a machine were in control. Certainly if in mechanical projects men had set to work with their naked hands, without the help and power of tools, just as in intellectual matters they have set to work with little but the naked forces of the intellect, even with their best collaborating efforts they wouldn't have achieved—or even attempted—much... Suppose that some enormous stone column had to be moved from its place (wanted elsewhere for some ceremonial purpose), and that men started trying to move it with their naked hands, wouldn't any sober spectator think them mad? If they then brought in more people, thinking that that might do it, wouldn't he think them even madder? If they then weeded out the weaker laborers, and used only the strong and vigorous ones, wouldn't he think them madder than ever? Finally, if they resolved to get help from the art of athletics, and required all their workers to come with hands, arms, and sinews properly oiled and medicated according to good athletic practice, wouldn't the onlooker think "My God, they are trying to show method in their madness!"? Yet that is exactly how men proceed in intellectual matters—with just the same kind of mad effort and useless combining of forces—when they hope to achieve great things either through their individual brilliance or through the sheer number of them who will co-operate in the work, and when they try through dialectics (which we can see as a kind of athletic art) to strengthen the sinews of the intellect. With all this study and effort, as anyone with sound judgment can see, they are merely applying the naked intellect; whereas in any great work to be done by the hand of man the only way to increase the force exerted by each and to co-ordinate the efforts of all is through instruments and machinery. Arising from those prefatory remarks, there are two more things I have to say; I want them to be known, and not forgotten. One concerns ancient philosophers, the other concerns modern philosophy (1) If I were to declare that I could set out on the same road as the ancient philosophers and come back with something better than they did, there would be no disguising the fact that I was setting up a rivalry between them and me, inviting a comparison in respect of our levels of excellence or intelligence or competence. There would nothing new in that, and nothing wrong with it either, for if the ancients got something wrong, why couldn't I—why couldn't anyone—point it out and criticize them for it? But that contest, however right or permissible it was, might have been an unequal one, casting an unfavourable light on my powers. So it is a good thing—good for avoiding conflicts and intellectual turmoil—that I can leave untouched the honour and reverence due to the ancients, and do what I plan to do while gathering the fruits of my modesty! There won't be any conflict here: my aim is to open up a new road for the intellect to follow, a road the ancients didn't know and didn't try. I shan't be taking a side or pressing a case. My role is merely that of a guide who points out the road—a lowly enough task, depending more on a kind of luck than on any ability or excellence. (2) That was a point about persons; the other thing I want to remind you of concerns the topic itself. Please bear this in mind: I'm not even slightly working to overthrow the philosophy [here = "philosophy and science"] that is flourishing these days, or any other more correct and complete philosophy that has been or will be propounded. I don't put obstacles in the way of this accepted philosophy or others like it; let them go on doing what they have long done so well—let them give philosophers something to argue about, provide decoration for speech, bring profit to teachers of rhetoric and civil servants! Let me be frank about it: the philosophy that I shall be advancing isn't much use for any of those purposes. It isn't ready to hand; you can't just pick it up as you go; it doesn't fit with preconceived ideas in a way that would enable it to slide smoothly into the mind; and the vulgar won't ever get hold of it except through its practical applications and its effects. [In this work, "vulgar" means "common, ordinary, run-of-the-mill" (as in "vulgar induction") or, as applied to people, "having little education and few intellectual interests".] So let there be two sources of doctrine, two disciplines, two groups of philosophers, and two ways of doing philosophy, with the groups not being hostile or alien to each other, but bound together by mutual services. In short, let there be one discipline for cultivating the knowledge we have, and another for discovering new knowledge. This may be pleasant and beneficial for both. Most men are in too much of a hurry, or too preoccupied with business affairs, to engage with my way of doing philosophy—or they don't have the mental powers needed to understand it. If for any of those reasons you prefer the other way—prefer cultivation to discovery—I wish you all success in your choice, and I hope you'll get what you are after. But if you aren't content to stick with the knowledge we already have, and want to penetrate further, to conquer nature by works, not conquer an adversary by argument, to look not for nice probable opinions but for sure proven knowledge, I invite you to join with me, if you see fit to do so. [In this context, "works" are experiments.] For ease of communication and to make my approach more familiar by giving it a name, I have chosen to call one of these approaches the mind's anticipation of nature, the other "the interpretation of nature". [Throughout this work, "anticipation" means something like "second-guessing, getting ahead of the data, jumping the gun". Bacon means it to sound rash and risky; no one current English word does the job.]

Aphorisms concerning the interpretation of nature—Book 2: 1 – 15

1. What **human power** does and is intended for is this: For a given body, to create and give to it a new nature (or new natures)—e.g. melting gold or cooking chicken or dissolving salt in water. What **human knowledge** does and is intended for is this: For a given nature, to discover its form, or true specific differentia... i.e. the features that a thing must have if it is to qualify as belonging to this or that natural kind, e.g. the features of gold that differentiate it from metal in general. Subordinate to these primary works are two secondary and less important ones. Under the "power" heading: turning concrete bodies into something different, so far as this is possible—e.g. turning lead into gold, if this can be done. Under the "knowledge" heading: (1) in every case of generation and motion, discovering the hidden process through which the end-state form results from the manifest efficient cause and the manifest material; and (2) discovering the hidden microstructure of bodies that are not changing. An example of (1): the wax around the wick of a lighted candle melts. Flame is the efficient cause, wax is the material, and meltedness is the end-state form. But "flame" and "wax" stand for items that are manifest, obvious, out there on the surface; we know that when you apply one to the other you get melting; but that isn't knowing what hidden process is involved—what is really basically going on at the sub-microscopic level when flame melts wax. An example of (2): discovering what the sub-microscopic structure is of wax when it isn't melting.

2. Human knowledge is in a poor state these days—how poor can be seen from things that are commonly said. Not that they are all wrong. True knowledge is knowledge by causes. Causes are of four kinds: material, formal, efficient, and final. [A coin's material cause is the metal, its formal cause is the property of being round-with-a-head-inscribed-on-it, etc., its immediate efficient cause is the stamping of a die on the metal, and its final cause is its purpose, use in commerce.] So far, so good; but the concept of final cause spoils the sciences rather than furthering them, except in contexts involving human action. The discovery of formal causes is

despaired of. Efficient and material causes are real and solid and important, but they are investigated and believed in only as they appear on things' surfaces, without reference to the hidden process through which the end-state form comes about; and, taken in that way, they are slight and superficial, and contribute little or nothing to true and active science. Earlier in this work I noted as an error of the human mind the opinion that to understand what exists you have to look at forms. It's true that nature really contains only individual bodies, performing individual pure actions according to a fixed law; but in science this law is what we inquire into, discover, and explain; it is at the root of our theorizing as well as of our practical applications. When I speak approvingly of "forms", what I'm talking about is this law; I use the word "form" because it has become familiar.

3. If someone knows the cause of a nature such as whiteness or heat in only some subjects, his knowledge is incomplete; and if he can produce a certain effect in only some of the substances that are capable of it, his power is incomplete. Now efficient and material causes are unstable causes, i.e. they can't be depended on to act in the same way in all cases; they are nothing but vehicles in which the operative hidden structures and causes are carried; they are causes that convey the end-state form in only some cases. If a man's knowledge is confined to them, he may arrive at new discoveries that hold generally about some pre-selected class of fairly similar substances; but he doesn't get to the fixed, deeper boundaries of things—"fixed" in contrast to the "unstable" nature of manifest causes. But someone who knows forms gets hold of the unity of nature in things that are superficially most unalike, and this enables him to discover and bring to light really new things—things that no one would ever have thought of, and that would never have come to light in the course of nature, or through deliberate experiments, or even by accident. So the discovery of forms leads to truth in theory-building and freedom in operation.

4. The roads to human power and to human knowledge lie extremely close together and are nearly the same. Still, because of the bad old habit of thinking in terms of abstractions, it is safer to get the sciences started and to carry them on from foundations that have to do with their practical part, and to let the practical part itself be a stamp of authenticity and also a limit-setter for the purely theoretical part. Well, then, let's think about a man who wants to confer some nature on a given body; he wants, for instance, to give a piece of silver the yellow colour that gold has or to make it heavier (subject to the laws of matter), or he wants to make an opaque stone transparent, or to make glass sticky, or to get something that isn't a plant to grow. Our question should be: what kind of rule or direction or guidance should he most wish for? And we should answer this in the simplest and plainest terms that we can find: (1) He will undoubtedly want to be shown something that won't let him down or fail when it is put to the test. (2) He will want a rule that won't tie him down to this or that particular means and mode of operation. Otherwise he may be stuck: he doesn't have the prescribed means, others are available and would do the job, but the rule he is to follow doesn't allow them. (3) He will want to be shown a procedure that isn't as difficult as the thing he wants to do—e.g. he won't want to be told "To make that silver yellow like gold, you must make it yellow like gold"; he'll want something more practicable than that. A true and complete rule of operation, then, will have to be a

proposition that is (1) certain, (2) not constricting and (3) practicable. And the same holds for the discovery of a true form. For the form of a nature is such that: given the form, the nature is sure to follow; so that the form is absent whenever the nature is absent and is also such that if the form is taken away, the nature is sure to vanish; so that the form is present whenever the nature is present. Lastly, the true form derives the given nature from some essence that many other also things have and that is better known to nature than the form we are discussing. Here, then, is the procedure that I urge you to follow to get a true and perfect axiom of knowledge concerning a nature N1: discover some other nature N2 that is convertible with N1 and is a special case of some more general nature N3, falling under it as a true species falls under a true and real genus. Now these two directions, the active rule of operation and the contemplative rule of discovery, are one and the same thing; what is most useful in operation is what is most true in knowledge.

5. There are two kinds of rule or axiom for the transformation of bodies. The first regards a body as a company or collection of simple natures. In gold, for example, the following properties meet:

- it is yellow in colour;
- it is heavy up to a certain weight;
- it is malleable and ductile up to a certain length;
- it doesn't vaporize or lose any of its substance through the action of fire;
- it turns into a liquid with a certain degree of fluidity;
- it is separated and dissolved by such-and-such means;

and so on for the other natures that come together in gold. This first kind of axiom derives the thing from the forms of its simple natures. Someone who knows the forms of yellowness, weight, ductility, fixity, fluidity, dissolving and so on, and the methods for giving them to bodies, and their intensities and varieties, will work to have them come together in some body which will thereby be transformed into gold. This kind of operation pertains to the primary kind of action; the fact that it involves many natures doesn't mean that it is a later, non-basic kind of event. For the principle of generating many simple natures is the same as that of generating just one; except that the investigator is more tightly constrained if more than one nature is involved, because of the difficulty of bringing together so many natures that don't easily combine except in the well-trodden ordinary paths of nature. Anyway, despite that drawback it must be said that this mode of operation that looks to simple natures in a compound body starts from what in nature is constant and eternal and universal, namely natures, and opens broad roads to human power—ones that in the present state of things human thought can scarcely take in. The second kind of axiom depends on the discovery of hidden processes. It doesn't start off from simple natures, but from compound bodies just as they are found in the ordinary course of nature. For example, one might be inquiring into the origins of gold or some other metal or stone—How does it start forming? What process takes it from its basic rudiments or elements right through to the completed mineral? Or, similarly, the question of how plants are generated—What process takes the plant from the first congealing of sap in the ground, or from seeds, right through to the formed plant? Similarly we might inquire into the process of development in the generation of animals from the beginning right through to birth; and similarly with other bodies. This investigation concerns not only the generation of bodies but also other motions and operations of nature. For example, we can inquire into nutrition, the whole continuous series of events leading from the swallowing of the food through to its complete assimilation. Or into voluntary motion in animals, from the first impression on the imagination and the continuous efforts of the spirits through to the flexing and moving of limbs. Or into what is involved in the motion of the tongue and lips and other organs right through to the uttering of articulate sounds. Each of these inquiries relates to natures that have been concertized, i.e. brought together into a single structure; they concern what may be called particular and special practices of nature, not its basic and universal laws that constitute forms. That drawback of this approach is balanced by an advantage that it has over the other. It has to be admitted that this second approach seems to have less baggage and to lie nearer at hand and to give more ground for hope than the first approach, i.e. the one described first in this aphorism. The practical-experimental approach corresponding to this second theoretical approach starts from ordinary familiar natural events and moves on from them to ones that are very like them or at least not too unlike. But the merits of the first approach mustn't be forgotten. Any deep and radical operations on nature depend entirely on the primary axioms, which are the business of the first approach. And then there are the matters where we have no power to operate but only to know, for example the heavenly bodies (for we can't operate on them, alter them, or turn them into something else). With these things, whether we are investigating the facts about what happens in the heavens or trying to understand why it happens, we have to depend on the primary and universal axioms concerning simple natures, such as the nature of spontaneous rotation, of attraction or magnetism, and of many others that apply to more things than just to the heavenly bodies. "Does the earth rotate daily, or do the heavens revolve around it?" Don't think you have a hope of answering this before you have understood the nature of spontaneous rotation.

6. The hidden process of which I speak is utterly different from anything that would occur to men in the present state of the human mind. For what I understand by it is not the different stages—different steps—that bodies can be seen to go through in their development but rather a perfectly continuous process which mostly escapes the senses. For instance: in all generation and transformation of bodies, we must inquire into

- what is lost and escapes, what remains, what is added;
- what is expanded, what is contracted;
- what is united, what is separated;
- what is continued, what is cut off;
- what pushes, what blocks;
- what predominates, what gives way;

and a variety of other particulars. And it's not just with the generation or transformation of bodies, but with all other alterations and motions we should inquire into

- what goes before, what comes after;
- what is quicker, what is slower;

· what produces motion, what merely guides it;
and so on. In the present state of the sciences no-one knows or does anything about any of these matters. For seeing that every natural action takes place per minima or at least by ones that are too small to strike the senses, no-one can hope to govern or change nature unless he understands and observes such action in the right way.

Questions

1. Why Bacon concludes that "Human knowledge is in a poor state these days"?
2. According to the 4th item, what does "the bad old habit of thinking" refer to? Why Bacon consider the old habit to be a bad one?
3. In your opinion, how many ways to obtain knowledge? Please illustrate with examples in your own words.
4. Do you think Bacon's approach to knowledge is as solid as he claims to be? Please illustrate with examples.

Questions for Further Reflection

1. According to the common knowledge nowadays, people would agree that a mathematical/physical research to be a scientific one. In what way a humanity study can be called a scientific one? Or how to carry out a scientific research in humanities?
2. Defend or attack following statement: "Meaning is calculating" by referring to your linguistic knowledge.

References and Further Reading

1. Donne, J. (1957). An Anatomy of the World. In Thomas S. Kuhn, *The Copernican Revolution: Planetary Astronomy in the Development of Western Thought*. Cambridge: Harvard University Press.

2. Hunt, S. D. (2003). *Controversy in Marketing Theory: For Reason, Realism, Truth, and Objectivity*. Armonk, N.Y.: M.E. Sharpe.

3. Butterfield, H. (1959). *The Origins of Modern Science, 1300 –1800*. New York: Macmillan Co.

4. Leibniz, G.W. (1996). *New Essays on Human Understanding*. (Peter Remnant & Jonathan Bennett, Trans. and Eds.). Cambridge: Cambridge University Press.

5. Bacon, Sir F. (1902). *Novum Organum*. (L. Bacon & J. Devey, Eds.). New York: P.F. Collier.

6. 科学革命大英百科全书词条 https://www.britannica.com/science/Scientific-Revolution

Chapter 6　French Enlightenment

This chapter presents two excerpts of the classic works in the *Age of Enlightenment*, the purpose of which is to give the readers a glimpse of the diverse ideas in this age.

The Enlightenment, known also as the *Age of Enlightenment* or the *Age of Reason*, was a philosophical and intellectual movement in Europe during the 18th century. At the very heart of it was a critical questioning of established institutions, customs, and morals and a belief that humanity's intellectual powers can lead to a better human existence.

In 1784, in his famous essay "What is Enlightenment?" (1784), German philosopher Immanuel Kant defined the Enlightenment as "man's leaving his self-caused immaturity" and proclaimed the motto of the Enlightenment as "Dare to know! Have the courage to use your own intelligence!" The Enlightenment was indeed a movement of intellectuals who dared to think for themselves and to rely on their intellectual capacities.

While the source of its ideas can be traced back to the Renaissance which revived humanity as creative beings and the Protestant Reformation which challenged the monolithic authority of the church, the movement was mostly influenced by the rational and empirical methods and accomplishments that were introduced by the scientific revolution. The very idea that scientific methods can be employed to understand all life, all institutions and all systems was gradually established. If Sir Issac Newton could capture the natural laws governing the world of nature, the intellectuals could too, discover the laws governing human society. And this led to a hope of freeing humanity from worthless tradition and superstition and of making progress toward a better society. *The Encyclopédie* best illustrated this. According to Denis Diderot, *the Encyclopédie's* aim was "to change the way people think" and for people to be able to inform themselves and to know things.

As science developed, more people began to question the accepted religious truths and values, as it could be seen from the skepticism of works of Pierre Bayle. Bayle criticized religious intolerance and maintained the existence of different religions. His famous work, the *Historical and Critical Dictionary* was well known to 18th century intellectuals.

John Locke's theory of knowledge especially influenced the Enlightenment thinkers too. In his "An Essay Concerning Human Understanding", John Locke probed into the foundation of human knowledge and understanding. The human mind, as he described in the essay, was a blank slate, a white paper, without any ideas and can only be filled through experience. Knowledge, then, is derived from environment instead of heredity; from reason rather than faith. The essay was one of the principal sources of empiricism in modern philosophy, and influenced many enlightenment philosophers, such as David Hume and George Berkeley.

Altogether the discoveries of Newton, the skepticism of Bayle, and the empiricism of Locke nurtured the leading figures of the Enlightenment who were called "Philosophes" in France. Although not all of them were French, in the mid-18th century, Paris became the center and most of the leaders of the Enlightenment were French, i.e. Voltaire, Montesquieu, Denis Diderot, Jean-Jacques Rousseau, and Condorcet.

Outside France, the Scottish philosophers and economists David Hume and Adam Smith, Immanuel Kant of Germany, and the American statesman Thomas Jefferson were notable Enlightenment thinkers.

The influence of Enlightenment ideas can be felt everywhere. The ideas of the Enlightenment undermined the authority of the monarchy and the Church and paved the way for the political revolutions of the 18th and 19th centuries. The French Revolution and the American Revolution were almost direct results of Enlightenment thinking.

In this chapter, the most outstanding philosopher Voltaire's first important work *Philosophical Letters* and the most controversial philosopher Rousseau's *Social Contract* are selected to give the readers a general idea of the grand subjects that fascinated the greatest minds of the 18th century.

Philosophical Letters

Voltaire

Pre-reading

Francois-Marie Arouet, known by his pen name Voltaire (1694 – 1778) was the greatest figure of the Enlightenment, famous for his challenge of authority, his advocacy of religious tolerance and his defenses of civil liberty. Voltaire published numerous books, plays, poems, and letters throughout his lifetime. There was seldom a subject of importance that he left untouched. In short, he greatly influenced 18th century European thought. As Victor Hugo said: "To name Voltaire is to characterize the entire eighteenth century."

Born in a prosperous middle-class family in Paris, he received a classical education and showed an early gift for languages. In his mid-twenties, he had already established his reputation as a poet and dramatist, and enjoyed great popularity among Parisian intellectuals. However, his attacks on the French government and the Catholic Church resulted in numerous exiles and imprisonments, keeping him away from the intellectual center of the country and Europe. It was until 1778 that he returned to Paris and died there at the age of 83.

Voltaire's philosophical and political views can be found in nearly all his writings. Especially well-known for his criticism of traditional religion, he is perhaps the most vocal and persistent critic of religion in France. Again and again Voltaire returned to the theme of the establishment of religious tolerance and a respect for the rights of man by the abolition of torture and abuses.

In his *Philosophical Letters*, Voltaire said, "If there were only one religion in England there would be danger of despotism; if there were two they would cut each other's throats. But there are thirty, and they live in peace and happiness." In his *Treatise on Toleration*, he argued that religious toleration introduced no problems for England and Holland, and thundered that "all men are brothers under God." In his private letters, he constantly referred to the word *l'infâme* and the expression *écrasez l'infâme* (crush the infamous thing)—the infamy being religious abuse, oppression, fanaticism and intolerance.

In this chapter, Voltaire's *Philosophical Letters* is selected to give the reader a glimpse to his attachment to the ideal of religious toleration. In 1726, Voltaire offended a nobleman and was issued to exile in England. Much impressed by the English society and government, its support of speech and religion freedom, and the philosophy of John Locke and the scientific works of Sir Isaac Newton as well, he wrote *Lettres Philosophiques* (*Philosophical Letters*), first published in English translation (London 1733) as the *Letters Concerning the English Nation*.

The book showed a great admiration of the country's religious toleration, freedom of thought, and its respect for scientists, merchants and philosophers. Although Voltaire exaggerated the English institutions from an outsider perspective, he did succeed in criticizing the absolute monarchy and the lack of religious freedom in France. The book caused a huge sensation soon after it was published, and was condemned and burnt publicly by the French authority. The author himself was forced again to leave Paris. Nevertheless, this small book shocked the intellectual culture of the French and ushered in a great movement that would someday spread to the whole Europe, even the world. As the *Encyclopedia Britannica* said, "This small, brilliant book is a landmark in the history of thought: not only does it embody the philosophy of the 18th century, but it also defines the essential direction of the modern mind."

The *Philosophical Letters* consists of 24 letters in which Voltaire first discusses about religion, especially about the Quakers, then about English political system, trade system, medicine, philosophers and art. In this chapter, three letters from the book are selected.

The first two letters are all about the Quakers. In Letter Ⅰ, Voltaire assumed a tone of innocent and pious French Catholic to introduce the seemingly weird and unorthodox Quakers and to show his readers how religiously tolerant the English people could be. In the description of Voltaire, the Quakers are humble, serious and virtuous. They retreated from the religious rituals (such as baptism and circumcision), discarded flattery and lies, saluted no person and treated beggars equally to a king. All these helped to provide French people a different perspective to examine their religious traditions.

Letter Ⅴ "On the Church of England" begins with an observation, "This is the country of sects. An Englishman, as a freeman, goes to Heaven by whatever road he pleases." Voltaire probed into the foundation of religious tolerance in England. However, neither political exclusion (the church of England being the dominant religion) nor zealous preachment promoted religious toleration. It is in Letter Ⅵ "On The Presbyterians", Voltaire answered the question, the free market. Taking the Royal Exchange in London, Voltaire lavished his praise on the air of toleration among people of different religions. "There the Jew, the Mahometan, and the Christian transact together, as though they all professed the same religion... There thee Presbyterian confides in the Anabaptist, and the Churchman depends on the Quaker's word... all are satisfied."

Voltaire's legacy is immense. His defense of religious toleration would find expressions in the future.

Now let's read the text and reflect on the questions that follow.

Text

Letter Ⅰ: On the Quakers

I was of opinion that the doctrine and history of so extraordinary a people were worthy the attention of the curious. To acquaint myself with them I made a visit to one of the most eminent Quakers in England, who, after having traded thirty years, had the wisdom to prescribe limits to his fortune and to his desires, and was settled in a little solitude not far from London. Being come into it, I perceived a small but regularly built house, vastly neat, but without the least pomp of furniture. The Quaker who owned it was a hale, ruddy complexioned old man, who had never been afflicted with sickness because he had always been insensible to passions, and a perfect stranger to intemperance. I never in my life saw a more noble or a more engaging aspect than his. He was dressed like those of his persuasion, in a plain coat without pleats in the sides, or buttons on the pockets and sleeves; and had on a beaver, the brims of which were horizontal like those of our clergy. He did not uncover himself when I appeared, and advanced towards me without once stooping his body; but there appeared more politeness in the open, humane air of his countenance, than in the custom of drawing one leg behind the other, and taking that from the head which is made to cover it. "Friend," says he to me, "I perceive thou art a stranger, but if I can do any thing for thee, only tell me." "Sir," said I to him, bending forwards and advancing, as is usual with us, one leg towards him, "I flatter myself that my just curiosity will not give you the least offense, and that you'll do me the honour to inform me of the particulars of your religion." "The people of thy country," replied the Quaker, "are too full of their bows and compliments, but I never yet met with one of them who had so much curiosity as thy self. Come in, and let us first dine together." I still continued to make some very unreasonable ceremonies, it not being easy to disengage one's self at once from habits we have been long used to; and after taking part in a frugal meal, which began and ended with a prayer to God, I began to question my courteous host. I opened with that which good Catholics have more than once made to Huguenots. "My dear sir," said I, "were you ever baptized?" "I never was," replied the Quaker, "nor any of my brethren." "Zounds!" said I to him, "you are not Christians, then." "Friend," replies the old man in a soft tone of voice, "swear not; we are Christians, and endeavour to be good Christians, but we are not of opinion that the sprinkling water on a child's head makes him a Christian." "Heavens!" said I, shocked at his impiety, "you have then forgot that Christ was baptised by St. John." "Friend," replies the mild Quaker once again, "swear not; Christ indeed was baptised by John, by He himself never baptised anyone. We are the disciples of Christ, not of John." I pitied very much the sincerity of my worthy Quaker, and was absolutely for forcing him to get himself christened. "Were that all," replied he very gravely, "we would submit cheerfully to baptism, purely in compliance with thy weakness, for we don't condemn any person who uses it; but then we think that those who profess a religion of so holy, so spiritual a nature as that of Christ, ought to abstain to the utmost of their power from the Jewish ceremonies." "O unaccountable!" said I: "what! baptism a Jewish ceremony?" "Yes, my friend," says he, "so truly Jewish, that a great many Jews use the baptism of John to this day. Look into ancient authors, and thou wilt find that John only revived this practice; and that it had been used by the Hebrews, long before his time, in like manner as the Mahometans imitated the Ishmaelites in their pilgrimages to Mecca. Jesus indeed submitted to the baptism of John, as He had suffered Himself to be circumcised; but circumcision and the washing with water ought to be abolished by the baptism of Christ, that baptism of the Spirit, that ablution of the soul, which is the salvation of mankind. Thus the forerunner said, 'I indeed baptise you with water unto repentance; but He that cometh after me is mightier that I, whose shoes I am not worthy to bear: He shall baptise you with the Holy Ghost and with fire.' Likewise Paul, the great apostle of the Gentiles, writes as follows to the Corinthians, 'Christ sent me not to baptise, but to preach the Gospel;' and indeed Paul never baptised but two persons with water, and that very much against his inclinations. He circumcised his disciple Timothy, and the other disciples likewise all who were willing to submit to that carnal ordinance. "But art thou circumcised?" added he. "I have not the honour to be so," said I. "Well, friend," continued the Quaker, "thou art a Christian without being circumcised, and I am one without being baptised." Thus did this pious man make a wrong, but very specious application of four or five texts of Scripture which seemed to favour the tenets of his sect; but at the same time forgot very sincerely a hundred texts which made directly against them. I had more sense than to contest with him, since there is no possibility of convincing an enthusiast. A man should never pretend to inform a lover of his mistress' faults, no more than one who is at law of the badness of his cause; nor attempt to win over a fanatic by strength of reasoning. Accordingly I waived the subject.

"Well", said I to him, "what sort of a communion have you?" "We have none like that thou hintest at among us," replied he. "How! no communion?" said I. "Only that spiritual one," replied he, "of hearts." He then began again to throw out his texts of Scripture; and preached a most eloquent sermon against that ordinance. He harangued in a tone as though he had been inspired, to prove that the sacraments were merely of human invention, and that the word "sacrament" was not once mentioned in the Gospel. "Excuse," said he, "my ignorance, for I have not employed a hundredth part of the arguments which might be brought to prove the truth of our religion, but these thou thyself mayest peruse in the Exposition of our Faith written by Robert Barclay. It is one of the best pieces that ever was penned by man; and as our adversaries confess it to be of dangerous tendency, the arguments in it must necessarily be very convincing." I promised to peruse this piece, and my Quaker imagined he had already made a convert of me. He afterwards gave me an account in few words of some singularities which make this sect the contempt of others. "Confess," said he, "that it was very difficult for thee to refrain from laughter, when I answered all thy civilities without uncovering my head, and at the same time said 'thee' and 'thou' to thee. However, thou appearest to me too well read not to know that in Christ's time no nation was so ridiculous as to put the plural number for the singular. Augustus Caesar himself was spoken to in such phrases as these: 'I love thee,' 'I beseech thee,' 'I thank thee;' but he did not allow any person to call him 'Domine,' sir. It was not till many ages after that men would have the word 'you,' as though they were double, instead of 'thou' employed in speaking to them; and usurped the flattering titles of lordship, of eminence, and of holiness, which mere worms bestow on other worms by assuring them that they are with a most profound respect, and an infamous falsehood, their most obedient humble servants. It is to secure ourselves more strongly from such a shameless traffic of lies and flattery, that we 'thee' and 'thou' a king with the same freedom as we do a beggar, and salute no person; we owing nothing to mankind but charity, and to the laws respect and obedience."

"Our apparel is also somewhat different from that of others, and this purely, that it may be a perpetual warning to us not to imitate them. Others wear the badges and marks of their several dignities, and we those of Christian humility. We fly from all assemblies of pleasure, from diversions of every kind, and from places where gaming is practised; and, indeed, our case would be very deplorable, should we fill with such levities as those I have mentioned the heart which ought to be the habitation of God. We never swear, not even in a court of justice, being of opinion that the most holy name of God ought not to be prostituted in the miserable contests betwixt man and man. When we are obliged to appear before a magistrate upon other people's account (for lawsuits are unknown among the Friends), we give evidence to the truth by sealing it with our yea or nay; and the judges believe us on our bare affirmation, whilst so many other Christians forswear themselves on the holy Gospels. We never war or fight in any case; but it is not that we are afraid, for so far from shuddering at the thoughts of death, we on the contrary bless themoment which unites us with the Being of Beings; but the reason of our not using the outward sword is, that we are neither wolves, tigers, nor mastiffs, but men and Christians. Our God, who has commanded us to love our enemies, and to suffer without repining, would certainly not permit us to cross the seas, merely because murderers clothed in scarlet, and wearing caps two foot high, enlist citizens by a noise made with two little sticks on an ass' skin extended. And when, after a victory is gained, the whole city of London is illuminated; when the sky is in a blaze with fireworks, and a noise is heard in the air, of thanksgivings, of bells, of organs, and of the cannon, we groan in silence, and are deeply affected with sadness of spirit and brokenness of heart, for the sad havoc which is the occasion of those public rejoicings."

Letter V: On the Church of England

England is properly the country of sectarists. Multae sunt mansiones in domo patrismei (in my Father's house are many mansions). An Englishman, as one to whom liberty is natural, may go to heaven his own way.

Nevertheless, though every one is permitted to serve God in whatever mode or fashion he thinks proper, yet their true religion, that in which a man makes his fortune, is the sect of

Episcopalians or Churchmen, called the Church of England, or simply the Church, by way of eminence. No person can possess an employment either in England or Ireland unless he be ranked among the faithful, that is, professes himself a member of the Church of England. This reason (which carries mathematical evidence with it) has converted such numbers of Dissenters of allpersuasions, that not a twentieth part of the nation is out of the pale of the Established Church. The English clergy have retained a great number of the Romish ceremonies, and especially that of receiving, with a most scrupulous attention, their tithes. They also have the pious ambition to aim at superiority.

Moreover, they inspire very religiously their flock with a holy zeal against Dissenters of all denominations. This zeal was pretty violent under the Tories in the four last years of Queen Anne; but was productive of no greater mischief than the breaking the windows of some meeting-houses and the demolishing of a few of them. For religious rage ceased in England with the civil wars, and was no more under Queen Anne than the hollow noise of a sea whose billows still heaved, though so long after the storm when the Whigs and Tories laid waste their native country, in the same manner as the Guelphs and Ghibellines formerly did theirs. It was absolutely necessary for both parties to call in religion on this occasion; the Tories declared for Episcopacy, and the Whigs, as some imagined, were for abolishing it; however, after these had got the upper hand, they contented themselves with only abridging it.

At the time when the Earl of Oxford and the Lord Bolingbroke used to drink healths to the Tories, the Church of England considered these noblemen as the defenders of its holy privileges. The lower House of Convocation (kind of House of Commons) composed wholly of the clergy, was in some credit at that time; at least the members of it had the liberty to meet, to dispute on ecclesiastical matters, to sentence impious books from time to time to the flames, that is, books written against themselves. The Ministry which is now composed of Whigs does not so much as allow those gentlemen to assemble, so that they are at this time reduced (in the obscurity of their respective parishes) to the melancholy occupation of praying for the prosperity of the Government whose tranquility they would willingly disturb. With regard to the bishops, who are twenty-six in all, they still have seats in the House of Lords in spite of the Whigs, because the ancient abuse of considering them as barons subsists to this day. There is a clause, however, in the oath which the Government requires from these gentlemen, that puts their Christian patience to a very great trial, viz., that they shall be of the Church of England as by law established. There are few bishops, deans, or other dignitaries, but imagine they are so jure divino; it is consequently a great mortification to them to be obliged to confess that they owe their dignity to a pitiful law enacted by a set of profane laymen. A learned monk (Father Courayer) wrote a book lately to prove the validity and succession of English ordinations. This book was forbid in France, but do you believe that the English Ministry were pleased with it? Far from it. Those damned Whigs don't care a straw whether the episcopal succession among them hath been interrupted or not, or whether Bishop Parker was consecrated (as it is pretended) in a tavern or a church; for these Whigs are much better pleased that the Bishops should derive their authority from the Parliament than from the Apostles. The Lord Bolingbroke observed that this notion of divine right would only make so many tyrants in lawn sleeves, but that the laws made so many citizens.

With regard to the morals of the English clergy, they are more regular than those of France, and for this reason. All the clergy (a very few excepted) are educated in the Universities of Oxford or Cambridge, far from the depravity and corruption which reign in the capital. They are not called to dignities till very late, at a time of life when men are sensible of no other passion but avarice, that is, when their ambition craves a supply. Employments are here bestowed both in the Church and the army, as a reward for long services; and we never see youngsters made bishops or colonels immediately upon their laying aside the academical gown; and besides most of the clergy are married. The stiff and awkward air contracted by them at the University, and the little familiarity the men of this country have with the ladies, commonly oblige a bishop to confine himself to, and rest contented with, his own. Clergymen sometimes take a glass at the tavern, custom giving them a sanction on this occasion; and if they fuddle themselves it is in a very serious manner, and without giving the least scandal.

That fable-mixed kind of mortal (not to be defined), who is neither of the clergy nor of the laity; in a word, the thing called Abbe in France; is a species quite unknown in England. All the clergy here are very much upon the reserve, and most of them pedants. When these are told that in France young fellows famous for their dissoluteness, and raised to the highest dignities of the Church by female intrigues, address the fair publicly in an amorous way, amuse themselves in writing tender love songs, entertain their friends very splendidly every night at their own houses, and after the banquet is ended withdraw to invoke the assistance of the Holy Ghost, and call themselves boldly the successors of the Apostles, they bless God for their being Protestants. But these are shameless heretics, who deserve to be blown hence through the flames toold Nick, as Rabelais says, and for this reason I don't trouble myself about them.

Letter VI: On the Presbyterians

The Church of England is confined almost to the kingdom whence it received its name, and to Ireland, for Presbyterianism is the established religion in Scotland. This Presbyterianism is directly the same with Calvinism, as it was established in France, and is now professed at Geneva. As the priests of this sect receive but very inconsiderable stipends from their churches, and consequently cannot emulate the splendid luxury of bishops, they exclaim very naturally against honours which they can never attain to. Figure to yourself the haughty Diogenes trampling under foot the pride of Plato. The Scotch Presbyterians are not very unlike that proud though tattered reasoner. Diogenes did not use Alexander half so impertinently as these treated King Charles II; for when they took up arms in his cause in opposition to Oliver, who had deceived them, they forced that poor monarch to undergo the hearing of three or four sermons every day, would not suffer him to play, reduced him to a state of penitence and mortification, so that Charles soon grew sick of these pedants, and accordingly eloped from them with as much joy as a youth does from school.

A Church of England minister appears as another Cato in presence of a juvenile, sprightly French graduate, who bawls for a whole morning together in the divinity schools, and hums a song in chorus with ladies in the evening; but this Cato is a very spark when before a Scotch Presbyterian. The latter affects a serious gait, puts on a sour look, wears a vastly broad-brimmed hat and a long cloak over a very short coat, preaches through the nose, and gives the name of the whore of Babylon to all churches where the ministers are so fortunate as to enjoy an annual revenue of five or six thousand pounds, and where the people are weak enough to suffer this, and to give them the titles of my lord, your lordship, or your eminence.

These gentlemen, who have also some churches in England, introduced there the mode of grave and severe exhortations. To them is owing the sanctification of Sunday in the three kingdoms. People are there forbidden to work or take any recreation on that day, in which the severity is twice as great as that of the Romish Church. No operas, plays, or concerts are allowed in London on Sundays, and even cards are so expressly forbidden that none but persons of quality, and those we call the genteel, play on that day; the rest of the nation go either to church, to the tavern, or to see their mistresses.

Though the Episcopal and Presbyterian sects are the two prevailing ones in Great Britain, yet all others are very welcome to come and settle in it, and live very sociably together, though most of their preachers hate one another almost as cordially as a Jansenist damns a Jesuit.

Take a view of the Royal Exchange in London, a place more venerable than many courts of justice, where the representatives of all nations meet for the benefit of mankind. There the Jew, the Mahometan, and the Christian transact together, as though they all professed the same religion, and give the name of infidel to none but bankrupts. Therethee Presbyterian confides in the Anabaptist, and the Churchman depends on the Quaker's word. At the breaking up of this pacific and free assembly, some withdraw to the synagogue, and others to take a glass. This man goes and is baptized in a great tub, in the name of the Father, Son, and Holy Ghost: that man has his son's foreskin cut off, whilst a set of Hebrew words (quite unintelligible to him) are mumbled over his child. Others retire to their churches, and there wait for the inspiration of heaven with their hats on, and all are satisfied.

If one religion only were allowed in England, the Government would very possibly become arbitrary; if there were but two, the people would cut one another's throats; but as there are such a multitude, they all live happy and in peace.

Questions

1. What is the typical image of a Quaker according to Letter Ⅰ?
2. What do the Quakers think of baptism and communion? How do they defend their practices?
3. How did Voltaire compare the English clergy with those in France? What was his conclusion?
4. What contributed to the tolerance among different sects in England according to Voltaire?

References and Further Reading

1. Durant, W. & Durant, A.(1980) [1965]. *The Story of Civilization: The Age of Voltaire*.

New York: Simon & Schuster.

2. Durant, W. & Durant, A.(1967) .*The Story of Civilization : Rousseau and Revolution* . New York: Simon & Schuster.

3. 英语文本 https://sourcebooks.fordham.edu/mod/1778voltaire-lettres.asp#Letter Ⅰ

4. 伏尔泰哲学思想 https://plato.stanford.edu/entries/voltaire/

5. 伏尔泰生平介绍 https://en.wikipedia.org/wiki/Voltaire#CITEREFDurantDurant1967

6. 伏尔泰生平介绍 https://www.britannica.com/biography/Voltaire

7. 伏尔泰生平介绍 https://www.philosophybasics.com/philosophers_voltaire.html

The Social Contract

Jean-Jacques Rousseau

Pre-reading

Born in the city of Geneva, Switzerland in 1712, Jean-Jacques Rousseau was a philosopher, writer, and a political theorist. As one of the most influential thinkers during the Enlightenment in the eighteenth century Europe, Rousseau's philosophy inspired the French Revolution and Romantic movement, and influenced the development of modern political and educational thought.

Few philosophers have aroused such varying interpretations as Rousseau. Although his major works span the latter part of 18th century and thus it is appropriate to consider him an Enlightenment thinker, there is dispute concerning whether his thought should be characterized as "Enlightenment" or "counter-Enlightenment". In 1750 he published his first important work, *Discourse on the Arts and Sciences*, in which he argued that the advancement in the arts and the sciences caused the corruption of virtue and morality.

Rousseau's political beliefs are presented in two discourses, the *Discourse on the Origin and Basis of Inequality Among Men* (usually known as the *Discourse on Inequality* or *Second Discourse*) and *The Social Contract*. In *Discourse on Inequality*, Rousseau first describes human beings in the pure state of nature, then explains a series of historical events that have moved humans from the state of nature to the state of civil society. Rousseau's natural man is essentially good, peaceful, content and free. It is the socialization that has caused inequality, competition and corruption.

One of the most influential works of political philosophy in the Western tradition,*The Social Contract* was first published as *On the Social Contract or Principles of Political Rights*. As the title has suggested, the object of the discourse is not to deal with the actual institutions, but to establish the essential principles that form the basis of every legitimate society. The *Social Contract* begins with the opening sentence: "Man is born free, and everywhere he is in chains." Rousseau founds his whole system on human freedom and makes the will of its members the basis of every society. To work out his theory, Rousseau introduces three conceptions: the Social Contract,

Sovereignty and the General Will. Rousseau argues that no one has natural authority over others. An agreement should be formed, in which all individuals give up their natural liberty to create a general will that in turn would represent the sovereign state. Rousseau refers to the agreement among the people as the Social Contract. By joining together into civil society under the social contract and exchanging their natural right for a better form of freedom, individuals can both preserve themselves and yet remain free, because submission to the general will of the people as a whole guarantees individuals against being subordinated to the wills of others, and also ensures that they themselves obey because they work collectively out the law.

A brilliant and unconventional thinker throughout his life, Rousseau's influence goes beyond political philosophy. His novel *Emile*, published in the same year with *The Social Contract*, is considered one of the Enlightenment's most important works on education. The work is more like a treatise on the education of the "natural man". His emphasis on the balance between heart and mind, sentiment and reason make him a precursor of the Romanticism movement. Rousseau was also a composer and music theorist, making important contributions to music.

In this section, five chapters of Book I in *The Social Contract* are selected. In Book I, Rousseau aims to determine the basis for a legitimate political authority. He declares that in Book I he intends to determine whether there can be any "sure and legitimate rule of administration" in the civil society and he will take both what is right and what is people's best interests, or put differently, "justice and utility", into consideration.

In Chapter II The First Societies, Rousseau uses the family as an analogy for society and implies the workings of human freedom are the same in different contexts. Children are attached to their father only as long as they depend on him for survival. Once a child no longer needs his father for preservation, their bond dissolves. If they choose to remain "united" with their parents, it is only by agreement. This is because self-preservation is human's most important drive. Similarly, in society, people can choose to give up their liberty to their ruler for their own advantage.

In Chapters III and IV, Rousseau argues that force cannot make the legitimate political authority and no man is entitled to a natural authority over other man. In Chapter III, according to Rousseau, force does not create right. People yield to those stronger than themselves out of necessity rather than of will. In addition, since strength is a relative form and there could be always a stronger force replacing the former one, all previous claims justified on the right of the strongest will be nullified. People should only obey legitimate powers. In Chapter IV, Rousseau refutes Grotius' justification of the legitimacy of authority on the basis of slavery and continues to argue that a government cannot control people without their consensus. But since people cannot be willing give up their freedom, their very nature and the basis of all morality, contracts based on absolute dominion for one party and absolute obedience for the other are not legitimate.

Thus there is a necessity to trace back to the first convention in society. In Chapter VI, Rousseau first states that when the obstacles people face in the state of nature become greater for any one person to handle, people form societies. Each person has to give up his natural liberty in exchange for the greater power of the community. Because everyone gives himself and all of his rights to the community, the conditions of the social contract are thus equal for all. Rousseau defines this contract in the following terms "Each of us puts his person and all his power in common under the supreme direction of the general will, and, in our corporate capacity, we receive each member as an indivisible part of the whole." This moral and collective body, formed by the union of all other persons, is called State when passive, and Sovereign when active, and Power when compared with others like itself.

Now let's read the first book of *The Social Contract* and get a glimpse of Rousseau's political philosophy.

Text

Book I

Chapter I : Subject of the first book

Man is born free; and everywhere he is in chains. One thinks himself the master of others, and still remains a greater slave than they. How did this change come about? I do not know. What can make it legitimate? That question I think I can answer.

If I took into account only force, and the effects derived from it, I should say: "As long as a people is compelled to obey, and obeys, it does well; as soon as it can shake off the yoke, and shakes it off, it does still better; for, regaining its liberty by the same right as took it away, either it is justified in resuming it, or there was no justification for those who took it away." But the social order is a sacred right which is the basis of all other rights. Nevertheless, this right does not come from nature, and must therefore be founded on conventions. Before coming to that, I have to prove what I have just asserted.

Chapter II : The first societies

The most ancient of all societies, and the only one that is natural, is the family: and even so the children remain attached to the father only so long as they need him for their preservation. As soon as this need ceases, the natural bond is dissolved. The children, released from the obedience they owed to the father, and the father, released from the care he owed his children, return equally to independence. If they remain united, they continue so no longer naturally, but voluntarily; and the family itself is then maintained only by convention.

This common liberty results from the nature of man. His first law is to provide for his own preservation, his first cares are those which he owes to himself; and, as soon as he reaches years of discretion, he is the sole judge of the proper means of preserving himself, and consequently becomes his own master.

The family then may be called the first model of political societies: the ruler corresponds to the father, and the people to the children; and all, being born free and equal, alienate their liberty only for their own advantage. The whole difference is that, in the family, the love of the father for his children repays him for the care he takes of them, while, in the State, the pleasure of commanding takes the place of the love which the chief cannot have for the peoples under him.

Grotius denies that all human power is established in favour of the governed, and quotes slavery as an example. His usual method of reasoning is constantly to establish right by fact. It would be possible to employ a more logical method, but none could be more favourable to tyrants.

It is then, according to Grotius, doubtful whether the human race belongs to a hundred men, or that hundred men to the human race: and, throughout his book, he seems to incline to the former alternative, which is also the view of Hobbes. On this showing, the human species is divided into so many herds of cattle, each with its ruler, who keeps guard over them for the purpose of devouring them.

As a shepherd is of a nature superior to that of his flock, the shepherds of men, i.e., their rulers, are of a nature superior to that of the peoples under them. Thus, Philo tells us, the Emperor Caligula reasoned, concluding equally well either that kings were gods, or that men were beasts.

The reasoning of Caligula agrees with that of Hobbes and Grotius. Aristotle, before any of them, had said that men are by no means equal naturally, but that some are born for slavery, and others for dominion.

Aristotle was right; but he took the effect for the cause. Nothing can be more certain than that every man born in slavery is born for slavery. Slaves lose everything in their chains, even the desire of escaping from them: they love their servitude, as the comrades of Ulysses loved their brutish condition. If then there are slaves by nature, it is because there have been slaves against nature. Force made the first slaves, and their cowardice perpetuated the condition.

I have said nothing of King Adam, or Emperor Noah, father of the three great monarchs who shared out the universe, like the children of Saturn, whom some scholars have recognised in them. I trust to getting due thanks for my moderation; for, being a direct descendant of one of these princes, perhaps of the eldest branch, how do I know that a verification of titles might not leave me the legitimate king of the human race? In any case, there can be no doubt that Adam was sovereign of the world, as Robinson Crusoe was of his island, as long as he was its only inhabitant; and this empire had the advantage that the monarch, safe on his throne, had no rebellions, wars, or conspirators to fear.

Chapter III: The right of the strongest

THE strongest is never strong enough to be always the master, unless he transforms strength into right, and obedience into duty. Hence the right of the strongest, which, though to all seeming meant ironically, is really laid down as a fundamental principle. But are we never to have an explanation of this phrase? Force is a physical power, and I fail to see what moral effect it can have. To yield to force is an act of necessity, not of will—at the most, an act of prudence. In what sense can it be a duty?

Suppose for a moment that this so-called "right" exists. I maintain that the sole result is a mass of inexplicable nonsense. For, if force creates right, the effect changes with the cause: every force that is greater than the first succeeds to its right. As soon as it is possible to disobey with impunity, disobedience is legitimate; and, the strongest being always in the right, the only thing that matters is to act so as to become the strongest. But what kind of right is that which perishes when force fails? If we must obey perforce, there is no need to obey because we ought; and if we are not forced to obey, we are under no obligation to do so. Clearly, the word "right" adds nothing to force: in this connection, it means absolutely nothing.

Obey the powers that be. If this means yield to force, it is a good precept, but superfluous: I can answer for its never being violated. All power comes from God, I admit; but so does all sickness: does that mean that we are forbidden to call in the doctor? A brigand surprises me at the edge of a wood: must I not merely surrender my purse on compulsion; but, even if I could withhold it, am I in conscience bound to give it up? For certainly the pistol he holds is also a power.

Let us then admit that force does not create right, and that we are obliged to obey only legitimate powers. In that case, my original question recurs.

Chapter IV: Slavery

Since no man has a natural authority over his fellow, and force creates no right, we must conclude that conventions form the basis of all legitimate authority among men.

If an individual, says Grotius, can alienate his liberty and make himself the slave of a master, why could not a whole people do the same and make itself subject to a king? There are in this passage plenty of ambiguous words which would need explaining; but let us confine ourselves to the word alienate. To alienate is to give or to sell. Now, a man who becomes the slave of another does not give himself; he sells himself, at the least for his subsistence: but for what does a people sell itself? A king is so far from furnishing his subjects with their subsistence that he gets his own only from them; and, according to Rabelais, kings do not live on nothing. Do subjects then give their persons on condition that the king takes their goods also? I fail to see what they have left to preserve.

It will be said that the despot assures his subjects civil tranquillity. Granted; but what do they gain, if the wars his ambition brings down upon them, his insatiable avidity, and the vexations conduct of his ministers press harder on them than their own dissensions would have done? What do they gain, if the very tranquillity they enjoy is one of their miseries? Tranquillity is found also in dungeons; but is that enough to make them desirable places to live in? The Greeks imprisoned in the cave of the Cyclops lived there very tranquilly, while they were awaiting their turn to be devoured.

To say that a man gives himself gratuitously, is to say what is absurd and inconceivable; such an act is null and illegitimate, from the mere fact that he who does it is out of his mind. To say the same of a whole people is to suppose a people of madmen; and madness creates no right.

Even if each man could alienate himself, he could not alienate his children: they are born men and free; their liberty belongs to them, and no one but they has the right to dispose of it. Before they come to years of discretion, the father can, in their name, lay down conditions for their preservation and well-being, but he cannot give them irrevocably and without conditions: such a gift is contrary to the ends of nature, and exceeds the rights of paternity. It would therefore be necessary, in order to legitimise an arbitrary government, that in every generation the people should be in a position to accept or reject it; but, were this so, the government would be no longer arbitrary.

To renounce liberty is to renounce being a man, to surrender the rights of humanity and even its duties. For him who renounces everything no indemnity is possible. Such a renunciation is incompatible with man's nature; to remove all liberty from his will is to remove all morality from his acts. Finally, it is an empty and contradictory convention that sets up, on the one side, absolute authority, and, on the other, unlimited obedience. Is it not clear that we can be under no obligation to a person from whom we have the right to exact everything? Does not this condition alone, in the absence of equivalence or exchange, in itself involve the nullity of the act? For what right can my slave have against me, when all that he has belongs to me, and, his right being mine, this right of mine against myself is a phrase devoid of meaning?

Grotius and the rest find in war another origin for the so-called right of slavery. The victor having, as they hold, the right of killing the vanquished, the latter can buy back his life at the price of his liberty; and this convention is the more legitimate because it is to the advantage of both parties.

But it is clear that this supposed right to kill the conquered is by no means deducible from the state of war. Men, from the mere fact that, while they are living in their primitive independence, they have no mutual relations stable enough to constitute either the state of peace or the state of war, cannot be naturally enemies. War is constituted by a relation between things, and not between persons; and, as the state of war cannot arise out of simple personal relations, but only out of real relations, private war, or war of man with man, can exist neither in the state of nature, where there is no constant property, nor in the social state, where everything is under the authority of the laws.

Individual combats, duels and encounters, are acts which cannot constitute a state; while the private wars, authorised by the Establishments of Louis IX, King of France, and suspended by the Peace of God, are abuses of feudalism, in itself an absurd system if ever there was one, and contrary to the principles of natural right and to all good polity.

War then is a relation, not between man and man, but between State and State, and individuals are enemies only accidentally, not as men, nor even as citizens, but as soldiers; not as members of their country, but as its defenders. Finally, each State can have for enemies only other States, and not men; for between things disparate in nature there can be no real relation.

Furthermore, this principle is in conformity with the established rules of all times and the constant practice of all civilised peoples. Declarations of war are intimations less to powers than to their subjects. The foreigner, whether king, individual, or people, who robs, kills or detains the subjects, without declaring war on the prince, is not an enemy, but a brigand. Even in real war, a just prince, while laying hands, in the enemy's country, on all that belongs to the public, respects the lives and goods of individuals: he respects rights on which his own are founded. The object of the war being the destruction of the hostile State, the other side has a right to kill its defenders, while they are bearing arms; but as soon as they lay them down and surrender, they cease to be enemies or instruments of the enemy, and become once more merely men, whose life no one has any right to take. Sometimes it is possible to kill the State without killing a single one of its members; and war gives no right which is not necessary to the gaining of its object. These principles are not those of Grotius: they are not based on the authority of poets, but derived from the nature of reality and based on reason.

The right of conquest has no foundation other than the right of the strongest. If war does not give the conqueror the right to massacre the conquered peoples, the right to enslave them cannot be based upon a right which does not exist. No one has a right to kill an enemy except when he cannot make him a slave, and the right to enslave him cannot therefore be derived from the right to kill him. It is accordingly an unfair exchange to make him buy at the price of his liberty his life, over which the victor holds no right. Is it not clear that there is a vicious circle in founding the right of life and death on the right of slavery, and the right of slavery on the right of life and death?

Even if we assume this terrible right to kill everybody, I maintain that a slave made in war, or a conquered people, is under no obligation to a master, except to obey him as far as he is compelled to do so. By taking an equivalent for his life, the victor has not done him a favour; instead of killing him without profit, he has killed him usefully. So far then is he from acquiring over him any authority in addition to that of force, that the state of war continues to subsist between them: their mutual relation is the effect of it, and the usage of the right of war does not imply a treaty of peace. A convention has indeed been made; but this convention, so far from destroying the state of war, presupposes its continuance.

So, from whatever aspect we regard the question, the right of slavery is null and void, not only as being illegitimate, but also because it is absurd and meaningless. The words slave and right contradict each other, and are mutually exclusive. It will always be equally foolish for a man to say to a man or to a people: "I make with you a convention wholly at your expense and wholly to my advantage; I shall keep it as long as I like, and you will keep it as long as I like."

Chapter VI: The social compact

I suppose men to have reached the point at which the obstacles in the way of their preservation in the state of nature show their power of resistance to be greater than the resources at the disposal of each individual for his maintenance in that state. That primitive condition can then subsist no longer; and the human race would perish unless it changed its manner of existence.

But, as men cannot engender new forces, but only unite and direct existing ones, they have no other means of preserving themselves than the formation, by aggregation, of a sum of forces great enough to overcome the resistance. These they have to bring into play by means of a single motive power, and cause to act in concert.

This sum of forces can arise only where several persons come together: but, as the force and liberty of each man are the chief instruments of his self-preservation, how can he pledge them without harming his own interests, and neglecting the care he owes to himself? This difficulty, in its bearing on my present subject, may be stated in the following terms:

"The problem is to find a form of association which will defend and protect with the whole common force the person and goods of each associate, and in which each, while uniting himself with all, may still obey himself alone, and remain as free as before." This is the fundamental problem of which the Social Contract provides the solution.

The clauses of this contract are so determined by the nature of the act that the slightest modification would make them vain and ineffective; so that, although they have perhaps never been formally set forth, they are everywhere the same and everywhere tacitly admitted and recognised, until, on the violation of the social compact, each regains his original rights and resumes his natural liberty, while losing the conventional liberty in favour of which he renounced it.

These clauses, properly understood, may be reduced to one—the total alienation of each associate, together with all his rights, to the whole community; for, in the first place, as each gives himself absolutely, the conditions are the same for all; and, this being so, no one has any interest in making them burdensome to others.

Moreover, the alienation being without reserve, the union is as perfect as it can be, and no associate has anything more to demand: for, if the individuals retained certain rights, as there would be no common superior to decide between them and the public, each, being on one point his own judge, would ask to be so on all; the state of nature would thus continue, and the association would necessarily become inoperative or tyrannical.

Finally, each man, in giving himself to all, gives himself to nobody; and as there is no associate over whom he does not acquire the same right as he yields others over himself, he gains an equivalent for everything he loses, and an increase of force for the preservation of what he has.

If then we discard from the social compact what is not of its essence, we shall find that it reduces itself to the following terms:

"Each of us puts his person and all his power in common under the supreme direction of the general will, and, in our corporate capacity, we receive each member as an indivisible part of the whole."

At once, in place of the individual personality of each contracting party, this act of association creates a moral and collective body, composed of as many members as the assembly contains votes, and receiving from this act its unity, its common identity, its life and its will. This public person, so formed by the union of all other persons formerly took the name of city, and now takes that of Republic or body politic; it is called by its members State when passive. Sovereign when active, and Power when compared with others like itself. Those who are associated in it take collectively the name of people, and severally are called citizens, as sharing in the sovereign power, and subjects, as being under the laws of the State. But these terms are often confused and taken one for another: it is enough to know how to distinguish them when they are being used with precision.

Questions

1. How do you understand Rousseau's argument that force does not create right?
2. How do you interpret Rousseau's analogy between family and political society?
3. What major arguments did Grotius use to justify the right of slavery? How did Rousseau rebut Grotius' claim?
4. In Chapter Ⅵ, Rousseau argued that "whoever refuses to obey the general will shall be compelled to do so by the whole body". How do you interpret this argument?

Questions for Further Reflection

1. What message can western readers get from Voltaire's *Philosophical Letters* when their society's increasingly split by different political and religious beliefs?
2. According to Voltaire, it seems that it is the free market, where people of different religions gather for interests, becomes the most tolerant place in London. What do you think of the relationship between religion and commerce?
3. Compare Rousseau's social contract theory with that of John Locke and Thomas Hobbes.
4. In what way did Rousseau's political philosophy influence the French Revolution?

References and Further Reading

1. 卢梭.卢梭全集.北京:商务印书馆,2012.
2. Rousseau, J.-J. (1923). *The Social Contract and Discourses by Jean-Jacques Rousseau*. (G. D. H. Cole, Trans.). London and Toronto: J.M. Dent and Sons.
3. 《社会契约论》简介
https://www.academia.edu/7255334/Rousseaus_Social_Contract_An_Introduction_Cambridge_University_Press_2014
4. 卢梭主要著作介绍 https://thegreatthinkers.org/rousseau/introduction/
5. 卢梭生平与著作 https://en.wikipedia.org/wiki/Jean-Jacques_Rousseau
6. 卢梭政治哲学思想 https://plato.stanford.edu/entries/rousseau/
7. 卢梭生平及政治哲学著作
https://www.britannica.com/biography/Jean-Jacques-Rousseau/Major-works-of-political-philosophy

Chapter 7 American Enlightenment

This chapter presents three excerpts of the classical works of American Enlightenment, the purpose of which is to facilitate the readers' understanding of the key ideas of the American Enlightenment.

The American Enlightenment was a period of intellectual movement in the 13 American colonies in the 17th to 18th century, which led to the American Revolution and the establishment of the American Republic. Despite its distinctive features, the American Enlightenment was much inspired by the ideas of the French Enlightenment. Many leading Enlightenment figures, for example, John Locke, Thomas Hobbes, Voltaire, Baron Montesquieu, Immanuel Kant, Adam Smith, Denis Diderot have been regarded as great influences on American thinking. The themes of deism, liberalism, republicanism, and religious toleration recurred in American context.

Deism is not a specific religion but rather a perspective on the nature of God. To most philosophes, God is merely the "first cause". Like a "clockmaker", after the "original act" to start the cosmic process, God left the universe run according to its own natural laws. Discarding the holy books, dogmas, revelation, prophecy and miracles, deists base their religious belief on reason and observation of the natural world. Deism greatly influenced the thought of intellectuals in American Enlightenment, as one can find from Thomas Pains' *The Age of Reason*.

Another idea important to American Enlightenment thinking is liberalism, which argues that humans have natural rights and that government authority is not absolute, but rather based on the will and consent of the governed. The claim that individuals have fundamental God-given rights, such as to property, life, and liberty can be traced back to English philosopher John Locke, and found new expression in Thomas Jefferson's drafting of the *Declaration of Independence*.

American Enlightenment promoted the idea that a nation should be governed as a republic, with its state's head being determined by a general election rather than through heredity. When the North American colonists became increasingly discontent with the British government and convinced its rule was against republican values, they formed an army and resisted. The thinking prompted the American Revolution.

Together with scientific rationality and experimental political ideas, religious toleration also had great effects on the fledgling nation. Inspired by European Enlightenment philosophes, for instance, John Locke, American Enlightenment thinkers believed their government ought to protect its citizens' right to worship the religion they choose (or not to worship any religion) without any fear of persecution by government.

Some of these beliefs are radical, and some moderate. Some can find their sources in Europe, while some take a unique American form. Who then were the thinkers of the American Enlightenment? Here is Paul Johnson in his book, *A History of the American People:*

"It is rare indeed for a nation to have such a group so variously gifted as Washington and Benjamin Franklin, Thomas Jefferson, Alexander Hamilton, James Madison, and John Adams...They were the Enlightenment made flesh."

In this chapter, Thomas Paine's *The Age of Reason* and *Rights of Man*, *The Declaration of Independence* are selected to give the readers a general idea of the significant political and religious themes of the American Enlightenment.

The Age of Reason & Rights of Man

Thomas Paine

Pre-reading

Born in Norfolk, England, Thomas Paine (1737 – 1809) was a political philosopher, writer, and pamphleteer who supported the revolutionary causes in America and Europe. His formal education was meagre. He withdrew from school at an early age and tried various occupations unsuccessfully until in 1774 he met Benjamin Franklin who persuaded him to seek his fortunes in America.

In 1775, Paine began to work on a pamphlet in which he argued that the cause of America should be not just against taxation but for independence. He published his *Common Sense* in 1776. Direct and clear, the 50-page pamphlet soon became a success. In the pamphlet, Paine denounced aristocracy and monarchy, promoted the idea of republicanism, and advocated separation from Britain. The pamphlet was so influential that John Adams once said that, "Without the pen of the author of *Common Sense*, the sword of Washington would have been raised in vain."

As the Revolutionary War began, Paine met General George Washington. Having witnessed the terrible condition of Washington's troops, he published a series of inspirational pamphlets known as *The American Crisis* in late 1776, which began with the famous line "These are the times that try men's souls." and established his reputation as a pamphleteer.

Paine published *Rights of Man* in two parts in 1791 and 1792, a rebuttal of an Irish political philosopher and his attack on the French Revolution. In the book, Paine argued in favor of republicanism and outlined a remedy for the evils of arbitrary government, poverty, illiteracy, unemployment and war.

Being prosecuted for sedition, Paine fled to France. There, he was first enthusiastically received then put into prison because of different political thoughts. While in prison, he began working on his next book, *The Age of Reason*. Though often mistaken as an atheist text, the book actually advocated deism and a belief in God. The first volume criticized Christian theology and organized religion in favor of reason and scientific inquiry while the second volume analyzed the Old Testament and the New Testament of the Bible, questioning the divinity of Jesus Christ.

Paine remained in France until 1802 before he moved to the United States. There he found his services to the country was all forgotten and that he was widely regarded only as an infidel. Despite his poverty and his poor health, Paine continued his attacks on privilege and religious superstitions. He died in New York City in 1809.

Paine expounded on a number of principles that later became central to a liberal-democratic culture. Few of his principles are original, however, unlike the formal style of his contemporaries, he managed to convey complex ideas in direct, clear and concise writing to reach a larger audience and thus secured his success and importance.

In this part, two chapters from *The Age of Reason* and one chapter from *Rights of Man* are selected. In the selection, you will learn about Paine's major religious belief and his attacks on religious institutions and supervisions as well, while from the selection of the conclusion of Rights of Man, you will learn about Paine's advocacy of natural rights, his attacks on mixed government and his defense of republicanism.

Now let's read the text and reflect on the questions that follow.

Text

The Age of Reason
Chapter I The author's profession of faith

IT has been my intention, for several years past, to publish my thoughts upon religion; I am well aware of the difficulties that attend the subject, and from that consideration, had reserved it to a more advanced period of life. I intended it to be the last offering I should make to my fellow-citizens of all nations, and that at a time when the purity of the motive that induced me to it could not admit of a question, even by those who might disapprove the work.

The circumstance that has now taken place in France, of the total abolition of the whole national order of priesthood, and of everything appertaining to compulsive systems of religion, and compulsive articles of faith, has not only precipitated my intention, but rendered a work of this kind exceedingly necessary, lest, in the general wreck of superstition, of false systems of government, and false theology, we lose sight of morality, of humanity, and of the theology that is true.

As several of my colleagues, and others of my fellow-citizens of France, have given me the example of making their voluntary and individual profession of faith, I also will make mine; and I do this with all that sincerity and frankness with which the mind of man communicates with itself.

I believe in one God, and no more; and I hope for happiness beyond this life.

I believe the equality of man, and I believe that religious duties consist in doing justice, loving mercy, and endeavoring to make our fellow-creatures happy.

But, lest it should be supposed that I believe many other things in addition to these, I shall, in the progress of this work, declare the things I do not believe, and my reasons for not believing them.

I do not believe in the creed professed by the Jewish church, by the Roman church, by the Greekchurch, by the Turkish church, by the Protestant church, nor by any church that I know of. My own mind is my own church.

All nationalinstitutions of churches, whether Jewish, Christian, or Turkish, appear to me no other than human inventions set up to terrify and enslave mankind, and monopolize power and profit.

I do not mean by this declaration to condemn those who believe otherwise; they have the same right to their belief as I have to mine. But it is necessary to the happiness of man, that he be mentally faithful to himself. Infidelity does not consist in believing, or in disbelieving; it consists in professing to believe what he does not believe.

It is impossible to calculate the moral mischief, if I may so express it, that mental lying has produced in society. When a man has so far corrupted and prostituted the chastity of his mind, as to subscribe his professional belief to things he does not believe, he has prepared himself for the commission of every other crime. He takes up the trade of a priest for the sake of gain, and, in order to qualify himself for that trade, he begins with a perjury. Can we conceive anything more destructive to morality than this?

Soon after I had published the pamphlet COMMON SENSE, in America, I saw the exceeding probability that a revolution in the system of government would be followed by a revolution in the system of religion. The adulterous connection of church and state, wherever it had taken place, whether Jewish, Christian, or Turkish, had so effectually prohibited, by pains and penalties, every discussion upon established creeds, and upon first principles of religion, that until the system of government should be changed, those subjects could not be brought fairly and openly before the world; but that whenever this should be done, a revolution in the system of religion would follow. Human inventions and priest-craft would be detected; and man would return to the pure, unmixed, and unadulterated belief of one God, and no more.

EVERY national church or religion has established itself by pretending some special mission from God, communicated to certain individuals. The Jews have their Moses; the Christians their Jesus Christ, their apostles and saints; and the Turks their Mahomet; as if the way to God was not open to every man alike.

Chapter Ⅱ Of missions and revelations

Each of those churches shows certain books, which they call revelation, or the Word of God. The Jews say that their Word of God was given by God to Moses face to face; the Christians say, that their Word of God came by divine inspiration; and the Turks say, that their Word of God (the Koran) was brought by an angel from heaven. Each of those churches accuses the other of unbelief; and, for my own part, I disbelieve them all.

As it is necessary to affix right ideas to words, I will, before I proceed further into the subject, offer some observations on the word "revelation." Revelation when applied to religion, means something communicated immediately from God to man.

No one will deny or dispute the power of the Almighty to make such a communication if he pleases. But admitting, for the sake of a case, that something has been revealed to a certain person, and not revealed to any other person, it is revelation to that person only. When he tells it to a second person, a second to a third, a third to a fourth, and so on, it ceases to be a revelation to all those persons. It is revelation to the first person only, and hearsay to every other, and, consequently, they are not obliged to believe it.

It is a contradiction in terms and ideas to call anything a revelation that comes to us at second hand, either verbally or in writing. Revelation is necessarily limited to the first communication. After this, it is only an account of something which that person says was a revelation made to him; and though he may find himself obliged to believe it, it cannot be incumbent on me to believe it in the same manner, for it was not a revelation made to me, and I have only his word for it that it was made to him.

When Moses told the children of Israel that he received the two tables of the commandments from the hand of God, they were not obliged to believe him, because they had no other authority for it than his telling them so; and I have no other authority for it than some historian telling me so, the commandments carrying no internal evidence of divinity with them. They contain some good moral precepts such as any man qualified to be a lawgiver or a legislator could produce himself, without having recourse to supernatural intervention. [NOTE: It is, however, necessary to except the declamation which says that God "visits the sins of the fathers upon the children". This is contrary to every principle of moral justice. —Author.]

When I am told that the Koran was written in Heaven, and brought to Mahomet by an angel, the account comes to near the same kind of hearsay evidence and second hand authority as the former. I did not see the angel myself, and therefore I have a right not to believe it.

When also I am told that a woman, called the Virgin Mary, said, or gave out, that she was with child without any cohabitation with a man, and that her betrothed husband, Joseph, said that an angel told him so, I have a right to believe them or not: such a circumstance required a much stronger evidence than their bare word for it: but we have not even this; for neither Joseph nor Mary wrote any such matter themselves. It is only reported by others that they said so. It is hearsay upon hearsay, and I do not chose to rest my belief upon such evidence.

It is, however, not difficult to account for the credit that was given to the story of Jesus Christ being the Son of God. He was born when the heathen mythology had still some fashion and repute in the world, and that mythology had prepared the people for the belief of such a story. Almost all the extraordinary men that lived under the heathen mythology were reputed to be the sons of some of their gods. It was not a new thing at that time to believe a man to have been celestially begotten; the intercourse of gods with women was then a matter of familiar opinion. Their Jupiter, according to their accounts, had cohabited with hundreds; the story therefore had nothing in it either new, wonderful, or obscene; it was conformable to the opinions that then prevailed among the people called Gentiles, or mythologists, and it was those people only that believed it. The Jews, who had kept strictly to the belief of one God, and no more, and who had always rejected the heathen mythology, never credited the story.

It is curious to observe how the theory of what is called the Christian Church, sprung out of the tail of the heathen mythology. A direct incorporation took place in the first instance, by making the reputed founder to be celestially begotten. The trinity of gods that then followed was no other than a reduction of the former plurality, which was about twenty or thirty thousand. The statue of Mary succeeded the statue of Diana of Ephesus. The deification of heroes changed into the canonization of saints. The Mythologists had gods for everything; the Christian Mythologists had saints for everything. The church became as crowded with the one, as the pantheon had been with the other; and Rome was the place of both. The Christian theory is little else than the idolatry of the ancient mythologists, accommodated to the purposes of power and revenue; and it yet remains to reason and philosophy to abolish the amphibious fraud.

NOTHING that is here said can apply, even with the most distant disrespect, to the real character of Jesus Christ. He was a virtuous and an amiable man. The morality that he preached and practiced was of the most benevolent kind; and though similar systems of morality had been preached by Confucius, and by some of the Greek philosophers, many years before, by the Quakers since, and by many good men in all ages, it has not been exceeded by any.

Rights of Man
Part The First
Being An Answer To Mr. Burke's Attack On The French Revolution
Conclusion
Reason and Ignorance, the opposites of each other, influence the great bulk of mankind. If either of these can be rendered sufficiently extensive in a country, the machinery of Government goes easily on. Reason obeys itself; and Ignorance submits to whatever is dictated to it.

The two modes of the Government which prevail in the world, are-

First, Government by election and representation.

Secondly, Government by hereditary succession.

The former is generally known by the name of republic; the latter by that of monarchy and aristocracy.

Those two distinct and opposite forms erect themselves on the two distinct and opposite bases of Reason and Ignorance.-As the exercise of Government requires talents and abilities, and as talents and abilities cannot have hereditary descent, it is evident that hereditary succession requires a belief from man to which his reason cannot subscribe, and which can only be established upon his ignorance; and the more ignorant any country is, the better it is fitted for this species of Government.

On the contrary, Government, in a well-constituted republic, requires no belief from man beyond what his reason can give. He sees the rationale of the whole system, its origin and its operation; and as it is best supported when best understood, the human faculties act with boldness, and acquire, under this form of government, a gigantic manliness.

As, therefore, each of those forms acts on a different base, the one moving freely by the aid of reason, the other by ignorance; we have next to consider, what it is that gives motion to that species of Government which is called mixed Government, or, as it is sometimes ludicrously styled, a Government of this, that and t' other.

The moving power in this species of Government is, of necessity, Corruption. However imperfect election and representation may be in mixed Governments, they still give exercise to a greater portion of reason than is convenient to the hereditary Part; and therefore it becomes necessary to buy the reason up. A mixed Government is an imperfect everything, cementing and soldering the discordant parts together by corruption, to act as a whole. Mr. Burke appears highly disgusted that France, since she had resolved on a revolution, did not adopt what he calls "A British Constitution"; and the regretful manner in which he expresses himself on this occasion implies a suspicion that the British Constitution needed something to keep its defects in countenance.

In mixed Governments there is no responsibility: the parts cover each other till responsibility is lost; and the corruption which moves the machine, contrives at the same time its own escape. When it is laid down as a maxim, that a King can do no wrong, it places him in a state of similar security with that of idiots and persons insane, and responsibility is out of the question with respect to himself. It then descends upon the Minister, who shelters himself under a majority in Parliament, which, by places, pensions, and corruption, he can always command; and that majority justifies itself by the same authority with which it protects the Minister. In this rotatory motion, responsibility is thrown off from the parts, and from the whole.

When there is a Part in a Government which can do no wrong, it implies that it does nothing; and is only the machine of another power, by whose advice and direction it acts. What is supposed to be the King in the mixed Governments, is the Cabinet; and as the Cabinet is always a part of the Parliament, and the members justifying in one character what they advise and act in another, a mixed Government becomes a continual enigma; entailing upon a country by the quantity of corruption necessary to solder the parts, the expense of supporting all the forms of government at once, and finally resolving itself into a Government by Committee; in which the advisers, the actors, the approvers, the justifiers, the persons responsible, and the persons not responsible, are the same persons.

By this pantomimical contrivance, and change of scene and character, the parts help each other out in matters which neither of them singly would assume to act. When money is to be obtained, the mass of variety apparently dissolves, and a profusion of parliamentary praises passes between the parts. Each admires with astonishment, the wisdom, the liberality, the disinterestedness of the other: and all of them breathe a pitying sigh at the burthens of the Nation.

But in a well-constituted republic, nothing of this soldering, praising, and pitying, can take place; the representation being equal throughout the country, and complete in itself, however it may be arranged into legislative and executive, they have all one and the same natural source. The parts are not foreigners to each other, like democracy, aristocracy, and monarchy. As there are no discordant distinctions, there is nothing to corrupt by compromise, nor confound by contrivance. Public measures appeal of themselves to the understanding of the Nation, and, resting on their own merits, disown any flattering applications to vanity. The continual whine of lamenting the burden of taxes, however successfully it may be practised in mixed Governments, is inconsistent with the sense and spirit of a republic. If taxes are necessary, they are of course advantageous; but if they require an apology, the apology itself implies an impeachment. Why, then, is man thus imposed upon, or why does he impose upon himself?

When men are spoken of as kings and subjects, or when Government is mentioned under the distinct and combined heads of monarchy, aristocracy, and democracy, what is it that reasoning man is to understand by the terms? If there really existed in the world two or more distinct and separate elements of human power, we should then see the several origins to which those terms would descriptively apply; but as there is but one species of man, there can be but one element of human power; and that element is man himself. Monarchy, aristocracy, and democracy, are but creatures of imagination; and a thousand such may be contrived as well as three.

From the Revolutions of America and France, and the symptoms that have appeared in other countries, it is evident that the opinion of the world is changing with respect to systems of Government, and that revolutions are not within the compass of political calculations. The progress of time and circumstances, which men assign to the accomplishment of great changes, is too mechanical to measure the force of the mind, and the rapidity of reflection, by which revolutions are generated: All the old governments have received a shock from those that already appear, and which were once more improbable, and are a greater subject of wonder, than a general revolution in Europe would be now.

When we survey the wretched condition of man, under the monarchical and hereditary systems of Government, dragged from his home by one power, or driven by another, and impoverished by taxes more than by enemies, it becomes evident that those systems are bad, and that a general revolution in the principle and construction of Governments is necessary.

What is government more than the management of the affairs of a Nation? It is not, and from its nature cannot be, the property of any particular man or family, but of the whole community, at whose expense it is supported; and though by force and contrivance it has been usurped into an inheritance, the usurpation cannot alter the right of things. Sovereignty, as a matter of right, appertains to the Nation only, and not to any individual; and a Nation has at all times an inherent indefeasible right to abolish any form of Government it finds inconvenient, and to establish such as accords with its interest, disposition and happiness. The romantic and barbarous distinction of men into Kings and subjects, though it may suit the condition of courtiers, cannot that of citizens; and is exploded by the principle upon which Governments are now founded. Every citizen is a member of the Sovereignty, and, as such, can acknowledge no personal subjection; and his obedience can be only to the laws.

When men think of what Government is, they must necessarily suppose it to possess a knowledge of all the objects and matters upon which its authority is to be exercised. In this view of Government, the republican system, as established by America and France, operates to embrace the whole of a Nation; and the knowledge necessary to the interest of all the parts, is to be found in the center, which the parts by representation form: But the old Governments are on a construction that excludes knowledge as well as happiness; government by Monks, who knew nothing of the world beyond the walls of a Convent, is as consistent as government by Kings.

What were formerly called Revolutions, were little more than a change of persons, or an alteration of local circumstances. They rose and fell like things of course, and had nothing in their existence or their fate that could influence beyond the spot that produced them. But what we now see in the world, from the Revolutions of America and France, are a renovation of the natural order of things, a system of principles as universal as truth and the existence of man, and combining moral with political happiness and national prosperity.

"Ⅰ. Men are born, and always continue, free and equal in respect of their rights. Civil distinctions, therefore, can be founded only on public utility.

"Ⅱ. The end of all political associations is the preservation of the natural and imprescriptible rights of man; and these rights are liberty, property, security, and resistance of oppression.

"Ⅲ. The nation is essentially the source of all sovereignty; nor can any Individual, or any body of men, be entitled to any authority which is not expressly derived from it."

In these principles, there is nothing to throw a Nation into confusion by inflaming ambition. They are calculated to call forth wisdom and abilities, and to exercise them for the public good, and not for the emolument or aggrandisement of particular descriptions of men or families. Monarchical sovereignty, the enemy of mankind, and the source of misery, is abolished; and the sovereignty itself is restored to its natural and original place, the Nation. Were this the case throughout Europe, the cause of wars would be taken away.

It is attributed to Henry the Fourth of France, a man of enlarged and benevolent heart, that he proposed, about the year 1610, a plan for abolishing war in Europe. The plan consisted in constituting an European Congress, or as the French authors style it, a Pacific Republic; by appointing delegates from the several Nations who were to act as a Court of arbitration in any disputes that might arise between nation and nation.

Had such a plan been adopted at the time it was proposed, the taxes of England and France, as two of the parties, would have been at least ten millions sterling annually to each Nation less than they were at the commencement of the French Revolution.

To conceive a cause why such a plan has not been adopted (and that instead of a Congress for the purpose of preventing war, it has been called only to terminate a war, after a fruitless expense of several years) it will be necessary to consider the interest of Governments as a distinct interest to that of Nations.

Whatever is the cause of taxes to a Nation, becomes also the means of revenue to Government. Every war terminates with an addition of taxes, and consequently with an addition of revenue; and in any event of war, in the manner they are now commenced and concluded, the power and interest of Governments are increased. War, therefore, from its productiveness, as it easily furnishes the pretence of necessity for taxes and appointments to places and offices, becomes a principal part of the system of old Governments; and to establish any mode to abolish war, however advantageous it might be to Nations, would be to take from such Government the most lucrative of its branches. The frivolous matters upon which war is made, show the disposition and avidity of Governments to uphold the system of war, and betray the motives upon which they act.

Why are not Republics plunged into war, but because the nature of their Government does not admit of an interest distinct from that of the Nation? Even Holland, though an ill-constructed Republic, and with a commerce extending over the world, existed nearly a century without war: and the instant the form of Government was changed in France, the republican principles of peace and domestic prosperity and economy arose with the new Government; and the same consequences would follow the cause in other Nations.

As war is the system of Government on the old construction, the animosity which Nations reciprocally entertain, is nothing more than what the policy of their Governments excites to keep up the spirit of the system. Each Government accuses the other of perfidy, intrigue, and ambition, as a means of heating the imagination of their respective Nations, and incensing them to hostilities. Man is not the enemy of man, but through the medium of a false system of Government. Instead, therefore, of exclaiming against the ambition of Kings, the exclamation should be directed against the principle of such Governments; and instead of seeking to reform the individual, the wisdom of a Nation should apply itself to reform the system.

Whether the forms and maxims of Governments which are still in practice, were adapted to the condition of the world at the period they were established, is not in this case the question. The older they are, the less correspondence can they have with the present state of things. Time, and change of circumstances and opinions, have the same progressive effect in rendering modes of Government obsolete as they have upon customs and manners.-Agriculture, commerce, manufactures, and the tranquil arts, by which the prosperity of Nations is best promoted, require a different system of Government, and a different species of knowledge to direct its operations, than what might have been required in the former condition of the world.

As it is not difficult to perceive, from the enlightened state of mankind, that hereditary Governments are verging to their decline, and that Revolutions on the broad basis of national sovereignty and Government by representation, are making their way in Europe, it would be an act of wisdom to anticipate their approach, and produce Revolutions by reason and accommodation, rather than commit them to the issue of convulsions.

From what we now see, nothing of reform in the political world ought to be held improbable. It is an age of Revolutions, in which everything may be looked for. The intrigue of Courts, by which the system of war is kept up, may provoke a confederation of Nations to abolish it: and an European Congress to patronise the progress of free Government, and promote the civilisation of Nations with each other, is an event nearer in probability, than once were the revolutions and alliance of France and America.

Questions

1. What major beliefs did Paine outline in the first chapter of *The Age of Reason*?
2. What did Paine think of the national institutions of churches?
3. According to Paine, what harm would a person do to the society if he subscribed his professional belief to things that he did not believe?
4. What are the differences between the government of republic and that of monarchy and aristocracy according to Paine?
5. What are the problems of the mixed government according to Paine?

References and Further Reading

1. 托马斯·潘恩.理性时代.田飞龙、徐维,译.北京:中国法制出版社,2011.
2. 托马斯·潘恩.人的权利.田飞龙,译.北京:中国法制出版社,2011.
3. 托马斯·潘恩.常识.曾尔恕、王铮,译.西安:陕西人民出版社,2011.
4. 《理性时代》文本 http://thomaspaine.org/major-works/the-age-of-reason-part-1.html
5. 潘恩生平介绍 https://www.history.com/topics/american-revolution/thomas-paine
6. 潘恩生平及著作 https://www.britannica.com/biography/Thomas-Paine
7. 潘恩哲学政治思想 http://www.thomaspaine.us/article_tepfer02.html
8. 政治理论 Philp, M., "Thomas Paine", The Stanford Encyclopedia of Philosophy (Fall 2017 Edition), Edward N. Zalta (ed.), https://plato.stanford.edu/archives/fall2017/entries/paine/
9. 美国启蒙运动思想 https://www.iep.utm.edu/amer-enl/

The Declaration of Independence

Pre-reading

When American colonists began to fight British soldiers in April 1775, the Americans were fighting only for their rights as subjects of the British crown. However, by the following summer, they had begun to fight for independence from Britain. In June 1776, a five-man committee including Thomas Jefferson, John Adams and Benjamin Franklin started to draft a formal statement to justify their decision. The Congress adopted *The Declaration of Independence* (written largely by Jefferson) on July 4, a date now regarded as the birth of American independence.

The Declaration of Independence was divided into five sections, including an introduction, a preamble, a body (divided into two sections) and a conclusion. The introduction first states that seeking independence from Britain had become "necessary" for the colonies. While the body of the document lists a series of grievances against the British crown, the preamble includes its most famous passage:

"We hold these truths to be self-evident; that all men are created equal; that they are endowed by their Creator with certain inalienable rights; that among these are life, liberty and the pursuit of happiness; that to secure these rights, governments are instituted among men, deriving their just powers from the consent of the governed."

The *Declaration* contains no novel ideas as Jefferson himself admitted. Its primary influences have long been regarded as the political thoughts of English political theorist John Locke whom Jefferson called one of "the three greatest men that have ever lived". For instance, Locke believed that all individuals are equal in the sense that they are born with certain natural rights. And these God-given rights can never be taken away. Among these fundamental natural rights, Locke said, are "life, liberty, and property." Jefferson adopted Locke's theory of natural rights to provide a reason for the *Declaration* and the revolution.

The Declaration of Independence is important for several reasons. It is the first formal statement of the American people to assert their right to choose their own government. It helped the original thirteen colonies break free from British rule and took the country into a new era of politics. Together with the *Constitution* and the *Bill of Rights*, *The Declaration of Independence* has become one of the three essential founding documents of the US government. For instance, 87 years later, in 1863, Abraham Lincoln delivered his Gettysburg Address and described the nation as "conceived in Liberty, and dedicated to the proposition that all men are created equal."

One, however, need not ignore the fact that Jefferson had to temporize when he drafted the *Declaration*. Native Americans, people without property, women and black slaves were considered neither equal nor endowed with rights. But the statement in the *Declaration* has since then exerted a profound influence to the American society.

Text

Declaration of Independence: A Transcription

Note: The following text is a transcription of the Stone Engraving of the parchment Declaration of Independence (the document on display in the Rotunda at the National Archives Museum.) The spelling and punctuation reflects the original.

In Congress   July 4, 1776.

The unanimous Declaration of the thirteen United States of America, when in the course of human events, it becomes necessary for one people to dissolve the political bands which have connected them with another, and to assume among the powers of the earth, the separate and equal station to which the Laws of Nature and of Nature's God entitle them, a decent respect to the opinions of mankind requires that they should declare the causes which impel them to the separation.

We hold these truths to be self-evident, that all men are created equal, that they are endowed by their Creator with certain unalienable Rights, that among these are Life, Liberty and the pursuit of Happiness.—That to secure these rights, Governments are instituted among Men, deriving their just powers from the consent of the governed, —That whenever any Form of Government becomes destructive of these ends, it is the Right of the People to alter or to abolish it, and to institute new Government, laying its foundation on such principles and organizing its powers in such form, as to them shall seem most likely to effect their Safety and Happiness. Prudence, indeed, will dictate that Governments long established should not be changed for light and transient causes; and accordingly all experience hath shewn, that mankind are more disposed to suffer, while evils are sufferable, than to right themselves by abolishing the forms to which they are accustomed. But when a long train of abuses and usurpations, pursuing invariably the same Object evinces a design to reduce them under absolute Despotism, it is their right, it is their duty, to throw off such Government, and to provide new Guards for their future security. —Such has been the patient sufferance of these Colonies; and such is now the necessity which constrains them to alter their former Systems of Government. The history of the present King of Great Britain is a history of repeated injuries and usurpations, all having in direct object the establishment of an absolute Tyranny over these States. To prove this, let Facts be submitted to a candid world.

He has refused his Assent to Laws, the most wholesome and necessary for the public good.

He has forbidden his Governors to pass laws of immediate and pressing importance, unless suspended in their operation till his assent should be obtained; and when so suspended, he has utterly neglected to attend to them.

He has refused to pass other laws for the accommodation of large districts of people, unless those people would relinquish the right of Representation in the legislature, a right inestimable to them and formidable to tyrants only.

He has called together legislative bodies at places unusual, uncomfortable, and distant from the depository of their public records, for the sole purpose of fatiguing them into compliance with his measures.

He has dissolved Representative Houses repeatedly, for opposing with manly firmness his invasions on the rights of the people.

He has refused for a long time, after such dissolutions, to cause others to be elected; whereby the Legislative powers, incapable of annihilation, have returned to the people at large for their exercise; the State remaining in the mean time exposed to all the dangers of invasion from without, and convulsions within.

He has endeavoured to prevent the population of these States; for that purpose obstructing the laws for naturalization of foreigners; refusing to pass others to encourage their migrations hither, and raising the conditions of new appropriations of lands.

He has obstructed the Administration of Justice, by refusing his assent to laws for establishing judiciary powers.

He has made judges dependent on his will alone, for the tenure of their offices, and the amount and payment of their salaries.

He has erected a multitude of new offices, and sent hither swarms of officers to harrass our people, and eat out their substance.

He has kept among us, in times of peace, standing armies without the consent of our legislatures.

He has affected to render the military independent of and superior to the civil power.

He has combined with others to subject us to a jurisdiction foreign to our constitution, and unacknowledged by our laws; giving his assent to their acts of pretended legislation:

For quartering large bodies of armed troops among us:

For protecting them, by a mock trial, from punishment for any murders which they should commit on the Inhabitants of these States:

· For cutting off our trade with all parts of the world;

· For imposing taxes on us without our consent;

· For depriving us in many cases, of the benefits of trial by jury;

· For transporting us beyond seas to be tried for pretended offences;

· For abolishing the free System of English Laws in a neighbouring province, establishing therein an arbitrary government, and enlarging its Boundaries so as to render it at once an example and fit instrument for introducing the same absolute rule into these colonies.

For taking away our charters, abolishing our most valuable laws, and altering fundamentally the Forms of our Governments.

For suspending our own legislatures, and declaring themselves invested with power to legislate for us in all cases whatsoever.

He has abdicated Government here, by declaring us out of his protection and waging War against us.

He has plundered our seas, ravaged our coasts, burnt our towns, and destroyed the lives of our people.

He is at this time transporting large armies of foreign Mercenaries to complete the works of death, desolation and tyranny, already begun with circumstances of cruelty & perfidy scarcely paralleled in the most barbarous ages, and totally unworthy the Head of a civilized nation.

He has constrained our fellow citizens taken captive on the high seas to bear arms against their Country, to become the executioners of their friends and Brethren, or to fall themselves by their hands.

He has excited domestic insurrections amongst us, and has endeavoured to bring on the inhabitants of our frontiers, the merciless Indian savages, whose known rule of warfare, is an undistinguished destruction of all ages, sexes and conditions.

In every stage of these oppressions we have petitioned for redress in the most humble terms: Our repeated petitions have been answered only by repeated injury. A prince whose character is thus marked by every act which may define a tyrant, is unfit to be the ruler of a free people.

Nor have we been wanting in attentions to our Brittish brethren. We have warned them from time to time of attempts by their legislature to extend an unwarrantable jurisdiction over us. We have reminded them of the circumstances of our emigration and settlement here. We have appealed to their native justice and magnanimity, and we have conjured them by the ties of our common kindred to disavow these usurpations, which would inevitably interrupt our connections and correspondence. They too have been deaf to the voice of justice and of consanguinity. We must, therefore, acquiesce in the necessity, which denounces our Separation, and hold them, as we hold the rest of mankind, enemies in war, in peace friends.

We, therefore, the representatives of the United States of America, in general congress, assembled, appealing to the Supreme Judge of the world for the rectitude of our intentions, do, in the name, and by authority of the good people of these colonies, solemnly publish and declare, that these United colonies are, and of right ought to be free and independent states; that they are absolved from all allegiance to the British Crown, and that all political connection between them and the State of Great Britain, is and ought to be totally dissolved; and that as free and independent states, they have full power to levy war, conclude peace, contract alliances, establish commerce, and to do all other acts and things which independent states may of right do. And for the support of this Declaration, with a firm reliance on the protection of divine Providence, we mutually pledge to each other our lives, our fortunes and our sacred honor.

Questions

1. According to Jefferson, what is the purpose of government? What does Jefferson suggest should happen whenever government becomes "destructive of the ends for which it was created?"
2. According to Jefferson, how do governments derive their powers?
3. Jefferson noted that "all men are created equal," suggesting that this was "self evident." Speculate as to what he meant by that statement. What sorts of conflicts and misconceptions may have stemmed from this statement?
4. Read the grievances that Jefferson lists as reasons that the King has violated the natural rights of the colonists. Then list the three grievances that you feel are the worst violations. Explain why you believe them to be important.

Questions for Further Reflection

1. What is deism? Analyze how its ideals influenced the American Revolution.
2. Paine argued that it would be impossible to calculate the moral mischief that mental lying has

produced. What do you think of this arguement? Think about the significance of building a society of credibility and integrity.
3. Compare the principles Paine listed in the conclusion of his *Rights of Man* Part I with the announcement in *The Declaration of Independence*.
4. John Locke died in 1704, over 70 years before Jefferson wrote *The Declaration of Independence*. In your estimate, would Locke *accept* the way Jefferson used his *Two Treatises* to justify independence from Britain, which was Locke' native country?
5. John Locke wrote about the natural rights of man including the right to life, liberty, and property. Why did Thomas Jefferson change "property" to "the pursuit of happiness" in the *Declaration*?

References and Further Reading

1. 约翰·洛克.政府论.北京:中国社会科学出版社,2009.
2. 卡尔·贝克尔.论《独立宣言》政治思想史研究.彭刚,译.北京:商务印书馆,2017.
3. 《独立宣言》文本 https://www.archives.gov/founding-docs/declaration-transcript
4. 贝克尔《独立宣言:政治思想史研究》Carl Lotus Becker, *The Declaration of Independence: A Study on the History of Political Ideas* [1922], https://oll.libertyfund.org/titles/becker-the-declaration-of-independence-a-study-on-the-history-of-political-ideas
5. 大英百科全书《独立宣言》词条
https://www.britannica.com/topic/Declaration-of-Independence
6. 《独立宣言》相关历史
https://www.history.com/topics/american-revolution/declaration-of-independence

Chapter 8   Liberalism

This chapter presents three excerpts of the classical works of liberalism to facilitate your understanding of the basic doctrines and framework in liberalism and promote a critical thinking of liberalism at the same time.

Liberalism became a distinct movement in the Age of Enlightenment. The development into maturity of classical liberalism took place before and after the French Revolution in Britain. Liberals sought to replace the norms of hereditary privilege, state religion, absolute monarchy, the divine right of kings and traditional conservatism with representative democracy and the rule of law. Leaders in the Glorious Revolution of 1688, the American Revolution of 1776 and the French Revolution of 1789 used liberal philosophy to justify the armed overthrow of royal tyranny. In general, liberalism supports limited government, individual rights (including civil rights and human rights), capitalism (free markets), secularism, gender equality, racial equality and internationalism.

Philosopher John Locke is often credited with founding liberalism as a distinct tradition, arguing that each man has a natural right to life, liberty and property, adding that governments must not violate these rights based on the social contract. After him, from the 17th century until the 19th century, liberals (from Adam Smith to John Stuart Mill) conceptualized liberty as the absence of interference from government and from other individuals, claiming that all people should have the freedom to develop their own unique abilities and capacities without being sabotaged by others. During the 20th century liberal ideas also spread even further—especially in Western Europe. Today, liberal parties in the western world continue to wield power and influence throughout the world. But it is undeniable that the liberal devotion to freedom does undermine traditional virtues and social order itself, and liberalism indeed has its own limitations or even fallacies. In today's global village, we all belong to "a Community of Shared Future for Mankind", which implies that the demands of belongingness and connection trump unlimited freedom, and we humankinds are interconnected to each other, thus a critical perspective is indispensable in our examination and exploration of liberalism.

Anti-liberalism is an intellectual position which rejects and censures the worldview of liberalism as an ideology centered on extreme individualism, an obsession with maximizing individual liberties in every possible area, and egalitarianism. Though anti-liberalism was itself based on and a furtherance of the ideals of classical liberalism, it was marked as a distrust for the enlightenment ideals of reason and science, and a return to the ideals of a simple, primitive society uncontaminated by modern civilization. Critiques of liberalism and liberal movements are very varied, usually differing based on the specific type of liberalism involved (most notably classical versus social liberalism), but are generally centered on arguments involving the reductionist view of human life.

The three works selected in this chapter are Adam Smith's *The Wealth of Nations*, John Stuart Mill's *On Liberty*, and Frederick Engels' *Socialism: Utopian and Scientific*. The first two works are considered as the classic texts in liberal philosophy. The first one, *The Wealth of Nations*, published in 1776, is a thorough criticism of the mercantile system that governed economic policy in Great Britain during Adam Smith's life. Smith charts the evolution of mercantile principles from the fall of Rome, through feudal times, and into the age of commerce in which he was born. The second one, *On Liberty*, published in 1859, is John Mill's finest argument for the principles he had espoused over his fifty years of life. The basic underlying theme is the lack of trust that can be placed in the government, which will need our critical reflection after reading. And this is why the third excerpt is selected from Frederick Engels' *Socialism: Utopian and Scientific*, which offers us a window for critical thinking of liberalism.

The Wealth of Nations
Adam Smith

Pre-reading

Adam Smith(1723 – 1790), known as "The Father of Economics", is a Scottish economist, philosopher and author as well as a moral philosopher, a pioneer of political economy and a key figure during the Scottish Enlightenment. Smith wrote two classic works, *The Theory of Moral Sentiments* (1759) and *An Inquiry into the Nature and Causes of the Wealth of Nations* (1776). The latter, often abbreviated as *The Wealth of Nations*, is considered his masterpiece. It is to provide most of the ideas of economics at least until the publication of John Stuart Mill's *Principles* in 1848.

In *The Wealth of Nations*, Smith addresses the motivation for economic activity, the causes of prices and the distribution of wealth and the policies the state should follow in order to maximize wealth. The book offers one of the world's first collected description of what builds nation's wealth. By reflecting upon the economics at the beginning of the Industrial Revolution, the book touches upon such broad topics as the division of labor, productivity, and free markets in its five Books.

Books One and Two focus on developing the idea of the division of labor, and describing how this division adds to the opulence of a given society by creating enormous surpluses, which can be exchanged among members. The division of labor also fuels technological innovation, by giving intense focus to certain tasks, and allowing workers to brainstorm ways to make these tasks more efficient. This, again, adds to efficiency and grows surpluses. Surpluses, Smith writes, may be either traded or re-invested. In the latter case, technologies are likely to improve, leading to even greater efficiencies. Adam Smith attaches great importance to efficiency and surpluses; therefore he advocates the division of labor. But Karl Marx thinks that the alienation of labor is but a negative and undesirable form when analyzing economic social phenomena, for it makes people loses any connection with the work they are involved in and thus has turned meaning work into boring labor. Today we're in knowledge economy instead of Industrial Revolution, so we need to develop a critical and updated view on the notions put forward by Adam Smith.

Book Three considers Great Britain in the context of the social evolution of society in general, which begins, according to Smith, with hunting and gathering societies and progresses through agricultural stages to arrive at a state of international commerce. According to Smith, the fall of Rome and the rise of feudalism retarded this progression by creating a system of decreased efficiency.

Book Four goes on to criticize the "mercantile commerce" that characterized much of Smith's Europe. Smith's first major criticism of mercantilism is that it conflates value and wealth with precious metals. According to Smith, the real measure of the wealth of a nation is the stream of goods and services that the nation creates. In making this point, Smith invents the idea of gross domestic product, which has become central to modern economics. The wealth of a nation is increased not by hoarding metals, but by increasing the productive capacity by expanding the market—by increasing trade.

The last part, Book Five, describes what Smith considers to be the appropriate roles of government, namely defense, justice, the creation and maintenance of public works that contribute to commerce, education, the maintenance of the "dignity of the sovereign,"—activities that are to be financed by fair and clear taxation.

Due to the length limit of this chapter, only parts of Books One, Three and Four are excerpted.

Now let's read the text and reflect on the questions that follow.

Text

Book One: Of the division of labor
Chapter VII
Of the natural and market price of commodities

There is in every society or neighbourhood an ordinary or average rate both of wages and profit in every different employment of labour and stock. This rate is naturally regulated, as I shall show hereafter, partly by the general circumstances of the society, their riches or poverty, their advancing, stationary, or declining condition; and partly by the particular nature of each employment.

There is likewise in every society or neighbourhood an ordinary or average rate of rent, which is regulated too, as I shall show hereafter, partly by the general circumstances of the society or neighbourhood in which the land is situated, and partly by the natural or improved fertility of the land.

These ordinary or average rates may be called the natural rates of wages, profit, and rent, at the time and place in which they commonly prevail.

When the price of any commodity is neither more nor less than what is sufficient to pay the rent of the land, the wages of the labour, and the profits of the stock employed in raising, preparing, and bringing it to market, according to their natural rates, the commodity is then sold for what may be called its natural price.

The commodity is then sold precisely for what it is worth, or for what it really costs the person who brings it to market; for though in common language what is called the prime cost of any commodity does not comprehend the profit of the person who is to sell it again, yet if he sell it at a price which does not allow him the ordinary rate of profit in his neighbourhood, he is evidently a loser by the trade; since by employing his stock in some other way he might have made that profit. His profit, besides, is his revenue, the proper fund of his subsistence. As, while he is preparing and bringing the goods to market, he advances to his workmen their wages, or their subsistence; so he advances to himself, in the same manner, his own subsistence, which is generally suitable to the profit which he may reasonably expect from the sale of his goods. Unless they yield him this profit, therefore, they do not repay him what they may very properly be said to have really cost him.

Though the price, therefore, which leaves him this profit is not always the lowest at which a dealer may sometimes sell his goods, it is the lowest at which he is likely to sell them for any considerable time; at least where there is perfect liberty, or where he may change his trade as often as he pleases.

The actual price at which any commodity is commonly sold is called its market price. It may either be above, or below, or exactly the same with its natural price.

The market price of every particular commodity is regulated by the proportion between the quantity which is actually brought to market, and the demand of those who are willing to pay the natural price of the commodity, or the whole value of the rent, labour, and profit, which must be paid in order to bring it thither. Such people may be called the effectual demanders, and their demand the effectual demand; since it may be sufficient to effectuate the bringing of the commodity to market. It is different from the absolute demand. A very poor man may be said in some sense to have a demand for a coach and six; he might like to have it; but his demand is not an effectual demand, as the commodity can never be brought to market in order to satisfy it.

When the quantity of any commodity which is brought to market falls short of the effectual demand, all those who are willing to pay the whole value of the rent, wages, and profit, which must be paid in order to bring it thither, cannot be supplied with the quantity which they want. Rather than want it altogether, some of them will be willing to give more. A competition will immediately begin among them, and the market price will rise more or less above the natural price, according as either the greatness of the deficiency, or the wealth and wanton luxury of the competitors, happen to animate more or less the eagerness of the competition. Among competitors of equal wealth and luxury the same deficiency will generally occasion a more or less eager competition, according as the acquisition of the commodity happens to be of more or less importance to them. Hence the exorbitant price of the necessaries of life during the blockade of a town or in a famine.

When the quantity brought to market exceeds the effectual demand, it cannot be all sold to those who are willing to pay the whole value of the rent, wages, and profit, which must be paid in order to bring it thither. Some part must be sold to those who are willing to pay less, and the low price which they give for it must reduce the price of the whole. The market price will sink more or less below the natural price, according as the greatness of the excess increases more or less the competition of the sellers, or according as it happens to be more or less important to them to get immediately rid of the commodity. The same excess in the importation of perishable, will occasion a much greater competition than in that of durable commodities; in the importation of oranges, for example, than in that of old iron.

When the quantity brought to market is just sufficient to supply the effectual demand, and no more, the market price naturally comes to be either exactly, or as nearly as can be judged of, the same with the natural price. The whole quantity upon hand can be disposed of for this price, and cannot be disposed of for more. The competition of the different dealers obliges them all to accept of this price, but does not oblige them to accept of less.

The quantity of every commodity brought to market naturally suits itself to the effectual demand. It is the interest of all those who employ their land, labour, or stock, in bringing any commodity to market, that the quantity never should exceed the effectual demand; and it is the interest of all other people that it never should fall short of that demand.

If at any time it exceeds the effectual demand, some of the component parts of its price must be paid below their natural rate. If it is rent, the interest of the landlords will immediately prompt them to withdraw a part of their land; and if it is wages or profit, the interest of the labourers in the one case, and of their employers in the other, will prompt them to withdraw a part of their labour or stock from this employment. The quantity brought to market will soon be no more than sufficient to supply the effectual demand. All the different parts of its price will rise to their natural rate, and the whole price to its natural price.

If, on the contrary, the quantity brought to market should at any time fall short of the effectual demand, some of the component parts of its price must rise above their natural rate. If it is rent, the interest of all other landlords will naturally prompt them to prepare more land for the raising of this commodity; if it is wages or profit, the interest of all other labourers and dealers will soon prompt them to employ more labour and stock in preparing and bringing it to market. The quantity brought thither will soon be sufficient to supply the effectual demand. All the different parts of its price will soon sink to their natural rate, and the whole price to its natural price.

The natural price, therefore, is, as it were, the central price, to which the prices of all commodities are continually gravitating. Different accidents may sometimes keep them suspended a good deal above it, and sometimes force them down even somewhat below it. But whatever may be the obstacles which hinder them from settling in this centre of repose and continuance, they are constantly tending towards it.

The whole quantity of industry annually employed in order to bring any commodity to market naturally suits itself in this manner to the effectual demand. It naturally aims at bringing always that precise quantity thither which may be sufficient to supply, and no more than supply, that demand.

But in some employments the same quantity of industry will in different years produce very different quantities of commodities; while in others it will produce always the same, or very nearly the same. The same number of labourers in husbandry will, in different years, produce very different quantities of corn, wine, oil, hops, etc. But the same number of spinners and weavers will every year produce the same or very nearly the same quantity of linen and woollen cloth. It is only the average produce of the one species of industry which can be suited in any respect to the effectual demand; and as its actual produce is frequently much greater and frequently much less than its average produce, the quantity of the commodities brought to market will sometimes exceed a good deal, and sometimes fall short a good deal, of the effectual demand. Even though that demand therefore should continue always the same, their market price will be liable to great fluctuations, will sometimes fall a good deal below, and sometimes rise a good deal above their natural price. In the other species of industry, the produce of equal quantities of labour being always the same, or very nearly the same, it can be more exactly suited to the effectual demand. While that demand continues the same, therefore, the market price of the commodities is likely to do so too, and to be either altogether, or as nearly as can be judged of, the same with the natural price. That the price of linen and woollen cloth is liable neither to such frequent nor to such great variations as the price of corn, every man's experience will inform him. The price of the one species of commodities varies only with the variations in the demand: that of the other varies, not only with the variations in the demand, but with the much greater and more frequent variations in the quantity of what is brought to market in order to supply that demand.

The occasional and temporary fluctuations in the market price of any commodity fall chiefly upon those parts of its price which resolve themselves into wages and profit. That part which resolves itself into rent is less affected by them. A rent certain in money is not in the least affected by them either in its rate or in its value. A rent which consists either in a certain proportion or in a certain quantity of the rude produce, is no doubt affected in its yearly value by all the occasional and temporary fluctuations in the market price of that rude produce; but it is seldom affected by them in its yearly rate. In settling the terms of the lease, the landlord and farmer endeavour, according to their best judgment, to adjust that rate, not to the temporary and occasional, but to the average and ordinary price of the produce.

Such fluctuations affect both the value and the rate either of wages or of profit, according as the market happens to be either overstocked or understocked with commodities or with labour; with work done, or with work to be done. A public mourning raises the price of black cloth (with which the market is almost always understocked upon such occasions), and augments the profits of the merchants who possess any considerable quantity of it. It has no effect upon the wages of the weavers. The market is understocked with commodities, not with labour; with work done, not with work to be done. It raises the wages of journeymen tailors. The market is here understocked with labour. There is an effectual demand for more labour, for more work to be done than can be had. It sinks the price of coloured silks and cloths, and thereby reduces the profits of the merchants who have any considerable quantity of them upon hand. It sinks, too, the wages of the workmen employed in preparing such commodities, for which all demand is stopped for six months, perhaps for a twelvemonth. The market is here over-stocked both with commodities and with labour.

But though the market price of every particular commodity is in this manner continually gravitating, if one may say so, towards the natural price, yet sometimes particular accidents, sometimes natural causes, and sometimes particular regulations of police, may, in many commodities, keep up the market price, for a long time together, a good deal above the natural price.

...

Book Three: Of the different progress of opulence in different nations
Chapter Ⅰ
Of the natural progress of opulence

The great commerce of every civilised society is that carried on between the inhabitants of the town and those of the country. It consists in the exchange of rude for manufactured produce, either immediately, or by the intervention of money, or of some sort of paper which represents money. The country supplies the town with the means of subsistence and the materials of manufacture. The town repays this supply by sending back a part of the manufactured produce to the inhabitants of the country. The town, in which there neither is nor can be any reproduction of substances, may very properly be said to gain its whole wealth and subsistence from the country. We must not, however, upon this account, imagine that the gain of the town is the loss of the country. The gains of both are mutual and reciprocal, and the division of labour is in this, as in all other cases, advantageous to all the different persons employed in the various occupations into which it is subdivided. The inhabitants of the country purchase of the town a greater quantity of manufactured goods, with the produce of a much smaller quantity of their own labour, than they must have employed had they attempted to prepare them themselves. The town affords a market for the surplus produce of the country, or what is over and above the maintenance of the cultivators, and it is there that the inhabitants of the country exchange it for something else which is in demand among them. The greater the number and revenue of the inhabitants of the town, the more extensive is the market which it affords to those of the country; and the more extensive that market, it is always the more advantageous to a great number. The corn which grows within a mile of the town sells there for the same price with that which comes from twenty miles distance. But the price of the latter must generally not only pay the expense of raising and bringing it to market, but afford, too, the ordinary profits of agriculture to the farmer. The proprietors and cultivators of the country, therefore, which lies in the neighbourhood of the town, over and above the ordinary profits of agriculture, gain, in the price of what they sell, the whole value of the carriage of the like produce that is brought from more distant parts, and they have, besides, the whole value of this carriage in the price of what they buy. Compare the cultivation of the lands in the neighbourhood of any considerable town with that of those which lie at some distance from it, and you will easily satisfy yourself how much the country is benefited by the commerce of the town. Among all the absurd speculations that have been propagated concerning the balance of trade, it has never been pretended that either the country loses by its commerce with the town, or the town by that with the country which maintains it.

As subsistence is, in the nature of things, prior to conveniency and luxury, so the industry which procures the former must necessarily be prior to that which ministers to the latter. The cultivation and improvement of the country, therefore, which affords subsistence, must, necessarily, be prior to the increase of the town, which furnishes only the means of conveniency and luxury. It is the surplus produce of the country only, or what is over and above the maintenance of the cultivators, that constitutes the subsistence of the town, which can therefore increase only with the increase of this surplus produce. The town, indeed, may not always derive its whole subsistence from the country in its neighbourhood, or even from the territory to which it belongs, but from very distant countries; and this, though it forms no exception from the general rule, has occasioned considerable variations in the progress of opulence in different ages and nations.

That order of things which necessity imposes in general, though not in every particular country, is, in every particular country, promoted by the natural inclinations of man. If human institutions had never thwarted those natural inclinations, the towns could nowhere have increased beyond what the improvement and cultivation of the territory in which they were situated could support; till such time, at least, as the whole of that territory was completely cultivated and improved. Upon equal, or nearly equal profits, most men will choose to employ their capitals rather in the improvement and cultivation of land than either in manufactures or in foreign trade. The man who employs his capital in land has it more under his view and command, and his fortune is much less liable to accidents than that of the trader, who is obliged frequently to commit it, not only to the winds and the waves, but to the more uncertain elements of human folly and injustice, by giving great credits in distant countries to men with whose character and situation he can seldom be thoroughly acquainted. The capital of the landlord, on the contrary, which is fixed in the improvement of his land, seems to be as well secured as the nature of human affairs can admit of. The beauty of the country besides, the pleasures of a country life, the tranquillity of mind which it promises, and wherever the injustice of human laws does not disturb it, the independency which it really affords, have charms that more or less attract everybody; and as to cultivate the ground was the original destination of man, so in every stage of his existence he seems to retain a predilection for this primitive employment.

Without the assistance of some artificers, indeed, the cultivation of land cannot be carried on but with great inconveniency and continual interruption. Smiths, carpenters, wheelwrights, and ploughwrights, masons, and bricklayers, tanners, shoemakers, and tailors are people whose service the farmer has frequent occasion for.

Such artificers, too, stand occasionally in need of the assistance of one another; and as their residence is not, like that of the farmer, necessarily tied down to a precise spot, they naturally settle in the neighbourhood of one another, and thus form a small town or village. The butcher, the brewer, and the baker soon join them, together with many other artificers and retailers, necessary or useful for supplying their occasional wants, and who contribute still further to augment the town. The inhabitants of the town and those of the country are mutually the servants of one another. The town is a continual fair or market, to which the inhabitants of the country resort in order to exchange their rude for manufactured produce. It is this commerce which supplies the inhabitants of the town both with the materials of their work, and the means of their subsistence. The quantity of the finished work which they sell to the inhabitants of the country necessarily regulates the quantity of the materials and provisions which they buy. Neither their employment nor subsistence, therefore, can augment but in proportion to the augmentation of the demand from the country for finished work; and this demand can augment only in proportion to the extension of improvement and cultivation.

Had human institutions, therefore, never disturbed the natural course of things, the progressive wealth and increase of the towns would, in every political society, be consequential, and in proportion to the improvement and cultivation of the territory or country.

In our North American colonies, where uncultivated land is still to be had upon easy terms, no manufactures for distant sale have ever yet been established in any of their towns. When an artificer has acquired a little more stock than is necessary for carrying on his own business in supplying the neighbouring country, he does not, in North America, attempt to establish with it a manufacture for more distant sale, but employs it in the purchase and improvement of uncultivated land. From artificer he becomes planter, and neither the large wages nor the easy subsistence which that country affords to artificers can bribe him rather to work for other people than for himself. He feels that an artificer is the servant of his customers, from whom he derives his subsistence; but that a planter who cultivates his own land, and derives his necessary subsistence from the labour of his own family, is really a master, and independent of all the world.

In countries, on the contrary, where there is either no uncultivated land, or none that can be had upon easy terms, every artificer who has acquired more stock than he can employ in the occasional jobs of the neighbourhood endeavours to prepare work for more distant sale. The smith erects some sort of iron, the weaver some sort of linen or woollen manufactory. Those different manufactures come, in process of time, to be gradually subdivided, and thereby improved and refined in a great variety of ways, which may easily be conceived, and which it is therefore unnecessary to explain any further.

In seeking for employment to a capital, manufactures are, upon equal or nearly equal profits, naturally preferred to foreign commerce, for the same reason that agriculture is naturally preferred to manufactures. As the capital of the landlord or farmer is more secure than that of the manufacturer, so the capital of the manufacturer, being at all times more within his view and command, is more secure than that of the foreign merchant. In every period, indeed, of every society, the surplus part both of the rude and manufactured produce, or that for which there is no demand at home, must be sent abroad in order to be exchanged for something for which there is some demand at home. But whether the capital, which carries this surplus produce abroad, be a foreign or a domestic one is of very little importance. If the society has not acquired sufficient capital both to cultivate all its lands, and to manufacture in the completest manner the whole of its rude produce, there is even a considerable advantage that rude produce should be exported by a foreign capital, in order that the whole stock of the society may be employed in more useful purposes. The wealth of ancient Egypt, that of China and Indostan, sufficiently demonstrate that a nation may attain a very high degree of opulence though the greater part of its exportation trade be carried on by foreigners. The progress of our North American and West Indian colonies would have been much less rapid had no capital but what belonged to themselves been employed in exporting their surplus produce.

According to the natural course of things, therefore, the greater part of the capital of every growing society is, first, directed to agriculture, afterwards to manufactures, and last of all to foreign commerce. This order of things is so very natural that in every society that had any territory it has always, I believe, been in some degree observed. Some of their lands must have been cultivated before any considerable towns could be established, and some sort of coarse industry of the manufacturing kind must have been carried on in those towns, before they could well think of employing themselves in foreign commerce.

But though this natural order of things must have taken place in some degree in every such society, it has, in all the modern states of Europe, been, in many respects, entirely inverted. The foreign commerce of some of their cities has introduced all their finer manufactures, or such as were fit for distant sale; and manufactures and foreign commerce together have given birth to the principal improvements of agriculture. The manners and customs which the nature of their original government introduced, and which remained after that government was greatly altered, necessarily forced them into this unnatural and retrograde order.

...

Book Four: Of systems of political economy
Chapter I
Of the principle of the commercial, or mercantile system

That wealth consists in money, or and silver, is a popular notion which naturally arises from the double function of money, as the instrument of commerce and as the measure of value. In consequence of its being the instrument of commerce, when we have money we can more readily obtain whatever else we have occasion for than by means of any other commodity. The great affair, we always find, is to get money. When that is obtained, there is no difficulty in making any subsequent purchase. In consequence of its being the measure of value, we estimate that of all other commodities by the quantity of money which they will exchange for. We say of a rich man that he is worth a great deal, and of a poor man that he is worth very little money. A frugal man, or a man eager to be rich, is said to love money; and a careless, a generous, or a profuse man, is said to be indifferent about it. To grow rich is to get money; and wealth and money, in short, are, in common language, considered as in every respect synonymous.

A rich country, in the same manner as a rich man, is supposed to be a country abounding in money; and to heap up gold and saver in any country is supposed to be the readiest way to enrich it. For some time after the discovery of America, the first inquiry of the Spaniards, when they arrived upon an unknown coast, used to be, if there was any gold or silver to be found in the neighbourhood. By the information which they received, they judged whether it was worth while to make a settlement there, or if the country was worth the conquering. Plano Carpino, a monk, sent ambassador from the King of France to one of the sons of the famous Genghis Khan, says that the Tartars used frequently to ask him if there was plenty of sheep and oxen in the kingdom of France. Their inquiry had the same object with that of the Spaniards. They wanted to know if the country was rich enough to be worth the conquering. Among the Tartars, as among all other nations of shepherds, who are generally ignorant of the use of money, cattle are the instruments of commerce and the measures of value. Wealth, therefore, according to them, consisted in cattle, as according to the Spaniards it consisted in gold and silver. Of the two, the Tartar notion, perhaps, was the nearest to the truth.

Mr. Locke remarks a distinction between money and other movable goods. All other movable goods, he says, are of so consumable a nature that the wealth which consists in them cannot be much depended on, and a nation which abounds in them one year may, without any exportation, but merely their own waste and extravagance, be in great want of them the next. Money, on the contrary, is a steady friend, which, though it may travel about from hand to hand, yet if it can be kept from going out of the country, is not very liable to be wasted and consumed. Gold and silver, therefore, are, according to him, the most solid and substantial part of the movable wealth of a nation, and to multiply those metals ought, he thinks, upon that account, to be the great object of its political economy.

Others admit that if a nation could be separated from all the world, it would be of no consequence how much, or how little money circulated in it. The consumable goods which were circulated by means of this money would only be exchanged for a greater or a smaller number of pieces; but the real wealth or poverty of the country, they allow, would depend altogether upon the abundance or scarcity of those consumable goods. But it is otherwise, they think, with countries which have connections with foreign nations, and which are obliged to carry on foreign wars, and to maintain fleets and armies in distant countries. This, they say, cannot be done but by sending abroad money to pay them with; and a nation cannot send much money abroad unless it has a good deal at home. Every such nation, therefore, must endeavour in time of peace to accumulate gold and silver that, when occasion requires, it may have wherewithal to carry on foreign wars.

In consequence of these popular notions, all the different nations of Europe have studied, though to little purpose, every possible means of accumulating gold and silver in their respective countries. Spain and Portugal, the proprietors of the principal mines which supply Europe with those metals, have either prohibited their exportation under the severest penalties, or subjected it to a considerable duty. The like prohibition seems anciently to have made a part of the policy of most other European nations. It is even to be found, where we should least of all expect to find it, in some old Scotch acts of Parliament, which forbid under heavy penalties the carrying gold or silver *forth of the kingdom*. The like policy anciently took place both in France and England.

When those countries became commercial, the merchants found this prohibition, upon many occasions, extremely inconvenient. They could frequently buy more advantageously with gold and silver than with any other commodity the foreign goods which they wanted, either to import into their own, or to carry to some other foreign country. They remonstrated, therefore, against this prohibition as hurtful to trade.

They represented, first, that the exportation of gold and silver in order to purchase foreign goods, did not always diminish the quantity of those metals in the kingdom. That, on the contrary, it might frequently increase that quantity; because, if the consumption of foreign goods was not thereby increased in the country, those goods might be re-exported to foreign countries, and, being there sold for a large profit, might bring back much more treasure than was originally sent out to purchase them. Mr. Mun compares this operation of foreign trade to the seed-time and harvest of agriculture. "If we only behold," says he, "the actions of the husbandman in the seed-time, when he casteth away much good corn into the ground, we shall account him rather a madman than a husbandman. But when we consider his labours in the harvest, which is the end of his endeavours, we shall find the worth and plentiful increase of his action."

They represented, secondly, that this prohibition could not hinder the exportation of gold and silver, which, on account of the smallness of their bulk in proportion to their value, could easily be smuggled abroad. That this exportation could only be prevented by a proper attention to, what they called, the balance of trade. That when the country exported to a greater value than it imported, a balance became due to it from foreign nations, which was necessarily paid to it in gold and silver, and thereby increased the quantity of those metals in the kingdom. But that when it imported to a greater value than it exported, a contrary balance became due to foreign nations, which was necessarily paid to them in the same manner, and thereby diminished that quantity. That in this case to prohibit the exportation of those metals could not prevent it, but only, by making it more dangerous, render it more expensive. That the exchange was thereby turned more against the country which owed the balance than it otherwise might have been; the merchant who purchased a bill upon the foreign country being obliged to pay the banker who sold it, not only for the natural risk, trouble, and expense of sending the money thither, but for the extraordinary risk arising from the prohibition. But that the more the exchange was against any country, the more the balance of trade became necessarily against it; the money of that country becoming necessarily of so much less value in comparison with that of the country to which the balance was due. That if the exchange between England and Holland, for example, was five per cent against England, it would require a hundred and five ounces of silver in England to purchase a bill for a hundred ounces of silver in Holland: that a hundred and five ounces of silver in England, therefore, would be worth only a hundred ounces of silver in Holland, and would purchase only a proportionable quantity of Dutch goods; but that a hundred ounces of silver in Holland, on the contrary, would be worth a hundred and five ounces in England, and would purchase a proportionable quantity of English goods: that the English goods which were sold to Holland would be sold so much cheaper; and the Dutch goods which were sold to England so much dearer by the difference of the exchange; that the one would draw so much less Dutch money to England, and the other so much more English money to Holland, as this difference amounted to: and that the balance of trade, therefore, would necessarily be so much more against England, and would require a greater balance of gold and silver to be exported to Holland.

Those arguments were partly solid and partly sophistical.

They were solid so far as they asserted that the exportation of gold and silver in trade might frequently be advantageous to the country. They were solid, too, in asserting that no prohibition could prevent their exportation when private people found any advantage in exporting them.

But they were sophistical in supposing that either to preserve or to augment the quantity of those metals required more the attention of government than to preserve or to augment the quantity of any other useful commodities, which the freedom of trade, without any such attention, never fails to supply in the proper quantity.

They were sophistical too, perhaps, in asserting that the high price of exchange necessarily increased what they called the unfavourable balance of trade, or occasioned the exportation of a greater quantity of gold and silver. That high price, indeed, was extremely disadvantageous to the merchants who had any money to pay in foreign countries. They paid so much dearer for the bills which their bankers granted them upon those countries. But though the risk arising from the prohibition might occasion some extraordinary expense to the bankers, it would not necessarily carry any more money out of the country. This expense would generally be all laid out in the country, in smuggling the money out of it, and could seldom occasion the exportation of a single sixpence beyond the precise sum drawn for. The high price of exchange too would naturally dispose the merchants to endeavour to make their exports nearly balance their imports, in order that they might have this high exchange to pay upon as small a sum as possible. The high price of exchange, besides, must necessarily have operated as a tax, in raising the price of foreign goods, and thereby diminishing their consumption. It would tend, therefore, not to increase but to diminish what they called the unfavourable balance of trade, and consequently the exportation of gold and silver.

Such as they were, however, those arguments convinced the people to whom they were addressed. They were addressed by merchants to parliaments and to the councils of princes, to nobles and to country gentlemen, by those who were supposed to understand trade to those who were conscious to themselves that they knew nothing about the matter. That foreign trade enriched the country, experience demonstrated to the nobles and country gentlemen as well as to the merchants; but how, or in what manner, none of them well knew. The merchants knew perfectly in what manner it enriched themselves. It was their business to know it. But to know in what manner it enriched the country was no part of their business. This subject never came into their consideration but when they had occasion to apply to their country for some change in the laws relating to foreign trade.

It then became necessary to say something about the beneficial effects of foreign trade, and the manner in which those effects were obstructed by the laws as they then stood. To the judges who were to decide the business it appeared a most satisfactory account of the matter, when they were told that foreign trade brought money into the country, but that the laws in question hindered it from bringing so much as it otherwise would do. Those arguments therefore produced the wished-for effect. The prohibition of exporting gold and silver was in France and England confined to the coin of those respective countries. The exportation of foreign coin and of bullion was made free. In Holland, and in some other places, this liberty was extended even to the coin of the country. The attention of government was turned away from guarding against the exportation of gold and silver to watch over the balance of trade as the only cause which could occasion any augmentation or diminution of those metals.

From one fruitless care it was turned away to another care much more intricate, much more embarrassing, and just equally fruitless. The title of Mun's book, *England's Treasure in Foreign Trade*, became a fundamental maxim in the political economy, not of England only, but of all other commercial countries. The inland or home trade, the most important of all, the trade in which an equal capital affords the greatest revenue, and creates the greatest employment to the people of the country, was considered as subsidiary only to foreign trade. It neither brought money into the country, it was said, nor carried any out of it. The country, therefore, could never become either richer or poorer by means of it, except so far as its prosperity or decay might indirectly influence the state of foreign trade.

A country that has no mines of its own must undoubtedly draw its gold and silver from foreign countries in the same manner as one that has no vineyards of its own must draw its wines. It does not seem necessary, however, that the attention of government should be more turned towards the one than towards the other object. A country that has wherewithal to buy wine will always get the wine which it has occasion for; and a country that has wherewithal to buy gold and silver will never be in want of those metals. They are to be bought for a certain price like all other commodities, and as they are the price of all other commodities, so all other commodities are the price of those metals. We trust with perfect security that the freedom of trade, without any attention of government, will always supply us with the wine which we have occasion for: and we may trust with equal security that it will always supply us with all the gold and silver which we can afford to purchase or to employ, either in circulating our commodities, or in other uses.

Questions

1. What is the market price of the commodity? How does it differ from its natural price?
2. What is Adam Smith's stance on the statement that the gain of the town is the loss of the country?
3. In Adam Smith's view, how should the greater part of the capital in a growing society be

directed, in priority order, to manufactures, foreign commerce, and agriculture?
4. According to Adam Smith, what is the double function of money?
5. In Adam Smith's words, what is the difference between money and other movable goods, according to Locke?

On Liberty

John Stuart Mill

Pre-reading

John Stuart Mill (1806–1873), a British philosopher, political economist, and civil servant, is one of the most influential thinkers in the history of classical liberalism. He contributed enormously to liberal thought by combining elements of classical liberalism with what eventually became known as the new liberalism. As a member of the Liberal Party, Mill was also the second Member of Parliament to call for women's suffrage after Henry Hunt in 1832. His substantial corpus of works includes texts in logic, epistemology, economics, social and political philosophy, ethics, metaphysics, religion, and current affairs. Among his most well-known and significant are *A System of Logic*, *Principles of Political Economy*, *On Liberty*, *Utilitarianism*, *The Subjection of Women*, *Three Essays on Religion*, and his *Autobiography*.

On Liberty (1859), one of the classic texts in liberal philosophy, addresses the nature and limits of the power that can be exercised by society over the individual. In perhaps his most passionate work, Mill writes about the rights of individuals to do what they wish with their own life as long as the ramifications from their actions don't harm other people. This type of advocacy for an autonomous life for all citizens is typical of Mill's utilitarian beliefs. Utilitarianism supports each person having the ability to maximize their own utility (happiness) as long as they don't negatively affect others on their path to happiness. And as to Mill's conception of happiness, he holds that "By happiness is intended pleasure, and the absence of pain; by unhappiness, pain, and the privation of pleasure." That statement has seemed to commit Mill, at a basic level, to hedonism as an account of happiness and a theory of value—that it is pleasurable sensations that are the ultimately valuable thing. From here, one can see the limitation or even fallacy of Mill's interpretation of both freedom and happiness. Thus, a critical perspective and reflection will be needed in our exploration of Mill's liberal ideas.

The essay *On Liberty* consists of five chapters. In Chapter I, Mill begins by explaining that his purpose is to discuss the maximum power that society can exercise over an individual and study the struggle between Liberty and Authority. And one can see Mill's strong and even extreme aversion to conformity in the first chapter, which will play an important role in the whole essay. Thus, critical thinking is a necessity during reading and analyzing Mill's extreme notions of liberty.

In Chapter II, Mill's ideas on society are tempered with his views on religion. Indeed, probably the most interesting aspect of Mill's work in this chapter is his views on religion. He doesn't believe that one should solely adhere to the doctrine of religion and ignore the importance of personal integrity standing on its own merit.

In Chapter III, Mill's argument strikes a balance between his utilitarian and liberal philosophies. And in Chapter IV, Mill anticipates and addresses some arguments against his theories. After his initial hard-line stance, Mill softens a bit as he attempts to clear up inconsistencies regarding his ideal of liberty and individuality. He finally makes a dependent connection between society and man, after denouncing the relationship in the early parts of the book. He makes people partially beholden to society and society responsible for the early development of their citizens-a strange thing for a man who sings the praises of autonomy.

Chapter V offers an overview of Mill's strategy, and through the application of his ideas to everyday events, a clearer view is obtained of what Mill's thoughts are about the direction society should go in. Mill suggests several protective measures that are used in modern-day society, and the foreshadowing of present-day America and the world is definitely notable in the last chapter.

Due to the length limit of this chapter, only parts of Chapters I and V are excerpted.

Now let's read the text and reflect on the questions that follow.

Text

Chapter I
Introductory

The subject of this Essay is not the so-called Liberty of the Will, so unfortunately opposed to the misnamed doctrine of Philosophical Necessity; but Civil, or Social Liberty: the nature and limits of the power which can be legitimately exercised by society over the individual. A question seldom stated, and hardly ever discussed, in general terms, but which profoundly influences the practical controversies of the age by its latent presence, and is likely soon to make itself recognized as the vital question of the future. It is so far from being new, that, in a certain sense, it has divided mankind, almost from the remotest ages, but in the stage of progress into which the more civilized portions of the species have now entered, it presents itself under new conditions, and requires a different and more fundamental treatment.

...

The object of this Essay is to assert one very simple principle, as entitled to govern absolutely the dealings of society with the individual in the way of compulsion and control, whether the means used be physical force in the form of legal penalties, or the moral coercion of public opinion. That principle is, that the sole end for which mankind are warranted, individually or collectively in interfering with the liberty of action of any of their number, is self-protection. That the only purpose for which power can be rightfully exercised over any member of a civilized community, against his will, is to prevent harm to others. His own good, either physical or moral, is not a sufficient warrant. He cannot rightfully be compelled to do or forbear because it will be better for him to do so, because it will make him happier, because, in the opinions of others, to do so would be wise, or even right. These are good reasons for remonstrating with him, or reasoning with him, or persuading him, or entreating him, but not for compelling him, or visiting him with any evil, in case he do otherwise. To justify that, the conduct from which it is desired to deter him must be calculated to produce evil to some one else. The only part of the conduct of any one, for which he is amenable to society, is that which concerns others. In the part which merely concerns himself, his independence is, of right, absolute. Over himself, over his own body and mind, the individual is sovereign.

It is, perhaps, hardly necessary to say that this doctrine is meant to apply only to human beings in the maturity of their faculties. We are not speaking of children, or of young persons below the age which the law may fix as that of manhood or womanhood. Those who are still in a state to require being taken care of by others, must be protected against their own actions as well as against external injury. For the same reason, we may leave out of consideration those backward states of society in which the race itself may be considered as in its nonage. The early difficulties in the way of spontaneous progress are so great, that there is seldom any choice of means for overcoming them; and a ruler full of the spirit of improvement is warranted in the use of any expedients that will attain an end, perhaps otherwise unattainable. Despotism is a legitimate mode of government in dealing with barbarians, provided the end be their improvement, and the means justified by actually effecting that end. Liberty, as a principle, has no application to any state of things anterior to the time when mankind have become capable of being improved by free and equal discussion. Until then, there is nothing for them but implicit obedience to an Akbar or a Charlemagne, if they are so fortunate as to find one. But as soon as mankind have attained the capacity of being guided to their own improvement by conviction or persuasion (a period long since reached in all nations with whom we need here concern ourselves), compulsion, either in the direct form or in that of pains and penalties for non-compliance, is no longer admissible as a means to their own good, and justifiable only for the security of others.

Chapter V
Applications

THE principles asserted in these pages must be more generally admitted as the basis for discussion of details, before a consistent application of them to all the various departments of government and morals can be attempted with any prospect of advantage. The few observations I propose to make on questions of detail, are designed to illustrate the principles, rather than to follow them out to their consequences. I offer, not so much applications, as specimens of application; which may serve to bring into greater clearness the meaning and limits of the two maxims which together form the entire doctrine of this Essay and to assist the judgment in holding the balance between them, in the cases where it appears doubtful which of them is applicable to the case.

The maxims are, first, that the individual is not accountable to society for his actions, in so far as these concern the interests of no person but himself. Advice, instruction, persuasion, and avoidance by other people, if thought necessary by them for their own good, are the only measures by which society can justifiably express its dislike or disapprobation of his conduct. Secondly, that for such actions as are prejudicial to the interests of others, the individual is accountable, and may be subjected either to social or to legal punishments, if society is of opinion that the one or the other is requisite for its protection.

In the first place, it must by no means be supposed, because damage, or probability of damage, to the interests of others, can alone justify the interference of society, that therefore it always does justify such interference. In many cases, an individual, in pursuing a legitimate object, necessarily and therefore legitimately causes pain or loss to others, or intercepts a good which they had a reasonable hope of obtaining. Such oppositions of interest between individuals often arise from bad social institutions, but are unavoidable while those institutions last; and some would be unavoidable under any institutions. Whoever succeeds in an overcrowded profession, or in a competitive examination; whoever is preferred to another in any contest for an object which both desire, reaps benefit from the loss of others, from their wasted exertion and their disappointment. But it is, by common admission, better for the general interest of mankind, that persons should pursue their objects undeterred by this sort of consequences. In other words, society admits no right, either legal or moral, in the disappointed competitors, to immunity from this kind of suffering; and feels called on to interfere, only when means of success have been employed which it is contrary to the general interest to permit—namely, fraud or treachery, and force.

Again, trade is a social act. Whoever undertakes to sell any description of goods to the public, does what affects the interest of other persons, and of society in general; and thus his conduct, in principle, comes within the jurisdiction of society: accordingly, it was once held to be the duty of governments, in all cases which were considered of importance, to fix prices, and regulate the processes of manufacture. But it is now recognized, though not till after a long struggle, that both the cheapness and the good quality of commodities are most effectually provided for by leaving the producers and sellers perfectly free, under the sole check of equal freedom to the buyers for supplying themselves elsewhere. This is the so-called doctrine of Free Trade, which rests on grounds different from, though equally solid with, the principle of individual liberty asserted in this Essay. Restrictions on trade, or on production for purposes of trade, are indeed restraints; and all restraint, qua restraint, is an evil: but the restraints in question affect only that part of conduct which society is competent to restrain, and are wrong solely because they do not really produce the results which it is desired to produce by them. As the principle of individual liberty is not involved in the doctrine of Free Trade so neither is it in most of the questions which arise respecting the limits of that doctrine: as for example, what amount of public control is admissible for the prevention of fraud by adulteration; how far sanitary precautions, or arrangements to protect work-people employed in dangerous occupations, should be enforced on employers. Such questions involve considerations of liberty, only in so far as leaving people to themselves is always better, caeteris paribus, than controlling them: but that they may be legitimately controlled for these ends, is in principle undeniable. On the other hand, there are questions relating to interference with trade which are essentially questions of liberty; such as the Maine Law, already touched upon; the prohibition of the importation of opium into China; the restriction of the sale of poisons; all cases, in short, where the object of the interference is to make it impossible or difficult to obtain a particular commodity. These interferences are objectionable, not as infringements on the liberty of the producer or seller, but on that of the buyer.

…

The right inherent in society, to ward off crimes against itself by antecedent precautions, suggests the obvious limitations to the maxim, that purely self-regarding misconduct cannot properly be meddled with in the way of prevention or punishment. Drunkennesses, for example, in ordinary cases, is not a fit subject for legislative interference; but I should deem it perfectly legitimate that a person, who had once been convicted of any act of violence to others under the influence of drink, should be placed under a special legal restriction, personal to himself; that if he were afterwards found drunk, he should be liable to a penalty, and that if when in that state he committed another offence, the punishment to which he would be liable for that other offence should be increased in severity. The making himself drunk, in a person whom drunkenness excites to do harm to others, is a crime against others. So, again, idleness, except in a person receiving support from the public, or except when it constitutes a breach of contract, cannot without tyranny be made a subject of legal punishment; but if either from idleness or from any other avoidable cause, a man fails to perform his legal duties to others, as for instance to support his children, it is no tyranny to force him to fulfil that obligation, by compulsory labor, if no other means are available.

Again, there are many acts which, being directly injurious only to the agents themselves, ought not to be legally interdicted, but which, if done publicly, are a violation of good manners, and coming thus within the category of offences against others, may rightfully be prohibited. Of this kind are offences against decency; on which it is unnecessary to dwell, the rather as they are only connected indirectly with our subject, the objection to publicity being equally strong in the case of many actions not in themselves condemnable, nor supposed to be so.

Questions

1. What is the subject and object of Mill's Essay?
2. Does Mill's doctrine of liberty apply to children and barbarians?
3. According to Mill, what possible impact will an individual, in pursuing a legitimate object, exert upon others?
4. What is the so-called doctrine of Free Trade? And is the principle of individual liberty involved in the doctrine of Free Trade?
5. Can the purely self-regarding misconduct be properly meddled with in the way of prevention of punishment?

Socialism: Utopian and Scientific

Frederick Engels

Pre-reading

Socialism: Utopian and Scientific is a short book first published in 1880 by German-born socialist Friedrich Engels. Intended as a popularization of Marxist ideas for a working class readership, the book was one of the fundamental publications of the international socialist movement during the late 19th and early 20th centuries, selling tens of thousands of copies.

The book explains the differences between utopian socialism and scientific socialism, which Marxism considers itself to embody. The book explains that whereas utopian socialism is idealist, reflecting the personal opinions of the authors and claims that society can be adapted based on these opinions, scientific socialism derives itself from reality. It focuses on the materialist conception of history, which is based on an analysis over history, and concludes that communism naturally follows capitalism. Engels begins the book by chronicling the thought of utopian socialists, starting with Saint-Simon. He then proceeds to Fourier and Robert Owen. In Chapter Two, he summarizes dialectics, and then chronicles the thought from the ancient Greeks to Hegel. Chapter Three summarizes dialectics in relation to economic and social struggles, essentially echoing the words of Marx, and will help the readers to develop a critical thinking of liberalism. This is why Chapter Three is excerpted. Now let's read the text and reflect on the questions that follow.

Text

III
Historical Materialism

The materialist conception of history starts from the proposition that the production of the means to support human life and, next to production, the exchange of things produced, is the basis of all social structure; that in every society that has appeared in history, the manner in which wealth is distributed and society divided into classes or orders is dependent upon what is produced, how it is produced, and how the products are exchanged. From this point of view, the final causes of all social changes and political revolutions are to be sought, not in men's brains, not in men's better insights into eternal truth and justice, but in changes in the modes of production and exchange. They are to be sought, not in the philosophy, but in the economics of each particular epoch. The growing perception that existing social institutions are unreasonable and unjust, that reason has become unreason, and right wrong, is only proof that in the modes of production and exchange changes have silently taken place with which the social order, adapted to earlier economic conditions, is no longer in keeping. From this it also follows that the means of getting rid of the incongruities that have been brought to light must also be present, in a more or less developed condition, within the changed modes of production themselves. These means are not to be invented by deduction from fundamental principles, but are to be discovered in the stubborn facts of the existing system of production.

What is, then, the position of modern Socialism in this connection?

The present situation of society—this is now pretty generally conceded—is the creation of the ruling class of today, of the bourgeoisie. The mode of production peculiar to the bourgeoisie, known, since Marx, as the capitalist mode of production, was incompatible with the feudal system, with the privileges it conferred upon individuals, entire social ranks and local corporations, as well as with the hereditary ties of subordination which constituted the framework of its social organization. The bourgeoisie broke up the feudal system and built upon its ruins the capitalist order of society, the kingdom of free competition, of personal liberty, of the equality, before the law, of all commodity owners, of all the rest of the capitalist blessings. Thenceforward, the capitalist mode of production could develop in freedom. Since steam, machinery, and the making of machines by machinery transformed the older manufacture into modern industry, the productive forces, evolved under the guidance of the bourgeoisie, developed with a rapidity and in a degree unheard of before. But just as the older manufacture, in its time, and handicraft, becoming more developed under its influence, had come into collision with the feudal trammels of the guilds, so now modern industry, in its complete development, comes into collision with the bounds within which the capitalist mode of production holds it confined. The new productive forces have already outgrown the capitalistic mode of using them. And this conflict between productive forces and modes of production is not a conflict engendered in the mind of man, like that between original sin and divine justice. It exists, in fact, objectively, outside us, independently of the will and actions even of the men that have brought it on. Modern Socialism is nothing but the reflex, in thought, of this conflict in fact; its ideal reflection in the minds, first, of the class directly suffering under it, the working class.

Now, in what does this conflict consist?

Before capitalist production—i.e., in the Middle Ages—the system of petty industry obtained generally, based upon the private property of the laborers in their means of production; in the country, the agriculture of the small peasant, freeman, or serf; in the towns, the handicrafts organized in guilds. The instruments of labor—land, agricultural implements, the workshop, the tool—were the instruments of labor of single individuals, adapted for the use of one worker, and, therefore, of necessity, small, dwarfish, circumscribed. But, for this very reason, they belonged as a rule to the producer himself. To concentrate these scattered, limited means of production, to enlarge them, to turn them into the powerful levers of production of the present day—this was precisely the historic role of capitalist production and of its upholder, the bourgeoisie. In the fourth section of Capital, Marx has explained in detail how since the 15th century this has been historically worked out through the three phases of simple co-operation, manufacture, and modern industry. But the bourgeoisie, as is shown there, could not transform these puny means of production into mighty productive forces without transforming them, at the same time, from means of production of the individual into social means of production only workable by a collectivity of men. The spinning wheel, the handloom, the blacksmith's hammer, were replaced by the spinning-machine, the power-loom, the steam-hammer; the individual workshop, by the factory implying the co-operation of hundreds and thousands of workmen. In like manner, production itself changed from a series of individual into a series of social acts, and the production from individual to social products. The yarn, the cloth, the metal articles that now come out of the factory were the joint product of many workers, through whose hands they had successively to pass before they were ready. No one person could say of them: "I made that; this is my product."

But where, in a given society, the fundamental form of production is that spontaneous division of labor which creeps in gradually and not upon any preconceived plan, there the products take on the form of commodities, whose mutual exchange, buying and selling, enable the individual producers to satisfy their manifold wants. And this was the case in the Middle Ages. The peasant, e.g., sold to the artisan agricultural products and bought from him the products of handicraft. Into this society of individual producers, of commodity producers, the new mode of production thrust itself. In the midst of the old division of labor, grown up spontaneously and upon no definite plan, which had governed the whole of society, now arose division of labor upon a definite plan, as organized in the factory; side by side with individual production appeared social production. The products of both were sold in the same market, and, therefore, at prices at least approximately equal. But organization upon a definite plan was stronger than spontaneous division of labor. The factories working with the combined social forces of a collectivity of individuals produced their commodities far more cheaply than the individual small producers. Individual producers succumbed in one department after another. Socialized production revolutionized all the old methods of production. But its revolutionary character was, at the same time, so little recognized that it was, on the contrary, introduced as a means of increasing and developing the production of commodities. When it arose, it found ready-made, and made liberal use of, certain machinery for the production and exchange of commodities: merchants' capital, handicraft, wage-labor. Socialized production thus introducing itself as a new form of the production of commodities, it was a matter of course that under it the old forms of appropriation remained in full swing, and were applied to its products as well.

In the medieval stage of evolution of the production of commodities, the question as to the owner of the product of labor could not arise. The individual producer, as a rule, had, from raw material belonging to himself, and generally his own handiwork, produced it with his own tools, by the labor of his own hands or of his family. There was no need for him to appropriate the new product. It belonged wholly to him, as a matter of course. His property in the product was, therefore, based upon his own labor. Even where external help was used, this was, as a rule, of little importance, and very generally was compensated by something other than wages. The apprentices and journeymen of the guilds worked less for board and wages than for education, in order that they might become master craftsmen themselves.

Then came the concentration of the means of production and of the producers in large workshops and manufactories, their transformation into actual socialized means of production and socialized producers. But the socialized producers and means of production and their products were still treated, after this change, just as they had been before—i.e., as the means of production and the products of individuals. Hitherto, the owner of the instruments of labor had himself appropriated the product, because, as a rule, it was his own product and the assistance of others was the exception. Now, the owner of the instruments of labor always appropriated to himself the product, although it was no longer his product but exclusively the product of the labor of others. Thus, the products now produced socially were not appropriated by those who had actually set in motion the means of production and actually produced the commodities, but by the capitalists. The means of production, and production itself, had become in essence socialized. But they were subjected to a form of appropriation which presupposes the private production of individuals, under which, therefore, every one owns his own product and brings it to market. The mode of production is subjected to this form of appropriation, although it abolishes the conditions upon which the latter rests.

This contradiction, which gives to the new mode of production its capitalistic character, contains the germ of the whole of the social antagonisms of today. The greater the mastery obtained by the new mode of production over all important fields of production and in all manufacturing countries, the more it reduced individual production to an insignificant residuum, the more clearly was brought out the incompatibility of socialized production with capitalistic appropriation.

The first capitalists found, as we have said, alongside of other forms of labor, wage-labor ready-made for them on the market. But it was exceptional, complementary, accessory, transitory wage-labor. The agricultural laborer, though, upon occasion, he hired himself out by the day, had a few acres of his own land on which he could at all events live at a pinch. The guilds were so organized that the journeyman of today became the master of tomorrow. But all this changed, as soon as the means of production became socialized and concentrated in the hands of capitalists. The means of production, as well as the product, of the individual producer became more and more worthless; there was nothing left for him but to turn wage-worker under the capitalist. Wage-labor, aforetime the exception and accessory, now became the rule and basis of all production; aforetime complementary, it now became the sole remaining function of the worker. The wage-worker for a time became a wage-worker for life. The number of these permanent was further enormously increased by the breaking-up of the feudal system that occurred at the same time, by the disbanding of the retainers of the feudal lords, the eviction of the peasants from their homesteads, etc. The separation was made complete between the means of production concentrated in the hands of the capitalists, on the one side, and the producers, possessing nothing but their labor-power, on the other. The contradiction between socialized production and capitalistic appropriation manifested itself as the antagonism of proletariat and bourgeoisie.

We have seen that the capitalistic mode of production thrust its way into a society of commodity-producers, of individual producers, whose social bond was the exchange of their products. But every society based upon the production of commodities has this peculiarity: that the producers have lost control over their own social inter-relations. Each man produces for himself with such means of production as he may happen to have, and for such exchange as he may require to satisfy his remaining wants. No one knows how much of his particular article is coming on the market, nor how much of it will be wanted. No one knows whether his individual product will meet an actual demand, whether he will be able to make good his costs of production or even to sell his commodity at all. Anarchy reigns in socialized production.

But the production of commodities, like every other form of production, has it peculiar, inherent laws inseparable from it; and these laws work, despite anarchy, in and through anarchy. They reveal themselves in the only persistent form of social inter-relations—i.e., in exchange—and here they affect the individual producers as compulsory laws of competition. They are, at first, unknown to these producers themselves, and have to be discovered by them gradually and as the result of experience. They work themselves out, therefore, independently of the producers, and in antagonism to them, as inexorable natural laws of their particular form of production. The product governs the producers.

In mediaeval society, especially in the earlier centuries, production was essentially directed toward satisfying the wants of the individual. It satisfied, in the main, only the wants of the producer and his family. Where relations of personal dependence existed, as in the country, it also helped to satisfy the wants of the feudal lord. In all this there was, therefore, no exchange; the products, consequently, did not assume the character of commodities. The family of the peasant produced almost everything they wanted: clothes and furniture, as well as the means of subsistence. Only when it began to produce more than was sufficient to supply its own wants and the payments in kind to the feudal lords, only then did it also produce commodities. This surplus, thrown into socialized exchange and offered for sale, became commodities.

The artisan in the towns, it is true, had from the first to produce for exchange. But they, also, themselves supplied the greatest part of their individual wants. They had gardens and plots of land. They turned their cattle out into the communal forest, which, also, yielded them timber and firing. The women spun flax, wool, and so forth. Production for the purpose of exchange, production of commodities, was only in its infancy. Hence, exchange was restricted, the market narrow, the methods of production stable; there was local exclusiveness without, local unity within; the mark in the country; in the town, the guild.

But with the extension of the production of commodities, and especially with the introduction of the capitalist mode of production, the laws of commodity-production, hitherto latent, came into action more openly and with greater force. The old bonds were loosened, the old exclusive limits broken through, the producers were more and more turned into independent, isolated producers of commodities. It became apparent that the production of society at large was ruled by absence of plan, by accident, by anarchy; and this anarchy grew to greater and greater height. But the chief means by aid of which the capitalist mode of production intensified this anarchy of socialized production was the exact opposite of anarchy. It was the increasing organization of production, upon a social basis, in every individual productive establishment. By this, the old, peaceful, stable condition of things was ended. Wherever this organization of production was introduced into a branch of industry, it brooked no other method of production by its side. The field of labor became a battle-ground. The great geographical discoveries, and the colonization following them, multiplied markets and quickened the transformation of handicraft into manufacture. The war did not simply break out between the individual producers of particular localities. The local struggles begat, in their turn, national conflicts, the commercial wars of the 17th and 18th centuries.

Finally, modern industry and the opening of the world-market made the struggle universal, and at the same time gave it an unheard-of virulence. Advantages in natural or artificial conditions of production now decide the existence or non-existence of individual capitalists, as well as of whole industries and countries. He that falls is remorselessly cast aside. It is the Darwinian struggle of the individual for existence transferred from Nature to society with intensified violence. The conditions of existence natural to the animal appear as the final term of human development. The contradiction between socialized production and capitalistic appropriation now presents itself as an antagonism between the organization of production in the individual workshop and the anarchy of production in society generally.

The capitalistic mode of production moves in these two forms of the antagonism immanent to it from its very origin. It is never able to get out of that "vicious circle" which Fourier had already discovered. What Fourier could not, indeed, see in his time is that this circle is gradually narrowing; that the movement becomes more and more a spiral, and must come to an end, like the movement of planets, by collision with the centre. It is the compelling force of anarchy in the production of society at large that more and more completely turns the great majority of men into proletarians; and it is the masses of the proletariat again who will finally put an end to anarchy in production. It is the compelling force of anarchy in social production that turns the limitless perfectibility of machinery under modern industry into a compulsory law by which every individual industrial capitalist must perfect his machinery more and more, under penalty of ruin.

But the perfecting of machinery is making human labor superfluous. If the introduction and increase of machinery means the displacement of millions of manual by a few machine-workers, improvement in machinery means the displacement of more and more of the machine-workers themselves. It means, in the last instance, the production of a number of available wage workers in excess of the average needs of capital, the formation of a complete industrial reserve army, as I called it in 1845, available at the times when industry is working at high pressure, to be cast out upon the street when the inevitable crash comes, a constant dead weight upon the limbs of the working-class in its struggle for existence with capital, a regulator for keeping of wages down to the low level that suits the interests of capital.

Thus it comes about, to quote Marx, that machinery becomes the most powerful weapon in the war of capital against the working-class; that the instruments of labor constantly tear the means of subsistence out of the hands of the laborer; that they very product of the worker is turned into an instrument for his subjugation.

Thus it comes about that the economizing of the instruments of labor becomes at the same time, from the outset, the most reckless waste of labor-power, and robbery based upon the normal conditions under which labor functions; that machinery, "the most powerful instrument for shortening labor time, becomes the most unfailing means for placing every moment of the laborer's time and that of his family at the disposal of the capitalist for the purpose of expanding the value of his capital."

Thus it comes about that the overwork of some becomes the preliminary condition for the idleness of others, and that modern industry, which hunts after new consumers over the whole world, forces the consumption of the masses at home down to a starvation minimum, and in doing thus destroys its own home market.

"The law that always equilibrates the relative surplus-population, or industrial reserve army, to the extent and energy of accumulation, this law rivets the laborer to capital more firmly than the wedges of Vulcan did Prometheus to the rock. It establishes an accumulation of misery, corresponding with the accumulation of capital. Accumulation of wealth at one pole is, therefore, at the same time accumulation of misery, agony of toil, slavery, ignorance, brutality, mental degradation, at the opposite pole, i.e., on the side of the class that produces its own product in the form of capital.

And to expect any other division of the products from the capitalist mode of production is the same as expecting the electrodes of a battery not to decompose acidulated water, not to liberate oxygen at the positive, hydrogen at the negative pole, so long as they are connected with the battery.

We have seen that the ever-increasing perfectibility of modern machinery is, by the anarchy of social production, turned into a compulsory law that forces the individual industrial capitalist always to improve his machinery, always to increase its productive force. The bare possibility of extending the field of production is transformed for him into a similarly compulsory law. The enormous expansive force of modern industry, compared with which that of gases is mere child's play, appears to us now as a necessity for expansion, both qualitative and quantative, that laughs at all resistance. Such resistance is offered by consumption, by sales, by the markets for the products of modern industry. But the capacity for extension, extensive and intensive, of the markets is primarily governed by quite different laws that work much less energetically. The extension of the markets cannot keep pace with the extension of production. The collision becomes inevitable, and as this cannot produce any real solution so long as it does not break in pieces the capitalist mode of production, the collisions become periodic. Capitalist production has begotten another "vicious circle".

As a matter of fact, since 1825, when the first general crisis broke out, the whole industrial and commercial world, production and exchange among all civilized peoples and their more or less barbaric hangers-on, are thrown out of joint about once every 10 years. Commerce is at a stand-still, the markets are glutted, products accumulate, as multitudinous as they are unsaleable, hard cash disappears, credit vanishes, factories are closed, the mass of the workers are in want of the means of subsistence, because they have produced too much of the means of subsistence; bankruptcy follows upon bankruptcy, execution upon execution. The stagnation lasts for years; productive forces and products are wasted and destroyed wholesale, until the accumulated mass of commodities finally filter off, more or less depreciated in value, until production and exchange gradually begin to move again. Little by little, the pace quickens. It becomes a trot. The industrial trot breaks into a canter, the canter in turn grows into the headlong gallop of a perfect steeplechase of industry, commercial credit, and speculation, which finally, after breakneck leaps, ends where it began—in the ditch of a crisis. And so over and over again. We have now, since the year 1825, gone through this five times, and at the present moment (1877), we are going through it for the sixth time. And the character of these crises is so clearly defined that Fourier hit all of them off when he described the first "crise plethorique", a crisis from plethora.

In these crises, the contradiction between socialized production and capitalist appropriation ends in a violent explosion. The circulation of commodities is, for the time being, stopped. Money, the means of circulation, becomes a hindrance to circulation. All the laws of production and circulation of commodities are turned upside down. The economic collision has reached its apogee. The mode of production is in rebellion against the mode of exchange.

The fact that the socialized organization of production within the factory has developed so far that it has become incompatible with the anarchy of production in society, which exists side by side with and dominates it, is brought home to the capitalist themselves by the violent concentration of capital that occurs during crises, through the ruin of many large, and a still greater number of small, capitalists. The whole mechanism of the capitalist mode of production breaks down under the pressure of the productive forces, its own creations. It is no longer able to turn all this mass of means of production into capital. They lie fallow, and for that very reason the industrial reserve army must also lie fallow. Means of production, means of subsistence, available laborers, all the elements of production and of general wealth, are present in abundance. But "abundance becomes the source of distress and want" (Fourier), because it is the very thing that prevents the transformation of the means of production and subsistence into capital. For in capitalistic society, the means of production can only function when they have undergone a preliminary transformation into capital, into the means of exploiting human labor-power. The necessity of this transformation into capital of the means of production and subsistence stands like a ghost between these and the workers. It alone prevents the coming together of the material and personal levers of production; it alone forbids the means of production to function, the workers to work and live. On the one hand, therefore, the capitalistic mode of production stands convicted of its own incapacity to further direct these productive forces. On the other, these productive forces themselves, with increasing energy, press forward to the removal of the existing contradiction, to the abolition of their quality as capital, to the practical recognition of their character as social production forces.

This rebellion of the productive forces, as they grow more and more powerful, against their quality as capital, this stronger and stronger command that their social character shall be recognized, forces the capital class itself to treat them more and more as social productive forces, so far as this is possible under capitalist conditions. The period of industrial high pressure, with its unbounded inflation of credit, not less than the crash itself, by the collapse of great capitalist establishments, tends to bring about that form of the socialization of great masses of the means of production which we meet with in the different kinds of joint-stock companies. Many of these means of production and of distribution are, from the outset, so colossal that, like the railways, they exclude all other forms of capitalistic expansion. At a further stage of evolution, this form also becomes insufficient. The producers on a large scale in a particular branch of an industry in a particular country unite in a "Trust", a union for the purpose of regulating production. They determine the total amount to be produced, parcel it out among themselves, and thus enforce the selling price fixed beforehand. But trusts of this kind, as soon as business becomes bad, are generally liable to break up, and on this very account compel a yet greater concentration of association. The whole of a particular industry is turned into one gigantic joint-stock company; internal competition gives place to the internal monopoly of this one company. This has happened in 1890 with the English alkali production, which is now, after the fusion of 48 large works, in the hands of one company, conducted upon a single plan, and with a capital of 6,000,000 pounds.

In the trusts, freedom of competition changes into its very opposite—into monopoly; and the production without any definite plan of capitalistic society capitulates to the production upon a definite plan of the invading socialistic society. Certainly, this is so far still to the benefit and advantage of the capitalists. But, in this case, the exploitation is so palpable, that it must break down. No nation will put up with production conducted by trusts, with so barefaced an exploitation of the community by a small band of dividend-mongers.

In any case, with trusts or without, the official representative of capitalist society—the state—will ultimately have to undertake the direction of production. This necessity for conversion into State property is felt first in the great institutions for intercourse and communication—the post office, the telegraphs, the railways.

If the crises demonstrate the incapacity of the bourgeoisie for managing any longer modern productive forces, the transformation of the great establishments for production and distribution into joint-stock companies, trusts, and State property, show how unnecessary the bourgeoisie are for that purpose. All the social functions of the capitalist has no further social function than that of pocketing dividends, tearing off coupons, and gambling on the Stock Exchange, where the different capitalists despoil one another of their capital. At first, the capitalistic mode of production forces out the workers. Now, it forces out the capitalists, and reduces them, just as it reduced the workers, to the ranks of the surplus-population, although not immediately into those of the industrial reserve army.

But, the transformation—either into joint-stock companies and trusts, or into State-ownership—does not do away with the capitalistic nature of the productive forces. In the joint-stock companies and trusts, this is obvious. And the modern State, again, is only the organization that bourgeois society takes on in order to support the external conditions of the capitalist mode of production against the encroachments as well of the workers as of individual capitalists. The modern state, no matter what its form, is essentially a capitalist machine—the state of the capitalists, the ideal personification of the total national capital. The more it proceeds to the taking over of productive forces, the more does it actually become the national capitalist, the more citizens does it exploit. The workers remain wage-workers—proletarians. The capitalist relation is not done away with. It is, rather, brought to a head. But, brought to a head, it topples over.

State-ownership of the productive forces is not the solution of the conflict, but concealed within it are the technical conditions that form the elements of that solution.

This solution can only consist in the practical recognition of the social nature of the modern forces of production, and therefore in the harmonizing with the socialized character of the means of production. And this can only come about by society openly and directly taking possession of the productive forces which have outgrown all control, except that of society as a whole. The social character of the means of production and of the products today reacts against the producers, periodically disrupts all production and exchange, acts only like a law of Nature working blindly, forcibly, destructively. But, with the taking over by society of the productive forces, the social character of the means of production and of the products will be utilized by the producers with a perfect understanding of its nature, and instead of being a source of disturbance and periodical collapse, will become the most powerful lever of production itself.

Active social forces work exactly like natural forces: blindly, forcibly, destructively, so long as we do not understand, and reckon with, them. But, when once we understand them, when once we grasp their action, their direction, their effects, it depends only upon ourselves to subject them more and more to our own will, and, by means of them, to reach our own ends. And this holds quite especially of the mighty productive forces of today. As long as we obstinately refuse to understand the nature and the character of these social means of action—and this understanding goes against the grain of the capitalist mode of production, and its defenders—so long these forces are at work in spite of us, in opposition to us, so long they master us, as we have shown above in detail.

But when once their nature is understood, they can, in the hands of the producers working together, be transformed from master demons into willing servants. The difference is as that between the destructive force of electricity in the lightning in the storm, and electricity under command in the telegraph and the voltaic arc; the difference between a conflagration, and fire working in the service of man. With this recognition, at last, of the real nature of the productive forces of today, the social anarchy of production gives place to a social regulation of production upon a definite plan, according to the needs of the community and of each individual. Then the capitalist mode of appropriation, in which the product enslaves first the producer, and then the appropriator, is replaced by the mode of appropriation of the products that is based upon the nature of the modern means of production; upon the one hand, direct social appropriation, as means to the maintenance and extension of production—on the other, direct individual appropriation, as means of subsistence and of enjoyment.

Whilst the capitalist mode of production more and more completely transforms the great majority of the population into proletarians, it creates the power which, under penalty of its own destruction, is forced to accomplish this revolution. Whilst it forces on more and more of the transformation of the vast means of production, already socialized, into State property, it shows itself the way to accomplishing this revolution. The proletariat seizes political power and turns the means of production into State property.

But, in doing this, it abolishes itself as proletariat, abolishes all class distinction and class antagonisms, abolishes also the State as State. Society, thus far, based upon class antagonisms, had need of the State. That is, of an organization of the particular class which was, pro tempore, the exploiting class, an organization for the purpose of preventing any interference from without with the existing conditions of production, and, therefore, especially, for the purpose of forcibly keeping the exploited classes in the condition of oppression corresponding with the given mode of production (slavery, serfdom, wage-labor). The State was the official representative of society as a whole; the gathering of it together into a visible embodiment. But, it was this only in so far as it was the State of that class which itself represented, for the time being, society as a whole:

in ancient times, the State of slave-owning citizens;
in the Middle Ages, the feudal lords;
in our own times, the bourgeoisie.

When, at last, it becomes the real representative of the whole of society, it renders itself unnecessary. As soon as there is no longer any social class to be held in subjection; as soon as class rule, and the individual struggle for existence based upon our present anarchy in production, with the collisions and excesses arising from these, are removed, nothing more remains to be repressed, and a special repressive force, a State, is no longer necessary. The first act by virtue of which the State really constitutes itself the representative of the whole of society—the taking possession of the means of production in the name of society—this is, at the same time, its last independent act as a State. State interference in social relations becomes, in one domain after another, superfluous, and then dies out of itself; the government of persons is replaced by the administration of things, and by the conduct of processes of production. The State is not "abolished". It dies out. This gives the measure of the value of the phrase: "a free State", both as to its justifiable use at times by agitators, and as to its ultimate scientific insufficiency; and also of the demands of the so-called anarchists for the abolition of the State out of hand.

Since the historical appearance of the capitalist mode of production, the appropriation by society of all the means of production has often been dreamed of, more or less vaguely, by individuals, as well as by sects, as the ideal of the future. But it could become possible, could become a historical necessity, only when the actual conditions for its realization were there. Like every other social advance, it becomes practicable, not by men understanding that the existence of classes is in contradiction to justice, equality, etc., not by the mere willingness to abolish these classes, but by virtue of certain new economic conditions. The separation of society into an exploiting and an exploited class, a ruling and an oppressed class, was the necessary consequences of the deficient and restricted development of production in former times. So long as the total social labor only yields a produce which but slightly exceeds that barely necessary for the existence of all; so long, therefore, as labor engages all or almost all the time of the great majority of the members of society—so long, of necessity, this society is divided into classes. Side by side with the great majority, exclusively bond slaves to labor, arises a class freed from directly productive labor, which looks after the general affairs of society: the direction of labor, State business, law, science, art, etc. It is, therefore, the law of division of labor that lies at the basis of the division into classes. But this does not prevent this division into classes from being carried out by means of violence and robbery, trickery and fraud. It does not prevent the ruling class, once having the upper hand, from consolidating its power at the expense of the working-class, from turning its social leadership into an intensified exploitation of the masses.

But if, upon this showing, division into classes has a certain historical justification, it has this only for a given period, only under given social conditions. It was based upon the insufficiency of production. It will be swept away by the complete development of modern productive forces. And, in fact, the abolition of classes in society presupposes a degree of historical evolution at which the existence, not simply of this or that particular ruling class, but of any ruling class at all, and, therefore, the existence of class distinction itself, has become an obsolete anachronism. It presupposes, therefore, the development of production carried out to a degree at which appropriation of the means of production and of the products, and, with this, of political domination, of the monopoly of culture, and of intellectual leadership by a particular class of society, has become not only superfluous but economically, politically, intellectually, a hindrance to development.

This point is now reached. Their political and intellectual bankruptcy is scarcely any longer a secret to the bourgeoisie themselves. Their economic bankruptcy recurs regularly every 10 years. In every crisis, society is suffocated beneath the weight of its own productive forces and products, which it cannot use, and stands helpless, face-to-face with the absurd contradiction that the producers have nothing to consume, because consumers are wanting. The expansive force of the means of production bursts the bonds that the capitalist mode of production had imposed upon them. Their deliverance from these bonds is the one precondition for an unbroken, constantly-accelerated development of the productive forces, and therewith for a practically unlimited increase of production itself. Nor is this all. The socialized appropriation of the means of production does away, not only with the present artificial restrictions upon production, but also with the positive waste and devastation of productive forces and products that are at the present time the inevitable concomitants of production, and that reach their height in the crises. Further, it sets free for the community at large a mass of means of production and of products, by doing away with the senseless extravagance of the ruling classes of today, and their political representatives. The possibility of securing for every member of society, by means of socialized production, an existence not only fully sufficient materially, and becoming day-by-day more full, but an existence guaranteeing to all the free development and exercise of their physical and mental faculties—this possibility is now, for the first time, here, but it is here.

With the seizing of the means of production by society, production of commodities is done away with, and, simultaneously, the mastery of the product over the producer. Anarchy in social production is replaced by systematic, definite organization. The struggle for individual existence disappears. Then, for the first time, man, in a certain sense, is finally marked off from the rest of the animal kingdom, and emerges from mere animal conditions of existence into really human ones. The whole sphere of the conditions of life which environ man, and which have hitherto ruled man, now comes under the dominion and control of man, who for the first time becomes the real, conscious lord of nature, because he has now become master of his own social organization. The laws of his own social action, hitherto standing face-to-face with man as laws of Nature foreign to, and dominating him, will then be used with full understanding, and so mastered by him. Man's own social organization, hitherto confronting him as a necessity imposed by Nature and history, now becomes the result of his own free action. The extraneous objective forces that have, hitherto, governed history, pass under the control of man himself. Only from that time will man himself, more and more consciously, make his own history—only from that time will the social causes set in movement by him have, in the main and in a constantly growing measure, the results intended by him. It is the ascent of man from the kingdom of necessity to the kingdom of freedom.

Let us briefly sum up our sketch of historical evolution.

Ⅰ. **Mediaeval Society**—Individual production on a small scale. Means of production adapted for individual use; hence primitive, ungainly, petty, dwarfed in action. Production for immediate consumption, either of the producer himself or his feudal lord. Only where an excess of production over this consumption occurs is such excess offered for sale, enters into exchange. Production of commodities, therefore, only in its infancy. But already it contains within itself, in embryo, anarchy in the production of society at large.

Ⅱ. **Capitalist Revolution**—transformation of industry, at first be means of simple cooperation and manufacture. Concentration of the means of production, hitherto scattered, into great workshops. As a consequence, their transformation from individual to social means of production—a transformation which does not, on the whole, affect the form of exchange. The old forms of appropriation remain in force. The capitalist appears. In his capacity as owner of the means of production, he also appropriates the products and turns them into commodities. Production has become a social act. Exchange and appropriation continue to be *individual* acts, the acts of individuals. The social product is appropriated by the individual capitalist. Fundamental contradiction, whence arise all the contradictions in which our present-day society moves, and which modern industry brings to light.

A. Severance of the producer from the means of production. Condemnation of the worker to wage-labor for life. *Antagonism between the proletariat and the bourgeoisie.*

B. Growing predominance and increasing effectiveness of the laws governing the production of commodities. Unbridled competition. *Contradiction between socialized organization in the individual factory and social anarchy in the production as a whole.*

C. On the one hand, perfecting of machinery, made by competition compulsory for each individual manufacturer, and complemented by a constantly growing displacement of laborers. Industrial reserve-army. On the other hand, unlimited extension of production, also compulsory under competition, for every manufacturer. On both sides, unheard-of development of productive forces, excess of supply over demand, over-production and products—excess there, of laborers, without employment and without means of existence. But these two levers of production and of social well-being are unable to work together, because the capitalist form of production prevents the productive forces from working and the products from circulating, unless they are first turned into capital—which their very superabundance prevents. The contradiction has grown into an absurdity. *The mode of production rises in rebellion against the form of exchange.*

D. Partial recognition of the social character of the productive forces forced upon the capitalists themselves. Taking over of the great institutions for production and communication, first by joint-stock companies, later in by trusts, then by the State. The bourgeoisie demonstrated to be a superfluous class. All its social functions are now performed by salaried employees.

Ⅲ. **Proletarian Revolution**—Solution of the contradictions. The proletariat seizes the public power, and by means of this transforms the socialized means of production, slipping from the hands of the bourgeoisie, into public property. By this act, the proletariat frees the means of production from the character of capital they have thus far borne, and gives their socialized character complete freedom to work itself out. Socialized production upon a predetermined plan becomes henceforth possible. The development of production makes the existence of different classes of society thenceforth an anachronism. In proportion as anarchy in social production vanishes, the political authority of the State dies out. Man, at last the master of his own form of social organization, becomes at the same time the lord over Nature, his own master—free.

To accomplish this act of universal emancipation is the historical mission of the modern proletariat. To thoroughly comprehend the historical conditions and thus the very nature of this act, to impart to the now oppressed proletarian class a full knowledge of the conditions and of the meaning of the momentous act it is called upon to accomplish, this is the task of the theoretical expression of the proletarian movement, scientific Socialism.

Questions

1. What major changes in the division of labour and productive forces have taken place in recent decades, and what political and social changes have been associated with these changes?
2. Engels defines the underlying contradiction in the development of capitalism in a series of different ways. Find all these different definitions: what does each mean, and is the sequence in which they are presented of any particular significance?
3. What does Engels mean by the "rebellion of the productive forces", and what are the "productive forces"?
4. Which different relations between the State and the community does Engels mention as having arisen down the ages?
5. What could it mean for the state to become "the real representative of the whole of society" and why would it then disappear?

Questions for Further Reflection

1. Do you agree with Adam Smith's view in the priority order of the distribution of capital in a growing society? Does it still apply to today's economy?
2. Both Adam Smith and Frederick Engels talked about the division of labour in the excerpts. What are the differences between their interpretations? Which one is more suitable in today's knowledge economy?
3. Frederick Engels mentions a couple of examples of a "vicious circle" in the development of capitalism. What are they? And how is this vicious circle associated with the notions of liberalism?
4. What are the inconsistencies of Adam Smith's liberal conception with the context of Economic Community?
5. John Mill says in his Essay that "in many cases, an individual, in pursuing a legitimate object, necessarily and therefore legitimately causes pain or loss to others, or intercepts a good which they had a reasonable hope of obtaining." Do you agree with this statement? Is it really impossible to reach a win-win situation and thereby maintain a harmonious relationship among individuals?
6. John Mill advocates an autonomous life for all citizens, which is typical of Mill's Utilitarian beliefs. But according to Karl Marx and Frederick Engels, freedom may be enjoyed by individuals but only in and through the community. What are the potential dangers or harms of Mill's Utilitarian beliefs in today's world? Whose elucidation of freedom do you support?
7. History will remember 2020 for the coronavirus pandemic. With dedication, ingenuity and collective efforts, the Chinese people are gaining the upper hand over the pandemic. The practice of China testifies one more time to the significance of "all for one and one for all". How does this value differ from the doctrine of liberalism? Which ideology can help people overcome this pandemic?
8. What is your understanding of the beliefs of "a Community of Shared Future for Mankind"? How does it diverge from the notions of liberalism ideologically? What would happen to the society if every individual had absolute freedom?

References and Further Reading

1. Smith, A.(1977).*The Wealth of Nations—An Inquiry into the Nature and Causes of the Wealth of Nations.* Chicago: University of Chicago Press.

2. https://www.gradesaver.com/the-wealth-of-nations/study-guide/summary

(The website offers a concise summary of each chapter in *The Wealth of Nation*, with introduction of themes, quizzes, and related links.)

3. https://www.gradesaver.com/on-liberty

(The website offers a concise summary of *On Liberty*, with introduction of themes, quizzes, and related links.)

4. https://www.adamsmith.org/the-wealth-of-nations

(The website is a link to Adam Smith Institute, with latest information related to the study of Adam Smith.)

5. https://www.marxists.org/archive/marx/works/

(The website offers a link to Marx and Engels library, with selected works, Marx quotes, study guides and Marxists Internet archive.)

Chapter 9   Evolutionism

"Evolutionism" means different things to different people. For example, there are theistic evolutionists and there are atheistic evolutionists. But the basic premise behind the evolutionary world-view is atheistic. Theistic evolutionists are those who have managed to reach a compromise between two very distinct world-views: creationism and evolutionism. Evolutionism, in its purer form, is the idea that this universe is the result of random cosmic accidents. Life arose spontaneously via chance chemical processes, and all life-forms are related and share a common ancestor—from bananas to birds, from fishes to flowers, apes to Adam, etc.

Evolutionism is a world-view, which seeks to explain every aspect of this world in which we live. It encompasses a wide variety of topics, from astronomy to chemistry to biology. At its core, it teaches that there were different stages in the evolution of our universe. Macro-evolution is the widely-held notion that all life is related and has descended from a common ancestor: the birds and the bananas, the fishes and the flowers—all related. From the goo, through the zoo, to you over millions of years! This is the stage of evolution which Charles Darwin popularized in his classic, *Origin of Species*, published in 1859. Darwin didn't invent the theory, but he gave it credence by supplying a plausible mechanism: natural selection.

Darwin's Theory of Evolution is the widely held notion that all life is related and has descended from a common ancestor: the birds and the bananas, the fishes and the flowers—all related. Darwin's general theory presumes the development of life from non-life and stresses a purely naturalistic (undirected) "descent with modification". That is, complex creatures evolve from more simplistic ancestors naturally over time. In a nutshell, as random genetic mutations occur within an organism's genetic code, the beneficial mutations are preserved because they aid survival—a process known as "natural selection." These beneficial mutations are passed on to the next generation.

Over time, beneficial mutations accumulate and the result is an entirely different organism (not just a variation of the original, but an entirely different creature).

While Darwin's Theory of Evolution is a relatively young archetype, the evolutionary world-view itself is as old as antiquity. Ancient Greek philosophers such as Anaximander postulated the development of life from non-life and the evolutionary descent of man from animal. Charles

Darwin simply brought something new to the old philosophy—a plausible mechanism called "natural selection." Natural selection acts to preserve and accumulate minor advantageous genetic mutations. Suppose a member of a species developed a functional advantage (it grew wings and learned to fly). Its offspring would inherit that advantage and pass it on to their offspring. The inferior (disadvantaged) members of the same species would gradually die out, leaving only the superior (advantaged) members of the species. Natural selection is the preservation of a functional advantage that enables a species to compete better in the wild. Natural selection is the naturalistic equivalent to domestic breeding. Over the centuries, human breeders have produced dramatic changes in domestic animal populations by selecting individuals to breed. Breeders eliminate undesirable traits gradually over time. Similarly, natural selection eliminates inferior species gradually over time.

Darwin's Theory of Evolution is a slow gradual process. Darwin wrote, "...Natural selection acts only by taking advantage of slight successive variations; she can never take a great and sudden leap, but must advance by short and sure, though slow steps." Thus, Darwin conceded that, "If it could be demonstrated that any complex organ existed, which could not possibly have been formed by numerous, successive, slight modifications, my theory would absolutely break down." Such a complex organ would be known as an "irreducibly complex system". An irreducibly complex system is one composed of multiple parts, all of which are necessary for the system to function. If even one part is missing, the entire system will fail to function. Every individual part is integral. Thus, such a system could not have evolved slowly, piece by piece. The common mousetrap is an everyday non-biological example of irreducible complexity. It is composed of five basic parts: a catch (to hold the bait), a powerful spring, a thin rod called "the hammer," a holding bar to secure the hammer in place, and a platform to mount the trap. If any one of these parts is missing, the mechanism will not work. Each individual part is integral. The mousetrap is irreducibly complex.

Darwin's Theory of Evolution is a theory in crisis in light of the tremendous advances we've made in molecular biology, biochemistry and genetics over the past fifty years. We now know that there are in fact tens of thousands of irreducibly complex systems on the cellular level. Specified complexity pervades the microscopic biological world. Molecular biologist Michael Denton wrote, "Although the tiniest bacterial cells are incredibly small, weighing less than $10-12$ grams, each is in effect a veritable micro-miniaturized factory containing thousands of exquisitely designed pieces of intricate molecular machinery, made up altogether of one hundred thousand million atoms, far more complicated than any machinery built by man and absolutely without parallel in the non-living world."

And we don't need a microscope to observe irreducible complexity. The eye, the ear and the heart are all examples of irreducible complexity, though they were not recognized as such in Darwin's day. Nevertheless, Darwin confessed, "To suppose that the eye with all its inimitable contrivances for adjusting the focus to different distances, for admitting different amounts of light, and for the correction of spherical and chromatic aberration, could have been formed by natural selection, seems, I freely confess, absurd in the highest degree."

The theory was outlined in Darwin's seminal work *On the Origin of Species*, published in 1859. Although Victorian England (and the rest of the world) was slow to embrace natural selection as the mechanism that drives evolution, the concept of evolution itself gained widespread traction by the end of Darwin's life.

On the Origin of Species
Charles Darwin

Pre-reading

Charles Darwin, in full Charles Robert Darwin (born February 12, 1809, Shrewsbury, Shropshire, England—died April 19, 1882, Downe, Kent), English naturalist whose scientific theory of evolution by natural selection became the foundation of modern evolutionary studies. An affable country gentleman, Darwin at first shocked religious Victorian society by suggesting that animals and humans shared a common ancestry. However, his nonreligious biology appealed to the rising class of professional scientists, and by the time of his death evolutionary imagery had spread through all of science, literature, and politics. Darwin, himself an agnostic, was accorded the ultimate British accolade of burial in Westminster Abbey, London.

Charles Darwin returned to England in 1836. In 1839, he was elected a Fellow of the Royal Society and, five days later, married to his cousin Emma Wedgwood, who bore him 10 children. In 1842, Darwin began drafting his *Origin of Species*. Darwin's work was heavily influenced by Lyell's *Principles of Geology* and Thomas Malthus' *An Essay on the Principle of Population* (1798). *Origin of Species* was ultimately published in 1859. Darwin's theory of evolution by natural selection is the foundation upon which modern evolutionary theory is built. Darwin didn't invent the evolutionary worldview. He simply brought something new to the old philosophy: a plausible mechanism called "natural selection."

Charles Darwin's theory of evolution had three main components: that variation occurred randomly among members of a species; that an individual's traits could be inherited by its progeny; and that the struggle for existence would allow only those with favorable traits to survive. Although many of his ideas have been borne out by modern science, Darwin didn't get everything right: traces of Jean-Baptiste Lamarck's outdated theory of evolution remained in Darwin's own. He was also unable to correctly establish how traits were inherited, which wasn't clarified until the rediscovery of Gregor Mendel's work with peas. In fact, with the tremendous advances we've made in molecular biology, biochemistry and genetics over the past fifty years, Darwin's theory has become "a theory in crisis."

However, Darwin's theories hugely impacted scientific thought. His ideas also affected the realms of politics, economics, and literature. More insidious were the ways that Darwin's ideas were used to support theories such as social Darwinism and eugenics, which used biological determinism to advocate for the elimination of people deemed socially unfit. Although Darwin himself was an abolitionist, the social Darwinist ideas inspired by his work contributed to some of the most racist and classist social programs of the last 150 years.

Now let's read the text and reflect on the questions that follow.

Text

Natural Selection—its power compared with man's selection—its power on characters of trifling importance—its power at all ages and on both sexes—Sexual Selection—On the generality of intercrosses between individuals of the same species—Circumstances favorable and unfavorable to Natural Selection, namely, intercrossing, isolation, number of individuals—Slow action—Extinction caused by Natural Selection—Divergence of Character, related to the diversity of inhabitants of any small area, and to naturalization—Action of Natural Selection, through Divergence of Character and Extinction, on the descendants from a common parent—explains the Grouping of all organic beings.

HOW will the struggle for existence, discussed too briefly in the last chapter, act in regard to variation? Can the principle of selection, which we have seen is so potent in the hands of man, apply in nature? I think we shall see that it can act most effectually. Let it be borne in mind in what an endless number of strange peculiarities our domestic productions, and, in a lesser degree, those under nature, vary; and how strong the hereditary tendency is. Under domestication, it may be truly said that the whole organization becomes in some degree plastic. Let it be borne in mind how infinitely complex and close-fitting are the mutual relations of all organic beings to each other and to their physical conditions of life. Can it, then, be thought improbable, seeing that variations useful to man have undoubtedly occurred, that other variations useful in some way to each being in the great and complex battle of life, should sometimes occur in the course of thousands of generations? If such do occur, can we doubt (remembering that many more individuals are born than can possibly survive) that individuals having any advantage, however slight, over others, would have the best chance of surviving and of procreating their kind? On the other hand, we may feel sure that any variation in the least degree injurious would be rigidly destroyed. This preservation of favourable variations and the rejection of injurious variations, I call Natural Selection. Variations neither useful nor injurious would not be affected by natural selection, and would be left a fluctuating element, as perhaps we see in the species called polymorphic.

We shall best understand the probable course of natural selection by taking the case of a country undergoing some physical change, for instance, of climate. The proportional numbers of its inhabitants would almost immediately undergo a change, and some species might become extinct. We may conclude, from what we have seen of the intimate and complex manner in which the inhabitants of each country are bound together, that any change in the numerical proportions of some of the inhabitants, independently of the change of climate itself, would most seriously affect many of the others. If the country were open on its borders, new forms would certainly immigrate, and this also would seriously disturb the relations of some of the former inhabitants. Let it be remembered how powerful the influence of a single introduced tree or mammal has been shown to be. But in the case of an island, or of a country partly surrounded by barriers, into which new and better adapted forms could not freely enter, we should then have places in the economy of nature which would assuredly be better filled up, if some of the original inhabitants were in some manner modified; for, had the area been open to immigration, these same places would have been seized on by intruders. In such case, every slight modification, which in the course of ages chanced to arise, and which in any way favored the individuals of any of the species, by better adapting them to their altered conditions, would tend to be preserved; and natural selection would thus have free scope for the work of improvement.

...

Summary of Chapter IV. If during the long course of ages and under varying conditions of life, organic beings vary at all in the several parts of their organisation, and I think this cannot be disputed; if there be, owing to the high geometrical powers of increase of each species, at some age, season, or year, a severe struggle for life, and this certainly cannot be disputed; then, considering the infinite complexity of the relations of all organic beings to each other and to their conditions of existence, causing an infinite diversity in structure, constitution, and habits, to be advantageous to them, I think it would be a most extraordinary fact if no variation ever had occurred useful to each being's own welfare, in the same way as so many variations have occurred useful to man. But if variations useful to any organic being do occur, assuredly individuals thus characterised will have the best chance of being preserved in the struggle for life; and from the strong principle of inheritance they will tend to produce offspring similarly characterised. This principle of preservation, I have called, for the sake of brevity, Natural Selection. Natural selection, on the principle of qualities being inherited at corresponding ages, can modify the egg, seed, or young, as easily as the adult. Amongst many animals, sexual selection will give its aid to ordinary selection, by assuring to the most vigorous and best adapted males the greatest number of offspring. Sexual selection will also give characters useful to the males alone, in their struggles with other males.

Whether natural selection has really thus acted in nature, in modifying and adapting the various forms of life to their several conditions and stations, must be judged of by the general tenour and balance of evidence given in the following chapters. But we already see how it entails extinction; and how largely extinction has acted in the world's history, geology plainly declares. Natural selection, also, leads to divergence of character; for more living beings can be supported on the same area the more they diverge in structure, habits, and constitution, of which we see proof by looking at the inhabitants of any small spot or at naturalised productions. Therefore during the modification of the descendants of any one species, and during the incessant struggle of all species to increase in numbers, the more diversified these descendants become, the better will be their chance of succeeding in the battle of life. Thus the small differences distinguishing varieties of the same species, will steadily tend to increase till they come to equal the greater differences between species of the same genus, or even of distinct genera.

We have seen that it is the common, the widely-diffused, and widely-ranging species, belonging to the larger genera, which vary most; and these will tend to transmit to their modified offspring that superiority which now makes them dominant in their own countries. Natural selection, as has just been remarked, leads to divergence of character and to much extinction of the less improved and intermediate forms of life. On these principles, I believe, the nature of the affinities of all organic beings may be explained. It is a truly wonderful fact—the wonder of which we are apt to overlook fromfamiliarity—that all animals and all plants throughout all time and space should be related to each other in group subordinate to group, in the manner which we everywhere behold-namely, varieties of the same species most closely related together, species of the same genus less closely and unequally related together, forming sections and sub-genera, species of distinct genera much less closely related, and genera related in different degrees, forming sub-families, families, orders, subclasses, and classes. The several subordinate groups in any class cannot be ranked in a single file, but seem rather to be clustered round points, and these round other points, and so on in almost endless cycles. On the view that each species has been independently created, I can see no explanation of this great fact in the classification of all organic beings; but, to the best of my judgment, it is explained through inheritance and the complex action of natural selection, entailing extinction and divergence of character, as we have seen illustrated in the diagram.

The affinities of all the beings of the same class have sometimes been represented by a great tree. I believe this simile largely speaks the truth. The green and budding twigs may represent existing species; and those produced during each former year may represent the long succession of extinct species. At each period of growth all the growing twigs have tried to branch out on all sides, and to overtop and kill the surrounding twigs and branches, in the same manner as species and groups of species have tried to overmaster other species in the great battle for life. The limbs divided into great branches, and these into lesser and lesser branches, were themselves once, when the tree was small, budding twigs; and this connexion of the former and present buds by ramifying branches may well represent the classification of all extinct and living species in groups subordinate to groups. Of the many twigs which flourished when the tree was a mere bush, only two or three, now grown into great branches, yet survive and bear all the other branches; so with the species which lived during long-past geological periods, very few now have living and modified descendants. From the first growth of the tree, many a limb and branch has decayed and dropped off; and these lost branches of various sizes may represent those whole orders, families, and genera which have now no living representatives, and which are known to us only from having been found in a fossil state. As we here and there see a thin straggling branch springing from a fork low down in a tree, and which by some chance has been favored and is still alive on its summit, so we occasionally see an animal like the Ornithorhynchus or Lepidosiren, which in some small degree connects by its affinities two large branches of life, and which has apparently been saved from fatal competition by having inhabited a protected station. As buds give rise by growth to fresh buds, and these, if vigorous, branch out and overtop on all sides many a feebler branch, so by generation I believe it has been with the great Tree of Life, which fills with its dead and broken branches the crust of the earth, and covers the surface with its ever branching and beautiful ramifications.

Questions

1. In *On the Origin of Species*, Darwin achieves two things that Lamarck does not. What are they?
2. How does natural selection lead to forming a new species?
3. What are Darwin's supporting arguments in *On the Origin of Species*?
4. What is the account of the development of reason in the work of Charles Darwin?
5. Does Darwin's view of reality instill optimism or pessimism at the prospect of solving environmental problems?

Questions for Further Reflection

1. What are your views on Charles Darwin's *On the Origin of Species*?
2. What are the conditions necessary within a population for Evolution by Natural Selection to occur?
3. Why do some people say Darwin's theory has become "a theory in crisis?"
4. What is Darwin's basic argument in *The Descent of Man*, and why did so many object to it?
5. How is Charles Darwin's theory of evolution the capstone of the "Enlightenment" conception of human beings?
6. What was the influence of Darwinism on English literature during the 19th century?

References and Further Reading

1. Clark, R. W.(1984). *The Survival of Charles Darwin : A Biography of a Man and an Idea*. New York: Random House.
2. Desmond, A. & Moore, J.(1991). *Darwin*. New York: Warner Books.

Chapter 10
Socialism and Communism

This chapter presents two excerpts of the classical works of socialism and communism, the purpose of which is to help readers establish a basic framework of this historical and philosophical trend.

Although the term communism did not come into use until the 1840s, socialist or communist ideas can certainly be traced back to as long ago as the 4th century BC. They play an important part in the ideas of the ancient Greek philosopher Plato, whose *Republic* depicts an austere society in which men and women of the "guardian" class share with each other not only their few material goods but also their spouses and children. The governing class of guardians devotes itself to serving the interests of the whole community. From then on, Thomas More's *Utopia*, Saint-Simon's belief in public control of property through central planning, Robert Owen's attempt to establish his "New Harmony", Fourier's vision of "phalanstery", Karl Marx and Friedrich Engels' *Manifesto of the Communist Party*, Lenin's revolutionary communism, and all the other philosophers' contributions have constituted the historical trend which exerts an unprecedented influence on the development of human society.

As is defined in Britannica, Socialism refers to social and economic doctrine that calls for public rather than private ownership or control of property and natural resources. According to the socialist view, individuals do not live or work in isolation but live in cooperation with one another. Furthermore, everything that people produce is in some sense a social product, and everyone who contributes to the production of a good is entitled to a share in it. Society as a whole, therefore, should own or at least control property for the benefit of all its members. Communism, as is defined, is a political and economic system that seeks to create a classless society in which the major means of production, such as mines and factories, are owned and controlled by the public. There is no government or private property or currency, and the wealth is divided among citizens equally or according to individual need. Accordingly, it is commonly seen as a form of socialism—a higher and more advanced form.

The two works selected in this chapter are *Critique of the Gotha Programme* and *Socialism: Utopian and Scientific*. The first one, mainly as the critique against the compromise to Lassalleanism, was written by Karl Marx in 1875 and later published in 1891 with a foreword written by Friedrich Engels. The second one was written by Friedrich Engels in 1880 where he pointed out that Utopian socialism served as the prelude of scientific socialism and demonstrated that dialectics and historical materialism were the two solid and powerful motors to push socialism upward from Utopian to Scientific level. Due to the length limit of this chapter, only Chapter Ⅱ was excerpted.

Critique of the Gotha Programme

Karl Marx

Pre-reading

In 1875, German Socialist Workers' Party (Sozialistische Arbeiterpartei Deutschlands) was formed in Gotha, German. The Party was composed of two parties of Germany: German Social Democratic Party (Sozial demokratische Partei Deutschlands) and General German Workers' Association (Allgemeiner Deutscher Arbeiterverein). Its new programme (later called The Gotha Programme) was featured with the compromises to Lassalleanism which, to Karl Marx, was a truly outrageous retrogression from the revolutionary cause and thus triggered Karl Marx to produce the "Marginal Notes to the Programme of the German Workers' Party" and some subsequent letters to Wilhelm Bracke, the leader of German Social Democratic Party at that time.

In this famous writing which lays the very foundation for the later development of socialism and communism, Marx pointed out that Lassalle had "conceived the workers' movement from the narrowest national standpoint"; that is, Lassalle had concentrated on converting Germany to socialism, whereas Marx thought that socialism had to be an international movement. Even worse, Lassalle and his followers had sought to gain control of the state through elections in hopes of using "state aid" to establish producers' cooperatives, which according to Marx was not feasible at all. To clarify the development path of communism, Marx identified two phases of communism that would follow the predicted overthrow of capitalism: the first would be a transitional system in which the working class would control the government and economy yet still find it necessary to pay people according to how long, hard, or well they worked; the second would be fully realized communism—a society without class divisions or government, in which the production and distribution of goods would be based upon the principle "From each according to his ability, to each according to his needs."

Critique of the Gotha Programme consists of four parts. The first part criticizes the Lassallean viewpoints about the relationship between labor and wealth—"Labor is the source of wealth and all culture" as well as "Fair distribution". By pointing out the illogic and infeasibility of so-called "fair distribution", Marx reveals its nature—the illusion of the bourgeoisie, since even if private ownership is eradicated, "Proceeds of labor" is not likely to be distributed evenly to all members of the society. Besides, to falsify the Lassallean claim "The emancipation of labor must be the work of the working class, relative to which all other classes are only one reactionary mass.", the first part also clarifies the revolutionary mass by indicating that besides the working class, "lower middle class" is becoming revolutionary "in view of [its] impending transfer to the proletariat". In the second part, the Lassallean Iron law of wages is criticized by Marx who states that "wages are not what they appear to be—namely, the value, or price, of labor—but only a masked form for the value, or price, of labor power." According to Marx, Iron law of wages, based upon the Malthusian theory of population, attributes the poverty to the reproduction of population. The third part illustrates the nature of "the establishment of producers' co-operative societies with state aid under the democratic control of the toiling people" by stating that it is "a retrograde step from the standpoint of a class movement to that of a sectarian movement". The fourth part disproves the Lasallean claim of the establishment of a Free State on the foundation of capitalist society by pointing out that between capitalist and communist society, there lies the period of the revolutionary transformation of the one into the other. To achieve the goal of revolutionary transformation, there is no other choice but a political transition period in which the state can be nothing but the revolutionary dictatorship of the proletariat.

Now let's read the text and reflect on the questions that follow.

Text

Foreword

The manuscript published here—the covering letter to Bracke as well as the critique of the draft programme—was sent in 1875, shortly before the Gotha Unity Congress, to Bracke for communication to Geib, Auer, Bebel, and Liebknecht and subsequent return to Marx. Since the Halle Party Congress has put the discussion of the Gotha Programme on the agenda of the Party, I think I would be guilty of suppression if I any longer withheld from publicity this important— perhaps the most important—document relevant to this discussion.

But the manuscript has yet another and more far-reaching significance. Here for the first time Marx's attitude to the line adopted by Lassalle in his agitation from the very beginning is clearly and firmly set forth, both as regards Lassalle's economic principles and his tactics.

The ruthless severity with which the draft programme is dissected here, the mercilessness with which the results obtained are enunciated and the shortcomings of the draft laid bare—all this today, after fifteen years, can no longer give offence. Specific Lassalleans now exist only abroad as isolated ruins, and in Halle the Gotha Programme was given up even by its creators as altogether inadequate.

Nevertheless, I have omitted a few sharp personal expressions and judgments where these were immaterial, and replaced them by dots. Marx himself would have done so if he had published the manuscript today. The violence of the language in some passages was provoked by two circumstances. In the first place, Marx and I had been more intimately connected with the German movement than with any other; we were, therefore, bound to be particularly perturbed by the decidedly retrograde step manifested by this draft programme. And secondly, we were at that time, hardly two years after the Hague Congress of the International, engaged in the most violent struggle against Bakunin and his anarchists, who made us responsible for everything that happened in the labour movement in Germany; hence we had to expect that we would also be addled with the secret paternity of this programme. These considerations do not now exist and so there is no necessity for the passages in question.

For reasons arising form the Press Law, also, a few sentences have been indicated only by dots. Where I have had to choose a milder expression this has been enclosed in square brackets. Otherwise the text has been reproduced word for word.

Part I
1. "Labor is the source of wealth and all culture, and since useful labor is possible only in society and through society, the proceeds of labor belong undiminished with equal right to all members of society."

First part of the paragraph: "Labor is the source of all wealth and all culture."

Labor is not the source of all wealth. Nature is just as much the source of use values (and it is surely of such that material wealth consists!) as labor, which itself is only the manifestation of a force of nature, human labor power. The above phrase is to be found in all children's primers and is correct insofar as it is implied that labor is performed with the appurtenant subjects and instruments. But a socialist program cannot allow such bourgeois phrases to pass over in silence the conditions that lone give them meaning. And insofar as man from the beginning behaves toward nature, the primary source of all instruments and subjects of labor, as an owner, treats her as belonging to him, his labor becomes the source of use values, therefore also of wealth. The bourgeois have very good grounds for falsely ascribing supernatural creative power to labor; since precisely from the fact that labor depends on nature it follows that the man who possesses no other property than his labor power must, in all conditions of society and culture, be the slave of other men who have made themselves the owners of the material conditions of labor. He can only work with their permission, hence live only with their permission.

Let us now leave the sentence as it stands, or rather limps. What could one have expected in conclusion? Obviously this:

"Since labor is the source of all wealth, no one in society can appropriate wealth except as the product of labor. Therefore, if he himself does not work, he lives by the labor of others and also acquires his culture at the expense of the labor of others."

Instead of this, by means of the verbal river "and since", a proposition is added in order to draw a conclusion from this and not from the first one.

Second part of the paragraph: "Useful labor is possible only in society and through society."

According to the first proposition, labor was the source of all wealth and all culture; therefore no society is possible without labor. Now we learn, conversely, that no "useful" labor is possible without society.

One could just as well have said that only in society can useless and even socially harmful labor become a branch of gainful occupation, that only in society can one live by being idle, etc., in short, once could just as well have copied the whole of Rousseau.

And what is "useful" labor? Surely only labor which produces the intended useful result. A savage—and man was a savage after he had ceased to be an ape—who kills an animal with a stone, who collects fruit, etc., performs "useful" labor.

Thirdly, the conclusion: "Useful labor is possible only in society and through society, the proceeds of labor belong undiminished with equal right to all members of society."

A fine conclusion! If useful labor is possible only in society and through society, the proceeds of labor belong to society and only so much therefrom accrues to the individual worker as is not required to maintain the "condition" of labor, society.

In fact, this proposition has at all times been made use of by the champions of the state of society prevailing at any given time. First comes the claims of the government and everything that sticks to it, since it is the social organ for the maintenance of the social order; then comes the claims of the various kinds of private property, for the various kinds of private property are the foundations of society, etc. One sees that such hollow phrases are the foundations of society, etc. One sees that such hollow phrases can be twisted and turned as desired.

The first and second parts of the paragraph have some intelligible connection only in the following wording:

"Labor becomes the source of wealth and culture only as social labor", or, what is the same thing, "in and through society".
This proposition is incontestably correct, for although isolated labor (its material conditions presupposed) can create use value, it can create neither wealth nor culture.
But equally incontestable is this other proposition:

"In proportion as labor develops socially, and becomes thereby a source of wealth and culture, poverty and destitution develop among the workers, and wealth and culture among the nonworkers."

This is the law of all history hitherto. What, therefore, had to be done here, instead of setting down general phrases about "labor" and "society", was to prove concretely how in present capitalist society the material, etc., conditions have at last been created which enable and compel the workers to lift this social curse.

In fact, however, the whole paragraph, bungled in style and content, is only there in order to inscribe the Lassallean catchword of the "undiminished proceeds of labor" as a slogan at the top of the party banner. I shall return later to the "proceeds of labor", "equal right", etc., since the same thing recurs in a somewhat different form further on.

2. "In present-day society, the instruments of labor are the monopoly of the capitalist class; the resulting dependence of the working class is the cause of misery and servitude in all forms."

This sentence, borrowed from the Rules of the International, is incorrect in this "improved" edition.

In present-day society, the instruments of labor are the monopoly of the landowners (the monopoly of property in land is even the basis of the monopoly of capital) and the capitalists. In the passage in question, the Rules of the International do not mention either one or the other class of monopolists. They speak of the "monopolizer of the means of labor, that is, the sources of life." The addition, "sources of life", makes it sufficiently clear that land is included in the instruments of labor.

The correction was introduced because Lassalle, for reasons now generally known, attacked only the capitalist class and not the landowners. In England, the capitalist class is usually not even the owner of the land on which his factory stands.

3. "The emancipation of labor demands the promotion of the instruments of labor to the common property of society and the co-operative regulation of the total labor, with a fair distribution of the proceeds of labor."

Promotion of the instruments of labor to the common property" ought obviously to read their "conversion into the common property"; but this is only passing.

What are the "proceeds of labor"? The product of labor, or its value? And in the latter case, is it the total value of the product, or only that part of the value which labor has newly added to the value of the means of production consumed?

"Proceeds of labor" is a loose notion which Lassalle has put in the place of definite economic conceptions.

What is "a fair distribution"?

Do not the bourgeois assert that the present-day distribution is "fair"? And is it not, in fact, the only "fair" distribution on the basis of the present-day mode of production? Are economic relations regulated by legal conceptions, or do not, on the contrary, legal relations arise out of economic ones? Have not also the socialist sectarians the most varied notions about "fair" distribution?

To understand what is implied in this connection by the phrase "fair distribution", we must take the first paragraph and this one together. The latter presupposes a society wherein the instruments of labor are common property and the total labor is cooperatively regulated, and from the first paragraph we learn that "the proceeds of labor belong undiminished with equal right to all members of society."

"To all members of society"? To those who do not work as well? What remains then of the "undiminished" proceeds of labor? Only to those members of society who work? What remains then of the "equal right" of all members of society?

But "all members of society" and "equal right" are obviously mere phrases. The kernel consists in this, that in this communist society every worker must receive the "undiminished" Lassallean "proceeds of labor".

Let us take, first of all, the words "proceeds of labor" in the sense of the product of labor; then the co-operative proceeds of labor are the total social product.

From this must now be deducted: First, cover for replacement of the means of production used up. Second, additional portion for expansion of production. Third, reserve or insurance funds to provide against accidents, dislocations caused by natural calamities, etc.

These deductions from the "undiminished" proceeds of labor are an economic necessity, and their magnitude is to be determined according to available means and forces, and partly by computation of probabilities, but they are in no way calculable by equity.

There remains the other part of the total product, intended to serve as means of consumption.

Before this is divided among the individuals, there has to be deducted again, from it: First, the general costs of administration not belonging to production. This part will, from the outset, be very considerably restricted in comparison with present-day society, and it diminishes in proportion as the new society develops. Second, that which is intended for the common satisfaction of needs, such as schools, health services, etc. From the outset, this part grows considerably in comparison with present-day society, and it grows in proportion as the new society develops. Third, funds for those unable to work, etc., in short, for what is included under so-called official poor relief today.

Only now do we come to the "distribution" which the program, under Lassallean influence, alone has in view in its narrow fashion—namely, to that part of the means of consumption which is divided among the individual producers of the cooperative society.

The "undiminished" proceeds of labor have already unnoticeably become converted into the "diminished" proceeds, although what the producer is deprived of in his capacity as a private individual benefits him directly or indirectly in his capacity as a member of society.

Just as the phrase of the "undiminished" proceeds of labor has disappeared, so now does the phrase of the "proceeds of labor" disappearaltogether.

Within the cooperative society based on common ownership of the means of production, the producers do not exchange their products; just as little does the labor employed on the products appear here as the value of these products, as a material quality possessed by them, since now, in contrast to capitalist society, individual labor no longer exists in an indirect fashion but directly as a component part of total labor. The phrase "proceeds of labor", objectionable also today on account of its ambiguity, thus loses all meaning.

What we have to deal with here is a communist society, not as it has developed on its own foundations, but, on the contrary, just as it emerges from capitalist society; which is thus in every respect, economically, morally, and intellectually, still stamped with the birthmarks of the old society from whose womb it emerges. Accordingly, the individual producer receives back from society-after the deductions have been made-exactly what he gives to it. What he has given to it is his individual quantum of labor. For example, the social working day consists of the sum of the individual hours of work; the individual labor time of the individual producer is the part of the social working day contributed by him, his share in it. He receives a certificate from society that he has furnished such-and-such an amount of labor (after deducting his labor for the common funds); and with this certificate, he draws from the social stock of means of consumption as much as the same amount of labor cost. The same amount of labor which he has given to society in one form, he receives back in another.

Here, obviously, the same principle prevails as that which regulates the exchange of commodities, as far as this is exchange of equal values. Content and form are changed, because under the altered circumstances no one can give anything except his labor, and because, on the other hand, nothing can pass to the ownership of individuals, except individual means of consumption. But as far as the distribution of the latter among the individual producers is concerned, the same principle prevails as in the exchange of commodity equivalents: a given amount of labor in one form is exchanged for an equal amount of labor in another form.

Hence, equal right here is still in principle—bourgeois right, although principle and practice are no longer at loggerheads, while the exchange of equivalents in commodity exchange exists only on the average and not in the individual case.

In spite of this advance, this equal right is still constantly stigmatized by a bourgeois limitation. The right of the producers is proportional to the labor they supply; the equality consists in the fact that measurement is made with an equal standard, labor.

But one man is superior to another physically, or mentally, and supplies more labor in the same time, or can labor for a longer time; and labor, to serve as a measure, must be defined by its duration or intensity, otherwise it ceases to be a standard of measurement. This equal right is an unequal right for unequal labor. It recognizes no class differences, because everyone is only a worker like everyone else; but it tacitly recognizes unequal individual endowment, and thus productive capacity, as a natural privilege. It is, therefore, a right of inequality, in its content, like every right. Right, by its very nature, can consist only in the application of an equal standard; but unequal individuals (and they would not be different individuals if they were not unequal) are measurable only by an equal standard insofar as they are brought under an equal point of view, are taken from one definite side only—for instance, in the present case, are regarded only as workers and nothing more is seen in them, everything else being ignored. Further, one worker is married, another is not; one has more children than another, and so on and so forth. Thus, with an equal performance of labor, and hence an equal in the social consumption fund, one will in fact receive more than another, one will be richer than another, and so on. To avoid all these defects, right, instead of being equal, would have to be unequal.

But these defects are inevitable in the first phase of communist society as it is when it has just emerged after prolonged birth pangs from capitalist society. Right can never be higher than the economic structure of society and its cultural development conditioned thereby.

In a higher phase of communist society, after the enslaving subordination of the individual to the division of labor, and therewith also the antithesis between mental and physical labor, has vanished; after labor has become not only a means of life but life's prime want; after the productive forces have also increased with the all-around development of the individual, and all the springs of cooperative wealth flow more abundantly-only then can the narrow horizon of bourgeois right be crossed in its entirety and society inscribe on its banners: From each according to his ability, to each according to his needs!

I have dealt more at length with the "undiminished" proceeds of labor, on the one hand, and with "equal right" and "fair distribution", on the other, in order to show what a crime it is to attempt, on the one hand, to force on our Party again, as dogmas, ideas which in a certain period had some meaning but have now become obsolete verbal rubbish, while again perverting, on the other, the realistic outlook, which it cost so much effort to instill into the Party but which has now taken root in it, by means of ideological nonsense about right and other trash so common among the democrats and French socialists.

Quite apart from the analysis so far given, it was in general a mistake to make a fuss about so-called distribution and put the principal stress on it.

Any distribution whatever of the means of consumption is only a consequence of the distribution of the conditions of production themselves. The latter distribution, however, is a feature of the mode of production itself. The capitalist mode of production, for example, rests on the fact that the material conditions of production are in the hands of nonworkers in the form of property in capital and land, while the masses are only owners of the personal condition of production, of labor power. If the elements of production are so distributed, then the present-day distribution of the means of consumption results automatically. If the material conditions of production are the cooperative property of the workers themselves, then there likewise results a distribution of the means of consumption different from the present one. Vulgar socialism (and from it in turn a section of the democrats) has taken over from the bourgeois economists the consideration and treatment of distribution as independent of the mode of production and hence the presentation of socialism as turning principally on distribution. After the real relation has long been made clear, why retrogress again?

Questions

1. How does Marx define "labor" and "member of the society"? In what way does his definition falsify the Lasallean "fair distribution"?
2. Why does Marx say the "Iron law of wages" is a retrograde step to Lasalleanism? What is the essence of wage according to Marx? What's your opinion?
3. Why does Marx say it is infeasible to establish a producers' co-operative society with state aid under the democratic control of the toiling people?
4. What's Marx's view of "Free state"? What is yours?
5. In what way does Marx say "lower middle class" is revolutionary?

Socialism: Utopian and Scientific

Friedrich Engels

Pre-reading

Socialism: Utopian and Scientific, written by Friedrich Engels in 1880, is a systematic exposition of socialism theories. This book consists of three chapters: Chapter I The Development of Utopian Socialism, Chapter II Dialectics, and Chapter III Historical Materialism. In this book Engels observes that Utopian socialism provides the immediate origin of thoughts for scientific socialism and paves the way to the later development of socialism and communism. Meanwhile, he also concludes that it is the doctrines of historical materialism and surplus value that lay the very foundation for scientific socialism.

At the very beginning of Chapter I, Engels points out that "modern Socialism originally appears ostensibly as a more logical extension of the principles laid down by the great French philosophers of the 18th century", which indicates the relationship between utopian socialism and scientific socialism. According to Engels, the philosophy of the bourgeois revolutions (such as the French Revolution) establishes Reason as the only thing capable of justifying the existence of things (enlightenment philosophy). The bourgeoisie's demands are limited to political equality, whereas certain movements at that time go beyond to demand economic equality, not just political rights. They pursue the liberation, not to a particular class, but to humanity as a whole. However, the harsh reality is Capitalism was still in its infancy without a developed proletariat or forces of production. Consequently, the solutions to the problems of capitalism would be inevitably utopian, derived solely from thought rather than material reality. As is summarized in this chapter, Saint-Simon recognized that the bourgeois revolution signaled nothing but the conquest of political power by the propertied bourgeoisie, leaving the workers and peasants open to continued exploitation in a new way by a different ruling class. Charles Fourier made similar criticisms and also recognized the development of history through ceaseless change and contradiction. Robert Owen adopted a materialist philosophy and set up experimental Communist communities. Great and meaningful as their attempts were, they were not founded upon material reality. Thus utopian socialists considered their ideas as absolute truths that could simply be discovered and put into practice.

In Chapter II, Engels focuses on the comparison between metaphysics and dialectics, through which he concludes that when dialectical reasoning is applied to history and society as a whole, the beginnings of capitalism and its continued existence can be explained, not just decried as "bad". Dialectics, first expounded by the ancient Greeks, consists of understanding the world as a mass of interconnections, changes and contradictions. According to Engels, metaphysics takes individual phenomena and places them under isolated examination, separating them out and contrasting them with all other things. It is necessary and useful for understanding phenomena, but is inadequate on its own because it fails to appreciate the connections between things in their change and motion. This justifies why dialectical thinking is important. He takes Natural science as an example. It makes extensive use of metaphysics, but a proper understanding of nature demonstrates that it only makes sense from a dialectical point of view. Hegel was the first to master the dialectical view of things, but his philosophy was limited by material factors and by his own idealism.

Chapter III talks about historical materialism. According to Engels, historical materialism consists of the understanding that the forces of production are the basis of all social structure.

The contradictions within economic systems lead inevitably to social contradictions. Under capitalism the major economic contradiction between socialized production and private appropriation is manifested in the social contradiction between proletariat and bourgeoisie. The further contradiction between organization in the individual workplace and anarchy in production as a whole leads to greater proletarianization as capitalism develops, through machinery and globalization. When these contradictions become too great, the forces of production are fettered by the social system them have created. This causes economic and therefore social crisis. The only way to resolve these crises is to recognize the socialized nature of production and reflect that with socialized appropriation i.e. take the forces of production out of private hands and place them under democratic public ownership. This is the nature of socialist revolution—the proletariat seizing political power and placing the productive forced under their control to be planned, organized and used to their full potential by the majority of people. Such a revolution is only possible once a certain stage in historical development has been reached. And finally Engels comes to the conclusion that we are now at that stage.

Now let's read the text and reflect on the questions that follow.

Text

Chapter Ⅱ Dialectics

In the meantime, along with and after the French philosophy of the 18th century, had arisen the new German philosophy, culminating in Hegel.

Its greatest merit was the taking up again of dialectics as the highest form of reasoning. The old Greek philosophers were all born natural dialecticians, and Aristotle, the most encyclopaedic of them, had already analyzed the most essential forms of dialectic thought. The newer philosophy, on the other hand, although in it also dialectics had brilliant exponents (e.g. Descartes and Spinoza), had, especially through English influence, become more and more rigidly fixed in the so-called metaphysical mode of reasoning, by which also the French of the 18th century were almost wholly dominated, at all events in their special philosophical work. Outside philosophy in the restricted sense, the French nevertheless produced masterpieces of dialectic. We need only call to mind Diderot's Le Neveu de Rameau, and Rousseau's Discourssurl'origineet les fondements de l'inegaliteparmi les hommes. We give here, in brief, the essential character of these two modes of thought.

When we consider and reflect upon Nature at large, or the history of mankind, or our own intellectual activity, at first we see the picture of an endless entanglement of relations and reactions, permutations and combinations, in which nothing remains what, where and as it was, but everything moves, changes, comes into being and passes away. We see, therefore, at first the picture as a whole, with its individual parts still more or less kept in the background; we observe the movements, transitions, connections, rather than the things that move, combine, and are connected. This primitive, naive but intrinsically correct conception of the world is that of ancient Greek philosophy, and was first clearly formulated by Heraclitus: everything is and is not, for everything is fluid, is constantly changing, constantly coming into being and passing away.①

But this conception, correctly as it expresses the general character of the picture of appearances as a whole, does not suffice to explain the details of which this picture is made up, and so long as we do not understand these, we have not a clear idea of the whole picture. In order to understand these details, we must detach them from their natural, special causes, effects, etc. This is, primarily, the task of natural science and historical research: branches of science which the Greek of classical times, on very good grounds, relegated to a subordinate position, because they had first of all to collect materials for these sciences to work upon. A certain amount of natural and historical material must be collected before there can be any critical analysis, comparison, and arrangement in classes, orders, and species. The foundations of the exact natural sciences were, therefore, first worked out by the Greeks of the Alexandrian period②, and later on, in the Middle Ages, by the Arabs. Real natural science dates from the second half of the 15th century, and thence onward it had advanced with constantly increasing rapidity. The analysis of Nature into its individual parts, the grouping of the different natural processes and objects in definite classes, the study of the internal anatomy of organized bodies in their manifold forms— these were the fundamental conditions of the gigantic strides in our knowledge of Nature that have been made during the last 400 years. But this method of work has also left us as legacy the habit of observing natural objects and processes in isolation, apart from their connection with the vast whole; of observing them in repose, not in motion; as constraints, not as essentially variables; in their death, not in their life. And when this way of looking at things was transferred by Bacon and Locke from natural science to philosophy, it begot the narrow, metaphysical mode of thought peculiar to the last century.

To the metaphysician, things and their mental reflexes, ideas, are isolated, are to be considered one after the other and apart from each other, are objects of investigation fixed, rigid, given once for all. He thinks in absolutely irreconcilable antitheses. His communication is 'yea, yea; nay, nay'; for whatsoever is more than these cometh of evil." For him, a thing either exists or does not exist; a thing cannot at the same time be itself and something else. Positive and negative absolutely exclude one another; cause and effect stand in a rigid antithesis, one to the other.

At first sight, this mode of thinking seems to us very luminous, because it is that of

---

① Unknown to the Western world until the 20th-century, the Chinese philosopher Lao Tzu was a predecessor of or possibly contemporary to Heraclitus. Lao Tzu wrote the renowned *Tao Te Ching* in which he also espouses the fundamental principles of dialectics.

② The Alexandrian period of the development of science comprises the period extending from the 3rd century BCE to the 17th century AD. It derives its name from the town of Alexandria in Egypt, which was one of the most important centers of international economic intercourses at that time. In the Alexandrian period, mathematics (Euclid and Archimedes), geography, astronomy, anatomy, physiology, etc., attained considerable development. China also been began development in natural sciences in the third century BCE.

so-called sound commonsense. Only sound commonsense, respectable fellow that he is, in the homely realm of his own four walls, has very wonderful adventures directly he ventures out into the wide world of research. And the metaphysical mode of thought, justifiable and necessary as it is in a number of domains whose extent varies according to the nature of the particular object of investigation, sooner or later reaches a limit, beyond which it becomes one-sided, restricted, abstract, lost in insoluble contradictions. In the contemplation of individual things, it forgets the connection between them; in the contemplation of their existence, it forgets the beginning and end of that existence; of their repose, it forgets their motion. It cannot see the woods for the trees.

For everyday purposes, we know and can say, e.g., whether an animal is alive or not. But, upon closer inquiry, we find that this is, in many cases, a very complex question, as the jurists know very well. They have cudgeled their brains in vain to discover a rational limit beyond which the killing of the child in its mother's womb is murder. It is just as impossible to determine absolutely the moment of death, for physiology proves that death is not an instantaneous, momentary phenomenon, but a very protracted process.

In like manner, every organized being is every moment the same and not the same; every moment, it assimilates matter supplied from without, and gets rid of other matter; every moment, some cells of its body die and others build themselves anew; in a longer or shorter time, the matter of its body is completely renewed, and is replaced by other molecules of matter, so that every organized being is always itself, and yet something other than itself.

Further, we find upon closer investigation that the two poles of an antithesis, positive and negative, e.g., are as inseparable as they are opposed, and that despite all their opposition, they mutually interpenetrate. And we find, in like manner, that cause and effect are conceptions which only hold good in their application to individual cases; but as soon as we consider the individual cases in their general connection with the universe as a whole, they run into each other, and they become confounded when we contemplate that universal action and reaction in which causes and effects are eternally changing places, so that what is effect here and now will be cause there and then, and vice versa.

None of these processes and modes of thought enters into the framework of metaphysical reasoning. Dialectics, on the other hand, comprehends things and their representations, ideas, in their essential connection, concatenation, motion, origin and ending. Such processes as those mentioned above are, therefore, so many corroborations of its own method of procedure.

Nature is the proof of dialectics, and it must be said for modern science that it has furnished this proof with very rich materials increasingly daily, and thus has shown that, in the last resort, Nature works dialectically and not metaphysically; that she does not move in the eternal oneness of a perpetually recurring circle, but goes through a real historical evolution. In this connection, Darwin must be named before all others. He dealt the metaphysical conception of Nature the heaviest blow by his proof that all organic beings, plants, animals, and man himself, are the products of a process of evolution going on through millions of years. But, the naturalists, who have learned to think dialectically, are few and far between, and this conflict of the results of discovery with preconceived modes of thinking, explains the endless confusion now reigning in theoretical natural science, the despair of teachers as well as learners, of authors and readers alike.

An exact representation of the universe, of its evolution, of the development of mankind, and of the reflection of this evolution in the minds of men, can therefore only be obtained by the methods of dialectics with its constant regard to the innumerable actions and reactions of life and death, of progressive or retrogressive changes. And in this spirit, the new German philosophy has worked. Kant began his career by resolving the stable Solar system of Newton and its eternal duration, after the famous initial impulse had once been given, into the result of a historical process, the formation of the Sun and all the planets out of a rotating, nebulous mass. From this, he at the same time drew the conclusion that, given this origin of the Solar system, its future death followed of necessity. His theory, half a century later, was established mathematically by Laplace, and half a century after that, the spectroscope proved the existence in space of such incandescent masses of gas in various stages of condensation.

This new German philosophy culminated in the Hegelian system. In this system—and herein is its great merit—for the first time the whole world, natural, historical, intellectual, is represented as a process—i.e., as in constant motion, change, transformation, development; and the attempt is made to trace out the internal connection that makes a continuous whole of all this movement and development. From this point of view, the history of mankind no longer appeared as a wild whirl of senseless deeds of violence, all equally condemnable at the judgment seat of mature philosophic reason and which are best forgotten as quickly as possible, but as the process of evolution of man himself. It was now the task of the intellect to follow the gradual march of this process through all its devious ways, and to trace out the inner law running through all its apparently accidental phenomena.

That the Hegelian system did not solve the problem it propounded is here immaterial. Its epoch-making merit was that it propounded the problem. This problem is one that no single individual will ever be able to solve. Although Hegel was—with Saint-Simon—the most encyclopaedic mind of his time, yet he was limited, first, by the necessary limited extent of his own knowledge and, second, by the limited extent and depth of the knowledge and conceptions of his age. To these limits, a third must be added; Hegel was an idealist. To him, the thoughts within his brain were not the more or less abstract pictures of actual things and processes, but, conversely, things and their evolution were only the realized pictures of the "Idea", existing somewhere from eternity before the world was. This way of thinking turned everything upside down, and completely reversed the actual connection of things in the world. Correctly and ingeniously as many groups of facts were grasped by Hegel, yet, for the reasons just given, there is much that is botched, artificial, labored, in a word, wrong in point of detail. The Hegelian system, in itself, was a colossal miscarriage—but it was also the last of its kind.

It was suffering, in fact, from an internal and incurable contradiction. Upon the one hand, its essential proposition was the conception that human history is a process of evolution, which, by its very nature, cannot find its intellectual final term in the discovery of any so-called absolute truth. But, on the other hand, it laid claim to being the very essence of this absolute truth. A system of natural and historical knowledge, embracing everything, and final for all time, is a contradiction to the fundamental law of dialectic reasoning.

This law, indeed, by no means excludes, but, on the contrary, includes the idea that the systematic knowledge of the external universe can make giant strides from age to age.

The perception of the fundamental contradiction in German idealism led necessarily back to materialism, but—nota bene—not to the simply metaphysical, exclusively mechanical materialism of the 18th century. Old materialism looked upon all previous history as a crude heap of irrationality and violence; modern materialism sees in it the process of evolution of humanity, and aims at discovering the laws thereof. With the French of the 18th century, and even with Hegel, the conception obtained of Nature as a whole—moving in narrow circles, and forever immutable, with its eternal celestial bodies, as Newton, and unalterable organic species, as Linnaeus, taught. Modern materialism embraces the more recent discoveries of natural science, according to which Nature also has its history in time, the celestial bodies, like the organic species that, under favorable conditions, people them, being born and perishing. And even if Nature, as a whole, must still be said to move in recurrent cycles, these cycles assume infinitely larger dimensions. In both aspects, modern materialism is essentially dialectic, and no longer requires the assistance of that sort of philosophy which, queen-like, pretended to rule the remaining mob of sciences. As soon as each special science is bound to make clear its position in the great totality of things and of our knowledge of things, a special science dealing with this totality is superfluous or unnecessary. That which still survives of all earlier philosophy is the science of thought and its law—formal logic and dialectics. Everything else is subsumed in the positive science of Nature and history.

Whilst, however, the revolution in the conception of Nature could only be made in proportion to the corresponding positive materials furnished by research, already much earlier certain historical facts had occurred which led to a decisive change in the conception of history. In 1831, the first working-class rising took place in Lyons; between 1838 and 1842, the first national working-class movement, that of the English Chartists, reached its height. The class struggle between proletariat and bourgeoisie came to the front in the history of the most advanced countries in Europe, in proportion to the development, upon the one hand, of modern industry, upon the other, of the newly-acquired political supremacy of the bourgeoisie. Facts more and more strenuously gave the lie to the teachings of bourgeois economy as to the identity of the interests of capital and labor, as to the universal harmony and universal prosperity that would be the consequence of unbridled competition. All these things could no longer be ignored, any more than the French and English Socialism, which was their theoretical, though very imperfect, expression. But the old idealist conception of history, which was not yet dislodged, knew nothing of class struggles based upon economic interests, knew nothing of economic interests; production and all economic relations appeared in it only as incidental, subordinate elements in the "history of civilization".

The new facts made imperative a new examination of all past history. Then it was seen that all past history, with the exception of its primitive stages, was the history of class struggles; that these warring classes of society are always the products of the modes of production and of exchange—in a word, of the economic conditions of their time; that the economic structure of society always furnishes the real basis, starting from which we can alone work out the ultimate explanation of the whole superstructure of juridical and political institutions as well as of the religious, philosophical, and other ideas of a given historical period. Hegel has freed history from metaphysics—he made it dialectic; but his conception of history was essentially idealistic. But now idealism was driven from its last refuge, the philosophy of history; now a materialistic treatment of history was propounded, and a method found of explaining man's "knowing" by his "being", instead of, as heretofore, his "being" by his "knowing".

From that time forward, Socialism was no longer an accidental discovery of this or that ingenious brain, but the necessary outcome of the struggle between two historically developed classes—the proletariat and the bourgeoisie. Its task was no longer to manufacture a system of society as perfect as possible, but to examine the historic-economic succession of events from which these classes and their antagonism had of necessity sprung, and to discover in the economic conditions thus created the means of ending the conflict. But the Socialism of earlier days was as incompatible with this materialist conception as the conception of Nature of the French materialists was with dialectics and modern natural science. The Socialism of earlier days certainly criticized the existing capitalistic mode of production and its consequences. But it could not explain them, and, therefore, could not get the mastery of them. It could only simply reject them as bad. The more strongly this earlier Socialism denounced the exploitations of the working-class, inevitable under Capitalism, the less able was it clearly to show in what this exploitation consisted and how it arose, but for this it was necessary —

> to present the capitalistic mode of production in its historical connection and its inevitableness during a particular historical period, and therefore, also, to present its inevitable downfall; and to lay bare its essential character, which was still a secret. This was done by the discovery of surplus-value.

It was shown that the appropriation of unpaid labor is the basis of the capitalist mode of production and of the exploitation of the worker that occurs under it; that even if the capitalist buys the labor power of his laborer at its full value as a commodity on the market, he yet extracts more value from it than he paid for; and that in the ultimate analysis, this surplus-value forms those sums of value from which are heaped up constantly increasing masses of capital in the hands of the possessing classes. The genesis of capitalist production and the production of capital were both explained.

These two great discoveries, the materialistic conception of history and the revelation of the secret of capitalistic production through surplus-value, we owe to Marx. With these discoveries, Socialism became a science. The next thing was to work out all its details and relations.

Questions

1. What is dialectics? What is the relationship between metaphysics and dialectics?
2. To what extent did Hegel's philosophical idealism limit his application of dialectics?
3. What constitutes the very foundation for socialism to develop into a science?
4. What does Engels mean when he says that socialism is "no longer an accidental discovery of this or that ingenious brain, but the necessary outcome of the struggle between two historically developed classes—the proletariat and the bourgeoisie"?
5. Combined with what you have learned in Chapter VIII on historical materialism, try to interpret Engels' saying that "Man, at last the master of his own form of social organization becomes at the same time the lord over Nature, his own master—free"? In what way is man free?

Questions for Further Reflection

1. To what extent would it be true to say that the bourgeois revolutions were philosophically dishonest?
2. In what way is Marx's view on socialism and communism different from the Utopian?
3. Defend or attack Marx's statement: "The executive of the modern State is but a committee for managing the common affairs of the whole bourgeoisie." Is this generally true?
4. Marx says that every class struggle is a political struggle. Is this true? If, yes, in what sense?

References and Further Reading

1. Eagleton, T. (2004). *The Ideology of Aesthetic*. Oxford: Blackwell Publishing Ltd.
2. Jacobus, L.A. (1983). *A World of Ideas*. New York: St. Martin's Press.
3. Selden, R., Widdowson, P. & Brooker, P. (2004). *A Reader's Guide to Contemporary Literary Theory*. London & Beijing: Pearson Education Limited & Foreign Language Teaching and Researcher Press.
4. 冯宪光."西方马克思主义"美学研究.重庆: 重庆出版社, 1997.
5. 马克思作品介绍 https://www.marxists.org/archive/marx/works/1875/gotha/ch02.htm
6. 社会主义乌托邦 https://www. marxists. org/archive/marx/works/1880/soc-utop/index.htm
7. 马克思主义介绍 http://marxiststudent.com/study-guide

Chapter 11   Existentialism

This chapter presents two excerpts of the classical works of existentialism, the purpose of which is to offer readers a basic and rough glimpse of this philosophical and literary phenomenon. Existentialism, as an intellectual movement most characteristic of European culture from about 1930 to the mid-20th century, interprets human existence in the world that stresses its concreteness and its problematic character from a perspective that is different from the previous philosophical thinking. In the philosophical context of existentialism, human existence is always particular and individual. Its philosophy of existence rejects the priority of the essence and considers man as a self-guided production, alone in a universe without God. For the purpose of uncovering the metaphysical meaning of man, existential philosophy interprets existence as the investigation of the meaning of Being. That investigation is continually faced with diverse possibilities, from among which the existent (i.e., the human individual) must make a selection, to which he must then commit himself. Because those possibilities are constituted by the individual's relationships with things and with other humans, existence is always a being-in-the-world—i.e., in a concrete and historically determinate situation that limits or conditions choice. Humans are therefore called, in Martin Heidegger's phrase, Dasein ("there being") because they are defined by the fact that they exist, or are in the world and inhabit it.

Among the major philosophers identified as existentialists (many of whom—for instance Camus and Heidegger—repudiated the label) were Karl Jaspers, Martin Heidegger, and Martin Buber in Germany, Jean Wahl and Jean-Paul Sartre in France, the Spaniards José Ortega y Gasset and Miguel de Unamuno, and the Russians Nikolai Berdyaev and Lev Shestov. The nineteenth century philosophers, Søren Kierkegaard and Friedrich Nietzsche are usually taken as precursors of the movement. But it is Jean-Paul Sartre and Martin Heidegger that carried it forward noticeably, thus standing out as the landmarks of existentialism.

For Kierkegaard, existence emerges as a philosophical problem in the struggle to think the paradoxical presence of God. According to Kierkegaard, the singularity of existence comes to light at the moment of conflict between ethics and religious faith. In his terms, there should be some standard to govern the dimension to individual being which is both meaningful and yet not governed by the rational standard of morality. For this purpose, he claimed that subjectivity is the truth, an idea that prefigures the existential concept of authenticity. By contrast, the crowd is untruth. The crowd is, roughly, public opinion in the widest sense—the ideas that a given age takes for granted; the ordinary and accepted way of doing things; the complacent attitude that comes from the conformity necessary for social life. Kierkegaard based his concept of subjectivity as truth on an equivocation: the objective truths of science and history, no matter how well-established, are in themselves matters of indifference; they belong to the crowd. It is not insofar as truth can be established objectively that it takes on meaning, but rather insofar as it is appropriated "passionately" in its very uncertainty. To "exist" is always to be confronted with this question of meaning. The truths that matter to who one is cannot be something to be attained only when objective science has completed its task.

For Nietzsche existence is to be found in the reverberations of the phrase "God is dead," in the challenge of nihilism. Responding in part to the cultural situation in nineteenth-century Europe—historical scholarship continuing to erode fundamentalist readings of the Bible, the growing cultural capital of the natural sciences, and Darwinism in particular—and in part driven by his own investigations into the psychology and history of moral concepts, Nietzsche sought to draw the consequences of the death of God, the collapse of any theistic support for morality. His overriding concern was to find a way to take the measure of human life in the modern world. Thus, for Nietzsche, existence emerges as a philosophical problem in his distinction between moral autonomy (as obedience to the moral law) and an autonomy "beyond good and evil." In Nietzsche's philosophical context, existence falls under such an imperative of style: to create meaning and value in a world from which all transcendent supports have fallen away is to give unique shape to one's immediate inclinations, drives, and passions; to interpret, prune, and enhance according to a unifying sensibility, a ruling instinct, that brings everything into a whole that satisfies the non-conceptual, aesthetic norm of what fits, what belongs, what is appropriate.

For Heidegger, to exist is to be historical. This does not mean that one simply finds oneself at a particular moment in history, conceived as a linear series of events. Rather, it means that selfhood has a peculiar temporal structure that is the origin of that "history" which subsequently comes to be narrated in terms of a series of events. Existential temporality is not a sequence of instants but instead a unified structure in which the "future" (that is, the possibility aimed at in any individual's project) recollects the "past" (that is, what no longer needs to be done, the completed) so as to give meaning to the "present" (that is, the things that take on significance in light of what currently needs doing). To act, therefore, is, in Heidegger's terms, to "historize" (geschehen), to constitute something like a narrative unity, with beginning, middle, and end, that does not so much take place in time as provides the condition for linear time. To exist "between birth and death," then, is not merely to be present in each of a discrete series of temporal instants but to constitute oneself in the unity of a history. Accordingly, human being is first and foremost not an isolated subject, cut off from a realm of objects that it wishes to know about. Instead, we human beings are rather beings who are always already in the world, outside and alongside a world from which, for the most part, we do not distinguish ourselves.

Sartre's slogan—"Existence precedes essence"— may serve to introduce what is most distinctive of existentialism, namely, the idea that no general, non-formal account of what it means to be human can be given, since that meaning is decided in and through existing itself. The fundamental contribution of existential thought lies in the idea that one's identity is constituted neither by nature nor by culture, since to "exist" is precisely to constitute such an identity. It is in light of this idea that key existential notions such as facticity, transcendence (project), alienation, and authenticity must be understood. Sartre came to hold that a philosophy of self-making could not content itself with highlighting the situation of individual choice; an authentic political identity could only emerge from a theory that situated such choice in a practically oriented analysis of its concrete situation. Thus it appeared to him that the "ideology of existence" was itself merely an alienated form of the deeper analysis of social and historical reality provided by Marx's dialectical approach.

To sum up, existentialism does not deny the validity of the basic categories of physics, biology, psychology, and the other sciences (categories such as matter, causality, force, function, organism, development, motivation, and so on). It claims only that human beings cannot be fully understood in terms of them. Nor can such an understanding be gained by supplementing our scientific picture with a moral one. Categories of moral theory such as intention, blame, responsibility, character, duty, virtue, and the like do capture important aspects of the human condition, but neither moral thinking (governed by the norms of the good and the right) nor scientific thinking (governed by the norm of truth) suffices. Existentialism is opposed to any doctrine that views human beings as the manifestation of an absolute or of an infinite substance. It is thus opposed to most forms of idealism, such as those that stress Consciousness, Spirit, Reason, Idea, or Over-soul. Similarly, it is opposed to any doctrine that sees in human beings some given and complete reality that must be resolved into its elements in order to be known or contemplated. It is thus opposed to any form of objectivism or scientism, since those approaches stress the crass reality of external fact. Furthermore, existentialism is opposed to any form of necessitarianism; for existence is constituted by possibilities from among which the individual may choose and through which he can project himself. And, finally, existentialism is opposed to any solipsism (holding that I alone exist) or any epistemological idealism (holding that the objects of knowledge are mental), because existence, which is the relationship with other beings, always extends beyond itself, toward the being of those entities; it is, so to speak, transcendence.

The two excerpts selected in this chapter are *Existentialism Is a Humanism* and *Being and Time*. The first one is a public lecture delivered by Jean-Paul Sartre to an enthusiastic Parisian crowd on October 28, 1945. Though short and oversimplified, it is taken as a quasi-manifesto for the Existentialist movement and has been the major introduction to his philosophy for the general public for decades. It exhibits the major tenets of existentialist and offers us a glimpse of Sartre's thought. Published in 1927, *Being and Time* is standardly hailed as one of the most significant texts in the canon of (what has come to be called) contemporary European (or Continental) Philosophy. It leads Heidegger to a position of international intellectual visibility and provides the philosophical impetus for a number of later programs and ideas in the contemporary European tradition, including Sartre's existentialism, Gadamer's philosophical hermeneutics, and Derrida's notion of "deconstruction". To be honest, it is extremely hard, if not impossible, to visualize a whole picture of what has been drawn in Heidegger's mind, and to follow his philosophical thinking merely through one excerpt, be it long or short. Clumsy as it may seem to be, the excerpts selected in this chapter intends to reveal the philosophical constitution of Dasein in Heidegger's term. Due to the length limit of this chapter, only the first two parts in Section IV, Division II "Temporality and Everydayness" were excerpted.

Existentialism Is a Humanism

Jean-Paul Sartre

Pre-reading

Jean-Paul Sartre (1905 – 1980) is arguably the best known philosopher of the twentieth century. He is best known as the main figurehead of the Existentialism movement. Along with his French contemporaries Albert Camus (1913 – 1960) and Simone de Beauvoir (1908 – 1986), he helped popularize the movement through his novels and plays as well as through his more academic works. He was a confirmed Atheist and a committed Communist and Marxist, and took a prominent role in many leftist political causes throughout his adult life. His indefatigable pursuit of philosophical reflection, literary creativity and, in the second half of his life, active political commitment gained him worldwide renown, if not admiration. He is commonly considered the father of Existentialist philosophy, whose writings set the tone for intellectual life in the decade immediately following the Second World War. His most notable works included *Nausea* (1938), *Being and Nothingness* (1943), and *Existentialism and Humanism* (1946).

Human consciousness, according to Sartre, is the power of nihilation and freedom: it is opposed to the in-itself, a being full, solid and opaque. Thus, condemned to absolute freedom, the man should invent himself, in other words, for-itself. He places human consciousness in opposition to being. In his philosophical context, consciousness is non-matter and thus escapes all determinism. In *Existentialism and Humanism* seen by many as one of the defining texts of the Existentialist movement, Sartre depicts this radical freedom as carrying with it a responsibility for the welfare of others. In this sense, freedom implies social responsibility. Freedom itself, which appears to be a gratuitous activity that needs no particular aim or purpose to be of value, becomes a tool for human struggle. As he said, "Man is nothing else but that which he makes of himself. That is the first principle of existentialism." Thus, freedom entails total responsibility, in the face of which we experience anguish, forlornness and despair, and genuine human dignity can be achieved only in our active acceptance of these emotions. Sartre concludes from his arguments that if God exists, then man is not free; by the same token, if man is free, then God does not exist. Atheism, then, is taken for granted in Sartre's philosophy, but he maintained that the "loss of God" is not to be mourned. On the contrary, in a godless universe, life has no meaning or purpose beyond the goals that each man sets for himself, and individuals must therefore detach themselves from things in order to give them meaning.

Now let's read the text and reflect on the questions that follow.

Text

My purpose here is to offer a defense of existentialism against several reproaches that have been laid against it.

First, it has been reproached as an invitation to people to dwell in quietism of despair. For if every way to a solution is barred, one would have to regard any action in this world as entirely ineffective, and one would arrive finally at a contemplative philosophy. Moreover, since contemplation is a luxury, this would be only another bourgeois philosophy. This is, especially, the reproach made by the Communists.

From another quarter we are reproached for having underlined all that is ignominious in the human situation, for depicting what is mean, sordid or base to the neglect of certain things that possess charm and beauty and belong to the brighter side of human nature: for example, according to the Catholic critic, Mlle. Mercier, we forget how an infant smiles. Both from this side and from the other we are also reproached for leaving out of account the solidarity of mankind and considering man in isolation. And this, say the Communists, is because we base our doctrine upon pure subjectivity—upon the Cartesian "I think": which is the moment in which solitary man attains to himself; a position from which it is impossible to regain solidarity with other men who exist outside of the self. The ego cannot reach them through the cogito.

From the Christian side, we are reproached as people who deny the reality and seriousness of human affairs. For since we ignore the commandments of God and all values prescribed as eternal, nothing remains but what is strictly voluntary. Everyone can do what he likes, and will be incapable, from such a point of view, of condemning either the point of view or the action of anyone else.

It is to these various reproaches that I shall endeavor to reply today; that is why I have entitled this brief exposition "Existentialism is a Humanism." Many may be surprised at the mention of humanism in this connection, but we shall try to see in what sense we understand it. In any case, we can begin by saying that existentialism, in our sense of the word, is a doctrine that does render human life possible; a doctrine, also, which affirms that every truth and every action imply both an environment and a human subjectivity. The essential charge laid against us is, of course, that of over-emphasis upon the evil side of human life. I have lately been told of a lady who, whenever she lets slip a vulgar expression in a moment of nervousness, excuses herself by exclaiming, "I believe I am becoming an existentialist." So it appears that ugliness is being identified with existentialism. That is why some people say we are "naturalistic," and if we are, it is strange to see how much we scandalize and horrify them, for no one seems to be much frightened or humiliated nowadays by what is properly called naturalism. Those who can quite well keep down a novel by Zola such as La Terre are sickened as soon as they read an existentialist novel. Those who appeal to the wisdom of the people—which is a sad wisdom—find ours sadder still. And yet, what could be more disillusioned than such sayings as "Charity begins at home" or "Promote a rogue and he'll sue you for damage, knock him down and he'll do you homage"? We all know how many common sayings can be quoted to this effect, and they all mean much the same—that you must not oppose the powers that be; that you must not fight against superior force; must not meddle in matters that are above your station. Or that any action not in accordance with some tradition is mere romanticism; or that any undertaking which has not the support of proven experience is foredoomed to frustration; and that since experience has shown men to be invariably inclined to evil, there must be firm rules to restrain them, otherwise we shall have anarchy. It is, however, the people who are forever mouthing these dismal proverbs and, whenever they are told of some more or less repulsive action, say "How like human nature!"—it is these very people, always harping upon realism, who complain that existentialism is too gloomy a view of things. Indeed, their excessive protests make me suspect that what is annoying them is not so much our pessimism, but, much more likely, our optimism. For at bottom, what is alarming in the doctrine that I am about to try to explain to you is—is it not?—that it confronts man with a possibility of choice. To verify this, let us review the whole question upon the strictly philosophic level. What, then, is this that we call existentialism?

Most of those who are making use of this word would be highly confused if required to explain its meaning. For since it has become fashionable, people cheerfully declare that this musician or that painter is "existentialist." A columnist in Clartes signs himself "The Existentialist," and, indeed, the word is now so loosely applied to so many things that it no longer means anything at all. It would appear that, for the lack of any novel doctrine such as that of surrealism, all those who are eager to join in the latest scandal or movement now seize upon this philosophy in which, however, they can find nothing to their purpose. For in truth this is of all teachings the least scandalous and the most austere: it is intended strictly for technicians and philosophers. All the same, it can easily be defined.

The question is only complicated because there are two kinds of existentialists. There are, on the one hand, the Christians, amongst whom I shall name Jaspers and Gabriel Marcel, both professed Catholics; and on the other the existential atheists, amongst whom we must place Heidegger as well as the French existentialists and myself. What they have in common is simply the fact that they believe that existence comes before essence—or, if you will, that we must begin from the subjective. What exactly do we mean by that?

If one considers an article of manufacture as, for example, a book or a paper-knife-one sees that it has been made by an artisan who had a conception of it; and he has paid attention, equally, to the conception of a paper-knife and to the pre-existent technique of production which is a part of that conception and is, at bottom, a formula. Thus the paper-knife is at the same time an article producible in a certain manner and one which, on the other hand, serves a definite purpose, for one cannot suppose that a man would produce a paper-knife without knowing what it was for. Let us say, then, of the paperknife that its essence—that is to say the sum of the formulae and the qualities which made its production and its definition possible—precedes its existence. The presence of such-and-such a paper-knife or book is thus determined before my eyes. Here, then, we are viewing the world from a technical standpoint, and we can say that production precedes existence.

When we think of God as the creator, we are thinking of him, most of the time, as a supernal artisan. Whatever doctrine we may be considering, whether it be a doctrine like that of Descartes, or of Leibnitz himself, we always imply that the will follows, more or less, from the understanding or at least accompanies it, so that when God creates he knows precisely what he is creating. Thus, the conception of man in the mind of God is comparable to that of the paperknife in the mind of the artisan: God makes man according to a procedure and a conception, exactly as the artisan manufactures a paper-knife, following a definition and a formula. Thus each individual man is the realization of a certain conception which dwells in the divine understanding. In the philosophic atheism of the eighteenth century, the notion of God is suppressed, but not, for all that, the idea that essence is prior to existence; something of that idea we still find everywhere, in Diderot, in Voltaire and even in Kant. Man possesses a human nature; that "human nature," which is the conception of human being, is found in every man; which means that each man is a particular example of a universal conception, the conception of Man. In Kant, this universality goes so far that the wild man of the woods, man in the state of nature and the bourgeois are all contained in the same definition and have the same fundamental qualities. Here again, the essence of man precedes that historic existence which we confront in experience.

Atheistic existentialism, of which I am a representative, declares with greater consistency that if God does not exist there is at least one being whose existence comes before its essence, a being which exists before it can be defined by any conception of it. That being is man or, as Heidegger has it, the human reality. What do we mean by saying that existence precedes essence? We mean that man first of all exists, encounters himself, surges up in the world-and defines himself afterwards. If man as the existentialist seeshim is not definable, it is because to begin with he is nothing. He will not be anything until later, and then he will be what he makes of himself. Thus, there is no human nature, because there is no God to have a conception of it. Man simply is. Not that he is simply what he conceives himself to be, but he is what he wills, and as he conceives himself after already existing-as he wills to be after that leap towards existence. Man is nothing else but that which he makes of himself. That is the first principle of existentialism. And this is what people call its "subjectivity," using the word as a reproach against us. But what do we mean to say by this, but that man is of a greater dignity than a stone or a table? For we mean to say that man primarily exists—that man is, before all else, something which propels itself towards a future and is aware that it is doing so. Man is, indeed, a project which possesses a subjective life, instead of being a kind of moss, or a fungus or a cauliflower. Before that projection of the self nothing exists; not even in the heaven of intelligence: man will only attain existence when he is what he purposes to be. Not, however, what he may wish to be. For what we usually understand by wishing or willing is a conscious decision taken—much more often than not—after we have made ourselves what we are. I may wish to join a party, to write a book or to marry-but in such a case what is usually called my will is probably a manifestation of a prior and more spontaneous decision. If, however, it is true that existence is prior to essence, man is responsible for what he is. Thus, the first effect of existentialism is that it puts every man in possession of himself as he is, and places the entire responsibility for his existence squarely upon his own shoulders. And, when we say that man is responsible for himself, we do not mean that he is responsible only for his own individuality, but that he is responsible for all men. The word "subjectivism" is to be understood in two senses, and our adversaries play upon only one of them. Subjectivism means, on the one hand, the freedom of the individual subject and, on the other, that man cannot pass beyond human subjectivity. It is the latter which is the deeper meaning of existentialism. When we say that man chooses himself, we do mean that every one of us must choose himself; but by that we also mean that in choosing for himself he chooses for all men. For in effect, of all the actions a man may take in order to create himself as he wills to be, there is not one which is not creative, at the same time, of an image of man such as he believes he ought to be. To choose between this or that is at the same time to affirm the value of that which is chosen; for we are unable ever to choose the worse. What we choose is always the better; and nothing can be better for us unless it is better for all. If, moreover, existence precedes essence and we will to exist at the same time as we fashion our image, that image is valid for all and for the entire epoch in which we find ourselves. Our responsibility is thus much greater than we had supposed, for it concerns mankind as a whole. If I am a worker, for instance, I may choose to join a Christian rather than a Communist trade union. And if, by that membership, I choose to signify that resignation is, after all, the attitude that best becomes a man, that man's kingdom is not upon this earth, I do not commit myself alone to that view. Resignation is my will for everyone, and my action is, in consequence, a commitment on behalf of all mankind. Or if, to take a more personal case, I decide to marry and to have children, even though this decision proceeds simply from my situation, from my passion or my desire, I am thereby committing not only myself, but humanity as a whole, to the practice of monogamy. I am thus responsible for myself and for all men, and I am creating a certain image of man as I would have him to be. In fashioning myself I fashion man.

...

But there is another sense of the word, of which the fundamental meaning is this: Man is all the time outside of himself: it is in projecting and losing himself beyond himself that he makes man to exist; and, on the other hand, it is by pursuing transcendent aims that he himself is able to exist. Since man is thus self-surpassing, and can grasp objects only in relation to his self-surpassing, he is himself the heart and center of his transcendence. There is no other universe except the human universe, the universe of human subjectivity. This relation of transcendence as constitutive of man (not in the sense that God is transcendent, but in the sense of self-surpassing) with subjectivity (in such a sense that man is not shut up in himself but forever present in a human universe)—it is this that we call existential humanism. This is humanism, because we remind man that there is no legislator but himself; that he himself, thus abandoned, must decide for himself; also because we show that it is not by turning back upon himself, but always by seeking, beyond himself, an aim which is one of liberation or of some particular realization, that man can realize himself as truly human.

You can see from these few reflections that nothing could be more unjust than the objections people raise against us. Existentialism is nothing else but an attempt to draw the full conclusions from a consistently atheistic position. Its intention is not in the least that of plunging men into despair. And if by despair one means as the Christians do—any attitude of unbelief, the despair of the existentialists is something different. Existentialism is not atheist in the sense that it would exhaust itself in demonstrations of the non-existence of God. It declares, rather, that even if God existed that would make no difference from its point of view. Not that we believe God does exist, but we think that the real problem is not that of His existence; what man needs is to find himself again and to understand that nothing can save him from himself, not even a valid proof of the existence of God. In this sense existentialism is optimistic. It is a doctrine of action, and it is only by self-deception, by confining their own despair with ours that Christians can describe us as without hope.

Questions

1. As Sartre said, Man is condemned to freedom. What does he want to convey? What is your interpretation of this viewpoint?
2. According to Sartre, Man is all the time outside of himself. Does it imply a dualistic relationship between subjectivity and objectivity? What's your opinion?
3. In what way can we say Sartre is atheistic?
4. How do you interpret the most viewpoint of Sartre, "existence precedes essence"? How can we define "essence"?
5. What's the difference between "being-in-itself" and "being-for-itself"?
6. How can we define the term "existentialism" in Sartre's philosophical dimension?
7. As Sartre said, the very heart of existentialism is the absolute character of the free commitment. Do you agree or disagree with him? What's your stance?

Being and Time

Martin Heidegger

Pre-reading

Martin Heidegger (1889 – 1976) was a 20th Century German philosopher. He was one of the most original and important philosophers of the 20th Century, but also one of the most controversial. He was born to a poor Catholic family in Messikirch, Germany. From 1909 to 1911, he started to study theology at the University of Freiburg, but then switched to studying philosophy, mathematics, and natural sciences. His teaching career was interrupted during the period of 1945 – 51 for his political involvement in the Nazi Party as an official member. He died in 1976 and is buried in his hometown.

Although often considered a founder of Existentialism, (mainly because his discussion of ontology is rooted in an analysis of the mode of existence of individual human beings), Heidegger vehemently rejected the association, just as he had rejected Husserl's Phenomenology. However, his works such as *Being and Time* and *What is Metaphysics*? are certainly a big influence on Jean-Paul Sartre (and especially on his *Being and Nothingness*, the title of which is a direct allusion to Heidegger's *Being and Time*).

His best known book, *Being and Time*, is generally considered to be one of the most important philosophical works of the 20th Century. Heidegger's writings are notoriously difficult and idiosyncratic, indulging in extended word play, employing his own spelling, vocabulary and syntax, and inventing new words for complex concepts. This is partly because the philosopher is discussing very specifically defined concepts (which he used in a very rigorous and consistent way) but it does make reading and understanding his work very difficult. *Being and Time* is a long and complex book. Once turning it open, the reader is bound to be struck by the huge quantities of "new" or "strange" words created by the philosopher himself. In any case, for many readers, the initially strange and difficult language of *Being and Time* is fully vindicated by the realization that Heidegger is struggling to say things for which the conventional terms and linguistic constructions are ultimately inadequate. Indeed, as is called by some thinkers, Heidegger's language has become the language of philosophy. In broad outline, *Being and Time* addresses a striking combination of ancient and modern themes. The central question of this book concerns the meaning of being. According to Heidegger, the question of being is a question about everything, or in a sense, about nothing. He gives an account of the distinctive features of human existence and claims that underlying all of these features is what he calls "original time".

In the first half of this book (Division one), Heidegger introduces the basic structures of the being of Dasein, which are named *existentials* in Heidegger's philosophical context. The most basic of the structures of the being of Dasein is *being-in-the-world*. Dasein is in the world in the sense of being engaged with things, but what Heidegger means by *world* is not itself an entity, not even the totality of entities, but the web of significance which makes it possible for entities to show themselves or be encountered. The *world* is not any one's private possession but a shared world. Being-in-the-world is being-with-others-in-the-world. Therefore, according to Heidegger, being alone is a possibility but it is only possible on the basis of being-with, which does not depend on inference from bodily appearance and behavior, nor on something inferential like empathy. The structures of being are structures of Dasein in what Heidegger calls its *everydayness*. Everyday existence is what he calls *inauthentic* existence. To exist authentically is to choose and own one's possibilities of existence and in this sense to be oneself; by contrast, to exist inauthentically is to have one's possibilities of existence determined by something, or other entities in the world. Authenticity, according to Heidegger, involves a certain mode of comportment towards death, the end of Dasein. In some sense, the being of Dasein is being towards death. In the case of inauthentic existence, Dasein covers up and disguises the features of death while in the case of authentic existence, Dasein faces up to death as the end of Dasein. Besides the question of being, Heidegger also reflects on time which possesses the following features:

datability, spannedness, publicness, and significance. Time as a uniform sequence of nows is an abstraction from time with these above-mentioned structures of being. But there is something more basic than this concrete time of everyday experience. This is called ecstatic temporality. In this sense, time is interpreted as something present-at-hand. The succession of nows is interpreted as a present-at-hand sequence. The nows may perish as other present-at-hand entities. Time must be brought to light as the horizon for all understanding and interpretation of being. It is in this sense that being and time are interwoven philosophically.

Now let's read the text and reflect on the questions that follow.

Text

Division Ⅱ Part Ⅳ Temporality and everydayness
68. The temporality of disclosedness in general

Resoluteness, which we have characterized with regard to its temporal meaning, represents an authentic disclosedness of Dasein—a disclosedness which constitutes an entity of such a kind that in existing, it can be its very "there". Care has been characterized with regard to its temporal meaning, but only in its basic features. To exhibit its concrete temporal Constitution, means to give a temporal Interpretation of the items of its structure, taking them each singly: understanding, state-of-mind, falling, and discourse. Every understanding has its mood. Every state-of-mind is one in which one understands. The understanding which one has in such a state-of-mind has the character of falling. The understanding which has its mood attuned in falling articulates itself with relation to its intelligibility in discourse. The current temporal Constitution of these phenomena leads back in each case to that one kind of temporality which serves as such to guarantee the possibility that understanding, state-of-mind, falling, and discourse, are united in their structure.

(a) The temporality of understanding

With the term "understanding" we have in mind a fundamental existentiale, which is neither a definite species of cognition distinguished, let us say, from explaining and conceiving, nor any cognition at all in the sense of grasping something thematically. Understanding constitutes rather the Being of the "there" in such a way that, on the basis of such understanding, a Dasein can, in existing, develop the different possibilities of sight, of looking around [Sichumsehens], and of just looking. In all explanation one uncovers understandingly that which one cannot understand; and all explanation is thus rooted in Dasein's primary understanding.

If the term "understanding" is taken in a way which is primordially existential, it means to be projecting towards a potentiality-for-Being for the sake of which any Dasein exists. In understanding, one's own potentiality-for-Being is disclosed in such a way that one's Dasein always knows understandingly what it is capable of. It 'knows' this, however, not by having discovered some fact, but by maintaining itself in an existentiell possibility. The kind of ignorance which corresponds to this, does not consist in an absence or cessation of understanding, but must be regarded as a deficient mode of the projectedness of one's potentiality-for-Being. Existence can be questionable. If it is to be possible for something "to be in question" [das "In-Frage-stehen"], a disclosedness is needed. When one understands oneself projectively in an existentiell possibility, the future underlies this understanding, and it does so as a coming-towards-oneself out of that current possibility as which one's Dasein exists. The future makes ontologically possible an entity which is in such a way that it exists understandingly in its potentiality-for-Being. Projection is basically futural; it does not primarily grasp the projected possibility thematically just by having it in view, but it throws itself into it as a possibility. In each case Dasein is understandingly in the way that it can be. Resoluteness has turned out to be a kind of existing which is primordial and authentic. Proximally and for the most part, to be sure, Dasein remains irresolute; that is to say, it remains closed off in its ownmost potentiality-for-Being, to which it brings itself only when it has been individualized. This implies that temporality does not temporalize itself constantly out of the authentic future. This inconstancy, however, does not mean that temporality sometimes lacks a future, but rather that the temporalizing of the future takes various forms.

...

Just as expecting is possible only on the basis of awaiting, remembering is possible only on that of forgetting, and not vice versa; for in the mode of having-forgotten, one's having been "discloses" primarily the horizon into which a Dasein lost in the "superficiality" of its object of concern, can bring itself by remembering. The awaiting which forgets and makes present is an ecstatical unity in its own right, in accordance with which inauthentic understanding temporalizes itself with regard to its temporality. The unity of these ecstases closes off one's authentic potentiality-for-Being, and is thus the existential condition for the possibility of irresoluteness. Though inauthentic concernful understanding determines itself in the light of making present the object of concern, the temporalizing of the understanding is performed primarily in the future.

(b) The temporality of state-of-mind

Understanding is never free-floating, but always goes with some state-of-mind. The "there" gets equiprimordially disclosed by one's mood in every case—or gets closed off by it. Having a mood brings Dasein face to face with its thrownness in such a manner that this thrownness is not known as such but disclosed far more primordially in "how one is". Existentially, "Being-thrown" means finding oneself in some state-of-mind or other. One's state-of-mind is therefore based upon thrownness. My mood represents whatever may be the way in which I am primarily the entity that has been thrown. How does the temporal Constitution of having-a-mood let itself be made visible? How will the ecstatical unity of one's current temporality give any insight into the existential connection between one's state-of-mind and one's understanding?

One's mood discloses in the manner of turning thither or turning away from one's own Dasein. Bringing Dasein face to face with the "that-it-is" of its own thrownness—whether authentically revealing it or inauthentically covering it up—becomes existentially possible only if Dasein'sBeing, by its very meaning, constantly is as having been. The "been" is not what first brings one face to face with the thrown entity which one is oneself; but the ecstasis of the "been" is what first makes it possible to find oneself in the way of having a state-of-mind.

Understanding is grounded primarily in the future; one's state-of-mind, however, temporalizes itself primarily in having been. Moods temporalize themselves—that is, their specific ecstasis belongs to a future and a Present in such a way, indeed, that these equiprimordial ecstases are modified by having been.

We have emphasized that while moods, of course, are ontically wellknown to us [bekannt], they are not recognized [erkannt] in their primordial existential function. They are regarded as fleeting Experiences which 'colour' one's whole "psychical condition". Anything which is observed to have the character of turning up and disappearing in a fleeting manner, belongs to the primordial constancy of existence. But all the same, what should moods have in common with "time"? That these "Experiences" come and go, that they run their course "in time", is a trivial thing to establish. Certainly. And indeed this can be established in an ontico-psychological manner. Our task, however, is to exhibit the ontological structure of having-a-mood in its existential-temporal Constitution. And of course this is proximally just a matter of first making the temporality of moods visible. The thesis that "one's state-of-mind is grounded primarily in having been" means that the existentially basic character of moods lies in bringing one back to something. This bringing-back does not first produce a having been; but in any state-of-mind some mode of having been is made manifest for existential analysis. So if we are toInterpret states-of-mind temporally, our aim is not one of deducing moods from temporality and dissolving them into pure phenomena of temporalizing. All we have to do is to demonstrate that except on the basis of temporality, moods are not possible in what they "signify" in an existentiell way or in how they "signify" it. Our temporal Interpretation will restrict itself to the phenomena of fear and anxiety, which we have already analysed in a preparatory manner.

...

The forgetting which is constitutive for fear, bewilders Dasein and lets it drift back and forth between "worldly" possibilities which it has not seized upon. In contrast to this making-present which is not held on to, the Present of anxiety is heldon to when one brings oneself back to one's ownmost thrownness. The existential meaning of anxiety is such that it cannot lose itself in something with which it might be concerned. If anything like this happens in a similar state-of-mind, this is fear, which the everyday understanding confuses with anxiety. But even though the Present of anxiety is held on to, it does not as yet have the character of the moment of vision, which temporalizes itself in a resolution. Anxiety merely brings one into the mood for a possible resolution. The Present of anxiety holds the moment of vision at the ready [auf dem Sprung]; as such a moment it itself, and only itself, is possible.

The temporality of anxiety is peculiar; for anxiety is grounded primordially in having been, and only out of this do the future and the Present temporalize themselves; in this peculiar temporality is demonstrated the possibility of that power which is distinctive for the mood of anxiety.. In this, Dasein is taken all the way back to its naked uncanniness, and becomes fascinated by it. This fascination, however, not only takes Dasein back from its "worldly" possibilities, but at the same time gives it the possibility of an authentic potentiality-for-Being.

Yet neither of these moods, fear and anxiety, ever "occurs" just isolated in the "stream of

Experiences"; each of them determines an understanding or determines itself in terms of one. Fear is occasioned by entities with which we concern ourselves environmentally. Anxiety, however, springs from Dasein itself. When fear assails us, it does so from what is within-the-world. Anxiety arises out of Being-in-the-world as thrown Being-towards-death. When understood temporally, this "mounting" of anxiety out of Dasein, means that the future and the Present of anxiety temporalize themselves out of a primordial Being-as-having-been in the sense of bringing us back to repeatability. But anxiety can mount authentically only in a Dasein which is resolute. He who is resolute knows no fear; but he understands the possibility of anxiety as the possibility of the very mood which neither inhibits nor bewilders him. Anxiety liberates him from possibilities which "count for nothing" ["nichtigen"], and lets him become free for those which are authentic.

Although both fear and anxiety, as modes of state-of-mind, are grounded primarily in having been, they each have different sources with regard to their own temporalization in the temporality of care. Anxiety springs from the future of resoluteness, while fear springs from the lost Present, of which fear is fearfully apprehensive, so that it falls prey to it more than ever.

Questions

1. In what way is the *world* in Heidegger's philosophical context different from the physical world we are living in?
2. What is the basic content of Dasein's *Existential Constitution?*
3. How does Heidegger define "Understanding" in his philosophical context? In what way is it different from the commonsense definition of this term?
4. What constitutes the Disclosedness? How are the components interrelated with each other?
5. How do you interpret the term "ecstatic temporality"? What does it refer to in Heidegger's Dasein system?
6. What is the difference between authenticity and inauthenticity according to Heidegger? What impact do they have upon Dasein?
7. As Heidegger said, Dasein gets dragged along in thrownness; that is to say, as something which has been thrown into the world, it loses itself in the "world" in its factical submission to that with which it is to concern itself. Does it imply that Dasein is passive, or submissive to something mysterious but powerful? If yes, what is it submissive to?

Questions for Further Reflection

1. Nietzsche claimed that God is dead; Sartre himself is also an atheist. What are the prior and subsequent links in the causal chain?
2. What implication does "Death" convey in Heidegger's philosophy? Is it the same or different from our Chinese concept of life and death?
3. Does what Heidegger calls "Dasein" have anything in common with the "Tao"(道) in Chinese

ancient philosophy, especially Taoism? If yes, in what way?

4. How can we interpret Heidegger's claim that to exist is to be historical? How is it different from the concept of history we learned in the previous chapters?

5. How can we interpret the famous line by Sartre: Hell is other people? In what way is it related with "free will"? Is it the same as what Immanuel Kant calls "the Categorical Imperative"?

References and Further Reading

1. Collins, T. (1952). *The Existentialists: A Critical Study*. Chicago: Henry Regnery Company.

2. Gordon, H. (1999). *Dictionary of Existentialism*. New York: Greenwood Press.

3. Heidegger, M. (1962). *Being and Time*. (John Macquarrie & Edward Robinson, Trans.). New York: Harper and Row.

4. Heidegger, M. (1998). Letter on Humanism. In Pathmarks (Ed.), *William McNeill*. Cambridge: Cambridge University Press.

5. Lee, A. J. (1983). *A World of Ideas: Essential Readings for College Writers*. New York: St. Martin's Press.

6. Gorner, P. (2007). *Heidegger's Being and Time An Introduction*. Cambridge: Cambridge University Press.

7. Sartre, J.-P. (2007). *Existentialism is a Humanism*. (Carol Macomber, Trans.). New Haven: Yale University Press.

8. Sartre, J.-P. (1988). *What is Literature?* Cambridge MA: Harvard University Press.

9. Kaufman, W. (1989). *Existentialism from Dostoyevsky to Sartre*. Utica, N.Y.: Meridian Publishing Company.

10. 吴格非.萨特与中国.徐州: 中国矿业大学出版社, 2004.

11. 萨特哲学思想介绍 https://www.the-philosophy.com/sartre-philosophy

12. 存在主义简介 https://plato.stanford.edu/entries/existentialism/

13. 萨特生平 https://plato.stanford.edu/entries/sartre/